Race and Probation

Race and Probation

edited by

Sam Lewis, Peter Raynor, David Smith and Ali Wardak

WILLAN
PUBLISHING

Willan Publishing
Culmcott House
Mill Street, Uffculme
Cullompton, Devon
EX15 3AT, UK
Tel: +44(0)1884 840337
Fax: +44(0)1884 840251
e-mail: info@willanpublishing.co.uk
website: www.willanpublishing.co.uk

Published simultaneously in the USA and Canada by

Willan Publishing
c/o ISBS, 920 NE 58th Ave, Suite 300
Portland, Oregon 97213-3786, USA
Tel: +001(0)503 287 3093
Fax: +001(0)503 280 8832
e-mail: info@isbs.com
website: www.isbs.com

First published 2006

ISBN-10: 1-84392-143-X Paperback
ISBN-13: 978-1-84392-143-1 Paperback

British Library Cataloguing-in-Publication Data

A catalogue record for this book is available from the British Library

Project management by Deer Park Productions, Tavistock, Devon
Typeset by GCS, Leighton Buzzard, Beds
Printed and bound by T.J. International, Padstow, Cornwall

Contents

Acknowledgements

The editors would like to thank all those people who assisted in the Home Office funded study of Black and Asian men on probation which provided the inspiration for this book. They include staff of the National Probation Service, in the Directorate and in the areas, who helped us with information and access; members of the steering group; and the project managers from Research Development and Statistics Directorate (RDS). We also wish to thank those people who commented on early drafts of the research report: particular thanks go to Coretta Phillips for her helpful observations and suggestions.

Some material in Chapters 2 and 11 is drawn from the findings of an Economic and Social Research Council (ESRC) funded research project which formed part of the Violence Research Programme (Ref. L13325019). The project also received support from the Greater Manchester Probation Service, and we are grateful to all involved for their support.

The editors also wish to thank Brian Willan for his advice and assistance.

Finally, our heartfelt thanks go to all of the probationers who allowed us and the other members of the research team to interview them for the original Home Office study, and who shared their views and experiences so readily. We sincerely hope that this book helps to achieve a better understanding of their needs and experiences amongst practitioners, academics, students, and in particular those responsible for setting policy objectives within the new National Offender Management Service (NOMS).

In all chapters, the views expressed are those of the authors and not of the Home Office or any other official body.

Sam Lewis, Peter Raynor, David Smith, Ali Wardak
October 2005

List of figures and tables

Figures

Tables

About the contributors

Adam Calverley has worked as a researcher at the University of Glamorgan and at the University of Keele. His research interests include race, ethnicity and crime, and why people stop offending. He has recently co-authored a book with Stephen Farrall entitled *Understanding Desistance from Crime* (Open University Press 2005). Adam is currently a postgraduate student at Keele, investigating what factors account for desistance among minority ethnic offenders.

Bankole Cole is Lecturer in Criminology and Director of Undergraduate Studies at the University of Hull. His teaching and research areas include criminal justice issues, with particular emphasis on developing countries, youth justice and theories of crime and punishment. He has published in the areas of post-colonial policing, crime and justice in developing countries. He is currently working on a book entitled *Globalisation, Citizenship and the War on Terror*.

Loraine Gelsthorpe is Reader in Criminology and Criminal Justice at the Institute of Criminology, and Fellow of Pembroke College, University of Cambridge. Her research and writing interests revolve around discretion and discrimination in the conception and delivery of criminal justice. She has published extensively in the field of community penalties, including *Community Penalties: Change and Challenges* (edited by Bottoms, Gelsthorpe and Rex) (Willan 2001). She is currently editing a *Handbook of Probation* (with Rod Morgan).

Gurpreet Kaur studied criminology and social policy at the University of Lincoln. She went on to work as a researcher at the University of Lincoln. Her main area of interest is probation and criminal justice issues relating to Asian offenders. Gurpreet's ambition is to train as a probation officer.

Sam Lewis is Lecturer in Criminology in the Centre for Criminal Justice Studies at the University of Leeds. In recent years she has undertaken research (with colleagues from other institutions) for the Home Office, local probation areas and youth offending services. Her research and publications focus on Black and Minority Ethnic experiences of criminal justice; youth crime and justice; prisoner resettlement; and Probation Service policy and practice.

Rod Morgan is Chairman of the Youth Justice Board, before which he was HM Chief Inspector of Probation, England and Wales. Previously he was Professor of Criminal Justice in the Faculty of Law, University of Bristol and he remains Professor Emeritus there. He is the author of many books and articles on aspects of policing, criminal justice and penal policy and during his academic career he led many empirical research studies on these topics. He is the co-editor of one of the principal texts in the field of criminology in the UK, *The Oxford Handbook of Criminology* (OUP 2002, 3rd edn) and is currently editing *Handbook of Probation* for publication by Willan in 2006 (with Loraine Gelsthorpe).

Jill Olumide is Lecturer in Social Science at Swansea University. She has worked as a school teacher and as a researcher. Her research interests are in children's participation in their health affairs and the sociology of mixed race. She has published in these areas and is the author of *Raiding the Gene Pool* (Pluto Press 2002) which is based on her PhD research on the social construction of mixed race.

Peter Raynor is Professor of Criminology and Criminal Justice at Swansea University. He is a former probation officer, probation committee member and probation board member. He has published widely on probation and criminal justice topics, and currently serves as an Accreditation Panel member for England and Wales and for Scotland.

Soheila Sadeghi is Senior Lecturer at Tehran University, Department of Sociology. She is also the director of the Centre for Women's

Studies at Tehran University. Her main areas of teaching and research are criminology, sociology, social problems, ethnic studies and gender studies.

David Smith is Professor of Criminology in the Department of Applied Social Science at Lancaster University, where he has worked since 1976. A former probation officer, he has researched and published extensively on issues of probation and youth justice policy and practice, and on racist violence.

Kate Stephens currently works as a researcher in the Home Office. She began her career in prison psychology, later working as a school teacher in the UK and Zimbabwe, a teacher educator and a researcher in education. She joined the Probation Service in West Yorkshire in 1999, where she worked on attrition from national accredited programmes and helped to design and implement an inter-agency approach to domestic violence. She has recently completed a short secondment to the voluntary sector.

Maurice Vanstone is Senior Lecturer in Criminal Justice and Criminology in the Centre for Criminal Justice and Criminology at Swansea University. His publications include *Effective Probation Practice* (with Peter Raynor and David Smith 1994), *Betrayal of Trust* (with Matthew Colton 1996), *Beyond Offending Behaviour* (with Mark Drakeford 1996), *Understanding Community Penalties* (with Peter Raynor 2002), and *Supervising Offenders in the Community: A History of Probation Theory and Practice* (Ashgate 2004) as well as numerous articles, chapters and reports. Recently, he has collaborated with Mike Maguire, Peter Raynor and Julie Vennard in research for the Home Office on prison after-care.

Rachel Walmsley is a Senior Research Officer in the Research Development and Statistics Directorate, National Offender Management Service at the Home Office. She has worked in the Home Office since 2001 conducting and managing research on interventions for offenders in custody and in the community.

Ali Wardak is Reader in Criminology at the University of Glamorgan, where he teaches criminological theory and comparative criminology. He has published widely on criminological and social issues. He is the author of *Social Control and Deviance* (Ashgate 2000), and has co-authored (with Johnson *et al.*) *Afghanistan's Political and Constitutional*

Development (ODI 2003). He has also co-edited (with Sheptycki) *Transnational and Comparative Criminology* (Cavendish 2005).

Patrick Williams is a co-founder of REClaim Northwest – a group committed to empowering community-based and not-for-profit organisations through the delivery of research and evaluation to strengthen their position in the provision of services to local people. He also works as a Research and Evaluation Officer for the Greater Manchester Probation Area and has made both national and local contributions to the design and development of interventions for minority ethnic offenders.

Introduction: race, crime and community penalties

Adam Calverley, Gurpreet Kaur and Soheila Sadeghi

The issue of minority ethnic groups' experiences of the criminal justice process, and in particular whether they are subject to disadvantageous treatment, has received much attention in recent years following high-profile events such as the publication of the Macpherson Report (1999) and the riots of, predominantly, British-born Asian youths in northern towns in 2001. Underlying the debate is consistent research evidence that Black and Minority Ethnic (BME) people are more likely to be stopped and searched than whites, more likely to be arrested as a result, more likely to be charged (and charged with more serious offences), and more likely to be remanded in custody (Hood 1992; Phillips and Brown 1998; Home Office 2005). The Home Office itself has argued that the differences 'are such that it would be implausible to argue that none are due to discrimination' (Home Office 2002: 10). BME individuals are also more likely than their white counterparts to be victims of crime (Kershaw *et al.* 2000), and specifically the targets of racial violence (Bowling 1999), while being 'under-represented in all police officer, prison officer and prison governor grades, as well as in various posts in criminal justice agencies' (Home Office 2005: viii). In light of this evidence, it is reasonable to assume that BME groups may experience different and possibly disadvantageous treatment within the criminal justice system.

The need for a greater awareness of what these different experiences might involve is important for all criminal justice agencies. However, it is arguably of particular importance for the Probation Service because of its position within the criminal justice structure, the nature of its work with offenders, and the context of the recent What Works policy. First, as the 'exit' agency situated at the end of the criminal justice process, the Probation Service supervises people whose perceptions of the fairness and legitimacy of the process have already been shaped by the actions of preceding agencies, be they the police, courts or prisons. If these are unfavourable then this may have implications for how they perceive the legitimacy of the justice system and their sentence. This, in turn, may affect motivation and compliance and, ultimately, the likelihood of whether they desist from crime. Second, there has also been concern that an inadequate understanding within the Probation Service of minority ethnic offenders' criminogenic needs, that is the factors directly associated with their offending, may mean that its officers are unable to address these groups' needs effectively. Thus the Probation Service could be guilty, albeit inadvertently, of compounding their disadvantage. Third, there has been concern that the 'evidence based' cognitive-behavioural programmes that were being rolled out nationally, which were largely based on studies involving white North American prisoners (Mair 2004), treat all offenders uniformly and may overlook the quite different needs of women and minority ethnic offenders (Shaw and Hannah-Moffat 2004).

Traditionally, however, the needs and experiences of BME offenders have been under-researched. Until recently there was simply no knowledge as to whether such offenders had different or greater criminogenic needs than white offenders. More specifically, there was little evidence concerning BME experiences of probation supervision and programmes. It was with the aim of addressing such questions that the Home Office commissioned the largest study of BME probationers ever conducted in Europe. A consortium of nine academics from four universities interviewed 483 BME men on probation from 17 probation areas. A full report of the findings is available elsewhere (see Calverley et al. 2004).

It is important to note the difficulties inherent in conducting such research. Access to information depends largely on the co-operation of busy practitioners with many other obligations, and of offenders for whom the research is unlikely to have high priority. In addition, researchers can only hope that the criminal justice databases used are accurate and up to date, and that information on ethnicity has been fully recorded. Such factors constituted a significant challenge to those involved in the study of BME men on probation: a fuller discussion of the difficulties encountered can be found in Appendix 1 of the Home Office report (Calverley et al. 2004).

In addition to the study by Calverley *et al.* (2004) and other relevant research (see, for example, Powis and Walmsley 2002), recent years have seen significant policy developments in relation to race, crime and community penalties, including efforts to develop and assess probation programmes specifically designed for BME offenders (Stephens *et al.* 2004), and research into understanding the behaviour of racially motivated offenders (see, for example, Webster 1996; Sibbitt 1997; Ray *et al.* 2003, 2004). At present, there is no single text that draws together the available evidence pertaining to race, crime and community penalties. The aim of *Race and Probation* is to provide that much needed text. Its contributors include academics and researchers with substantial experience of work on issues of race and racism, but, importantly, there are also chapters by the former Chief Inspector of Probation and specialist researchers in the Home Office and the National Probation Service. This diversity of authorship, and the fact that much of the book is based on recent and innovative research, makes the book relevant to a wide readership, beyond as well as within the academic community.

It is important, at the outset, to explain the title of the book. *Race and Probation* is intended to give potential readers an immediate impression of the book's content, concerned, as it is, with the Probation Service's work with BME and racially motivated offenders. It should be noted, however, that talk of 'race' is inherently problematic. Race is not a fact of nature. Rather, it is a social construct which may be deployed to legitimise social relations of subjugation, or used reactively in resistance to such social relations. Ethnicity, on the other hand, is about belonging to or identifying with a particular group in the population, characterised by common national, geographical or cultural origin. Any categorisition by race or ethnicity will involve oversimplifications. That is, they obscure hybrid identities (such as Black British, British Asian, etc.), and inevitably overgeneralise (for example 'Asian' in this country usually includes 'Indians', 'Pakistanis', 'Bangladeshis', and more besides).

The book is organised into three parts. The first three chapters, making up Part One, set out the context of recent policy, research and practice initiatives. In Chapter 1, Maurice Vanstone provides a critical history of the Probation Service's engagement with BME offenders. He identifies two distinct approaches: 'minimal managerial anti-racism and equal opportunities strategies' (recruitment of Black staff, equality of treatment and ethnic monitoring) and a 'more politicised anti-racist project' (liberation and Black empowerment groups). Vanstone charts the motivation and reasoning behind these two approaches and explains why, over time, policy and practice have taken the direction they have. In Chapter 2, David Smith similarly provides a history and context for the Probation Service's efforts to make sense of work with racially motivated offenders. Drawing largely on writing by practitioners, he shows that probation staff, with some notable exceptions, have tended to avoid a full acknowledgement of the racist element in offending, seeing it as difficult and threatening to the development of constructive relationships with those under their supervision. Rod Morgan returns to this theme in Chapter 3, from the perspective of the Probation Inspectorate. In the wake of the Macpherson Report (1999), with its critique of institutional racism, the Inspectorate examined the Probation Service's responses to race issues, in relation both to work with offenders and to its employment practice. Morgan discusses the findings of this report, and of its follow-up in 2003–4, and outlines the implications they have for operational practice.

Part Two of the book focuses on the needs and experiences of minority ethnic offenders. Three of the four chapters draw on the research by Calverley *et al.* (2004), and discuss its findings in the context of the broader themes addressed in the book. In Chapter 4, Peter Raynor and Sam Lewis outline the characteristics of the 483 offenders who took part in the study and compare these with what is known from other studies of predominantly white probation populations. They also discuss in detail one of the key findings of the study: that contrary to preconceptions in some quarters, the interviewees had fewer 'criminogenic needs' and lower levels of self-reported social and personal problems than offenders in the predominantly white matched comparison samples. In Chapter 5, Bankole Cole and Ali Wardak examine the views and experiences of the sample more generally. They discuss the nature and extent of their social exclusion (economic, geographical/environmental, and educational) and their views of the criminal justice system. They explore offenders' experiences of racism and discrimination, and conclude by analysing the impact of these experiences on their sense of the legitimacy of the justice system as a whole. Chapter 6, by Loraine Gelsthorpe, discusses the under-researched topic of Black and Asian women's experiences of probation. The author was considerably hampered by a general failure to consider both race and gender issues in the same research study or set of statistics, and the dearth of evidence is notable in itself. Gelsthorpe critiques culturally neutral theories of pathways into crime and makes the case that, if service delivery is to be effective, intervention programmes must reflect institutional racism, sexism and classism and be based on models of offending behaviour that theorise power and social justice. Chapter 7, by Sam Lewis and Jill Olumide, also focuses on a neglected theme, the experiences of mixed heritage offenders. In the study by Calverley *et al.* (2004), the mixed heritage interviewees regularly fared worse, particularly in relation to social exclusion and deprivation, than the Black and Asian interviewees. Lewis and Olumide review the evidence from this study and other sources concerning the distinctive needs and experiences of this group, and consider the implications for practice.

The chapters in Part Three discuss aspects of recent practice and policy. In Chapter 8, Patrick Williams discusses the challenges involved in designing and delivering programmes specifically for BME offenders. He outlines the rationale for such programmes and the practical and theoretical challenges they involve, and explores the meaning of 'effectiveness' in this context, noting the possible tensions between local initiatives and national policy. In Chapter 9, Rachel Walmsley and Kate Stephens explore the work conducted by the Home Office on developing programmes for BME offenders. They report findings from research on the effectiveness of interventions with these groups in the probation context, and the ways in which these might inform practice. Chapter 10, by Sam Lewis, returns to the research by Calverley *et al.* (2004), focusing on offenders' experiences of case management, individual supervision, and probation programmes, and comparing their experiences with those of their white counterparts. Particular attention is paid to the extent to which supervisors and the content of programmes addressed the distinct needs and experiences of BME offenders. In Chapter 11, David Smith returns to the issues raised in Chapter 2, and discusses the most recent developments in probation practice with racist offenders. Drawing on research on racist violence, Smith argues that practitioners need to recognise the emotions of distress and neglect that often underpin racist resentment and hostility. The short concluding chapter by the editors that makes up Part Four of the book summarises what has gone before and suggests some 'next steps' for policy and practice.

The book makes the findings of the Home Office study by Calverley *et al.* (2004) easily accessible and explores them thematically; it pays attention to the needs of women and mixed heritage offenders; it explores possibilities for work with racist offenders; and it presents recent developments in research, theory and practice against the background of the Probation Service's history and traditions. We believe that in these ways the book makes an important contribution to increased understanding of the meanings of 'race' for the development of practice in community penalties.

References

Bowling, B. (1999) *Violent Racism: Victimisation, Policing and Social Context*. Oxford: Clarendon Press.

Calverley, A., Cole, B., Kaur, G., Lewis, S., Raynor, P., Sadeghi, S., Smith, D., Vanstone, M. and Wardak, A. (2004) *Black and Asian offenders on Probation*, Home Office Research Study 277. London: Home Office.

Home Office (2002) *Statistics on Race and the Criminal Justice System 2002*. London: Home Office.

Home Office (2005) *Statistics on Race and the Criminal Justice System 2004*. London: Home Office. Available online at: http://www.homeoffice.gov.uk/rds/pdfs05/s95race04.pdf

Hood, R. (1992) *Race and Sentencing*. Oxford: Clarendon Press.

Kershaw, C., Budd, T., Kinshott, G., Mayhew, P. and Myhill, A. (2000) *The 2000 British Crime Survey (England and Wales)*, Home Office Statistical Bulletin, 18/00. London: Home Office.

Macpherson, W. (1999) *The Stephen Lawrence Inquiry: Report of an Inquiry by Sir William Macpherson of Cluny*. Cm. 4262-1. London: Home Office.

Mair, G. (2004) 'The Origins of What Works in England and Wales: A House Built on Sand?' in G. Mair (ed.) *What Matters in Probation*. Cullompton: Willan.

Phillips, C. and Brown, D. (1998) *Entry into the Criminal Justice System: A Study of Police Arrests and their Outcomes*, Home Office Research Study 185. London: Home Office.

Powis, B. and Walmsley, R. K. (2002) *Programmes for Black and Asian Offenders on Probation: Lessons for Developing Practice*, Home Office Research Study 250. London: Home Office.

Ray, L., Smith, D. and Wastell, L. (2003) 'Understanding Racist Violence', in E. A. Stanko (ed.) *The Meanings of Violence*. London and New York: Routledge, 112–29.

Ray, L., Smith, D. and Wastell, L. (2004) 'Shame, Rage and Racist Violence', *British Journal of Criminology*, 44 3, 350–68.

Shaw, M. and Hannah-Moffat, K. (2004) 'How Cognitive Skills Forgot About Gender and Diversity', in G. Mair (ed.) *What Matters in Probation*. Cullompton: Willan.

Sibbitt, R. (1997) *The Perpetrators of Racial Harassment and Racial Violence*, Home Office Research Study 176. London: Home Office.

Stephens, K., Coombs, J. and Debidin, M. (2004) *Black and Asian offenders Pathfinder: Implementation Report*, Home Office Development and Practice Report 24. London: Home Office.

Webster, C. (1996) 'Local Heroes: Violent Racism, Spacism and Localism Among White and Asian Young People', *Youth and Policy*, 53, 15–27.

Part One

Background

Chapter 1

Room for improvement: a history of the Probation Service's response to race

Maurice Vanstone

In as much as awareness of the needs and problems of offenders drawn from minority ethnic groups only began to develop in ways that had impact on policy and practice during the last quarter of the twentieth century, the history of the Probation Service's awareness of, and engagement with, the issue of race mirrors that of the country and culture in which it has developed. As Denney (1992: 140) has persuasively argued, as late as the end of the 1960s policy aspirations paid little heed to the effects of discrimination, and the 'post Second World War recruitment of Black people from the New Commonwealth and Pakistan by the British government does not appear to have influenced probation policy until the early 1980s'. Even then that influence has been encompassed by what Denney describes as the *externality* of racism: thus racism is individualised, punitive policies likely to have disproportionate impact on minority ethnic groups are introduced at the same time as equal opportunities policies, and managerialism dominates policy (1992: 157). Admittedly, the period since the early 1980s has been positive and characterised by honest attempts to confront the Service's own contribution to discrimination and unfairness. For example, from the time that Walker and Beaumont (1981) focused on the issue of oppression of Black women and men, the Service and the National Association of Probation Officers (NAPO) encouraged and supported a range of initiatives aimed at improving the quality of provision to those people. Nevertheless, it is also a patchy and inconsistent history; a thematic inspection in 2000 acknowledged the fact that some Probation Services had been in the vanguard of anti-racism policy development, but highlighted the low priority given to race equality in other Services (HMIP 2000). Moreover, even as late as 2002, Powis and Walmsley, in their survey of probation policy and practice, found little research data on criminogenic factors, no evidence based programmes, ambivalence about special provision, and inconsistency over ethnic definitions.

This chapter traces the history of the Service's response to the needs of minority ethnic groups and its engagement with the issue of race. With necessary caution, it attempts to explain how and why policy and practice have taken the direction they have. While doing so, it acknowledges that the meaning of terms such as 'race', 'ethnicity' and 'Black' has been highly contested in a number of political and organisational arenas, and that in probation there has been inconsistent use of ethnic definitions (Powis and Walmsley 2002). Accordingly, this will be reflected in a historical summary that takes account of Denney's view that probation's approach to anti-racism has been affected as much as national politics by 'deficient cultural assumptions', and Jeffers' (1995) classification of two characteristic probation approaches. These are 'minimal managerial anti-racism and equal opportunities strategies' (recruitment of Black staff, equality of treatment and ethnic monitoring), on the one hand, the 'more politicised anti-racist project' (empowerment, liberation and Black empowerment groups) on the other. Throughout, it attempts to provide a critical examination of both research findings and the main policy and practice initiatives while keeping an eye on general trends in the treatment of these groups in the criminal justice system. It is a story from the perspective of a white historian to be read in conjunction with others, and it begins with a short account of the early historical context.

Historical context

The roots of probation are entangled with the symbolism of colonisation and imperialism. Probation officers' forebears were missionaries spreading the civilising doctrine of Christianity to the poor in this country in the same ways as their counterparts were doing in the colonies. Indeed, the Howard Association (a significant influence in the emergence of probation) equated the Church's fight against crime with missionary work (Howard Association 1878), and the early work of the missionaries was described as a 'crusade' with all that word's connotations of imperialism and racial superiority (Church of England Temperance Chronicle 1873). Self-evidently, the

Howard Association, like the Police Court Mission (PCM) and some missionaries, merely reflected prevailing cultural and social attitudes: Thomas Holmes, for example, described an attack by 'a well-educated young stalwart' on the shop of a tailor who had black mannequins in his window as 'patriotism plus a dose of alcohol' (Holmes 1900: 276). These dominant attitudes did not go unchallenged, however, and Holmes, the PCM and the Association may have been exposed to the influence of an emergent Pan Africanism because one of its pioneers, Trinidadian Henry Sylvester Williams, gave lectures to the Church of England Temperance Society (Fryer 1984). (It perhaps goes without saying, though, that the first Pan African conference held in Westminster Hall in 1900 attracted little attention from the press except for W. T. Stead, who, as Fryer (1984: 286) points out, was 'one of the few journalists of the day who could rise above the prevailing jingoism and imperial arrogance'.)

Early probation officers who put pen to paper manifested the same imperialist assumptions. One, in an address on the nature of the child, argued that to be successful the probation officer must 'see as the natives see, hear as they hear, think as they think', and, indeed, he must be all the time 'thinking black' (Taylor 1921: 15).[1] The colonial construct underlying such thinking was flavoured also by the trend towards eugenic analysis that influenced thinking about crime at that time (Vanstone 2004), and was most starkly illustrated when 12 years later a paper on the biological aspects of crime by a previous General Secretary of the Eugenics Society was published in Probation, declaring that 'we are increasingly to realise that a great deal of law-breaking rests ultimately on the inborn make-up of the individual concerned' (Hodson 1932: 151). Now there is nothing remarkable about such beliefs: they permeate much of the writing of probation officers and psychologists involved in probation thinking during this period. Their significance flows from the fact that they emanate from a person who in the 1930s supported National Socialists in Germany, and promulgated the view that alien races, while being all right if they kept themselves to themselves, must be prevented from 'poison[ing] good German blood' (http://www.africa2000.com).[2] None of this, however, fatally undermines the humanitarian tradition of probation history; rather, it serves to underline the point that the humanitarianism of probation developed within a social, political and cultural context, and that awareness and understanding of the significance of race and ethnicity in probation work did so too. So even much later, for example, just as the attempts to counter racism in the 1960s and the 1976 Race Relations Act paid little heed to the empowerment of Black people, neither did the dominant therapeutic probation intervention of that period.[3]

The criminal justice context

Despite racial unrest in places as diverse as Cadoxton, Cardiff, Liverpool and London (Fryer 1984), it was not until the last quarter of the twentieth century that concern about the possibility that minority ethnic groups, if not being overtly discriminated against, were being disadvantaged at each stage of the criminal justice process become apparent (Phillips and Brown 1998). Thus, in the 1970s for example, the radical Case Con had a special issue on race (Case Con 1977);[4] McCulloch *et al.* (1974) explored the nature and distribution of crime between Asians and non-Asians, and discovered a 'remarkably low crime rate for Asians' (1974: 16); and Smith *et al.* (1975a; 1975b) compared what they termed coloured, half-coloured and white boys going through classifying school, and found that 'delinquency [was] neither qualitatively nor quantitatively a serious problem among the coloured juveniles' (1975a: 121). Although a few years later, McConville and Baldwin could assert confidently, that 'no empirical research has ever been conducted in this country into the relationship between the race of an offender and the severity of the sentence received' (1982: 652), these examples describe not only the elucidation of race as a factor in the implementation of criminal justice but also the initial stages of a deconstruction of commonly held beliefs. Moreover, they provide some of the first indicators of a concern that would culminate a few decades later in the first political move (through the auspices of Section 95 of the 1991 Criminal Justice Act) to ensure the annual publication of evidence or otherwise of the performance of those agencies involved in the system in combating discrimination, and the unequivocal statement in the foreword to a recent report, *Race and the Criminal Justice System*:

> A modern, fair, effective criminal justice system is not possible whilst significant sections of the population perceive it as dis-criminatory and lack confidence in it delivering justice. (Home Office 2002: 1)

This rhetorical position is largely the result of analysis of (and argument about) the issue of discrimination against Black women and men in the process of implementing criminal justice by a number of researchers and commentators (for example, Agozino 1997; Chesney-Lind 1997; Chigwada-Bailey 1997; Crowe 1987; Fitzgerald 1993; Home Office 1998; Mair 1986; Phillips and Brown 1998; Shallice and Gordon 1990; Willis 1983). We know from those studies and other research that men and women from minority ethnic groups are disproportionately represented in the prison population (Home Office 1994, 2002), and that they face different experiences in their contact with criminal justice agencies. Kalunta-Crumpton (1999), for instance, in her seven-month field study of 104 drug offence cases involving Black and white defendants, concludes that white and Black defendants did not have their cases viewed in the same way and that the presentation of Black defendants' cases was permeated by stereotypical and racially imbued knowledge and ideology. Waters (1988) in his report on the scrutiny of Social Inquiry Reports (SIRs) identified three perspectives operating: first, culture conflict; second, racial marginality (race not central in decision making); and third, 'alien' offender (race prominent in the decision making process).

Despite these findings, we do know that providing incontrovertible evidence of overt racism is problematical. For example, as Smith has pointed out, generalised notions of racism cannot explain the high rate of imprisonment of Afro-Caribbean offenders (1997: 726–8); indeed, others (Phillips and Bowling 2003) have predicted that empirical proof of discrimination will continue to be elusive. Certainly, the varied and sometimes contradictory conclusions of research studies support these views. On the one hand, evidence is weighted against the existence of bias in the process of administering justice (Crowe and Cove 1984; McConville and Baldwin 1982; Moxon 1988), and on the other hand, it is weighted towards bias, albeit at various points in the process (Brown and Hullin 1992; Hood 1992; Walker 1988). A more recent study suggests that there has been some improvement in as far as the level of perceived racial bias by Black and Asian defendants in magistrates' court and Crown Court has diminished (Hood et al. 2003). Yet even that study expresses concern about the fact that one in five Black defendants and one in eight Asian defendants still believe that they have been discriminated against in court.

So how can current understandings best be summarised? The 2000 British Crime Survey (BCS) shows that people from minority ethnic groups view aspects of the administration of the efficacy of the criminal justice system (such as bringing offenders to justice) more favourably than do white people, but they are less confident about the system's (and in particular the police's) ability to treat people fairly and with respect (Mirrlees-Black 2001). This might well be because the BCS also found that people from minority ethnic groups were more likely to be stopped by the police, thus increasing their chances of being drawn into the criminal justice system; and they are less likely to view their subsequent treatment by the police as fair or respectful (Clancy and Hough 2001). Once stopped and brought into the system, minority ethnic people are exposed to different decisions that make them more vulnerable to subsequent custody. Moreover, they have less chance of being cautioned, more chance of facing a serious charge, and if convicted of a violent offence more chance of being imprisoned (Phillips and Brown 1998; Bowling and Phillips 2002). They are more worried about becoming victims of crime, and when victims are less likely to report satisfaction with the response of the police. As indicated above, there is a significant over-representation of Black men and women in the prison population, estimated as about nine times as high as that for white males, and about 15 times as high for Black as for white females, and only some of this is explained by the imprisonment of foreign nationals (Home Office 2002). Black people experience disadvantage in relation to employment, money and education – all of which can be described as criminogenic problems which place them at higher risk of involvement in crime (Home Office 2000a). While not regarding it as proven that this situation is caused by discrimination, the Home Office itself has emphasised the implausibility of any assumption that discrimination does not offer at least a partial explanation (Home Office 2002).

There has been some political response to these new understandings: first, the Race Relations (Amendment) Act 2001, under which most criminal justice agencies come within the ambit of legislation that legally proscribes race discrimination; second, the formal scrutiny of possible discrimination within the Crown Prosecution Service and the Department of Constitutional Affairs; third, the attempts to enhance good practice in the National Probation Service and the Youth Justice Board; and finally, a new unit within the Home Office to expand understanding of the nature of disproportionate representation of minority ethnic groups in the criminal justice system, and improve practice and data collection and dissemination (Home Office 2002). These demonstrate that issues of racism and discrimination in criminal justice are recognised as important, and go beyond what Jeffers (1995) terms minimum managerialist anti-racism policies, but perhaps not as far as direct empowerment of minority ethnic people.

The probation context

Probation currently operates, therefore, within the context of much greater understanding and awareness of the impact of criminal justice processes on ethnicity, but it has not always been so; in fact, as argued above, the growth of such understanding and awareness in the Probation Service has been relatively recent. One of the earliest efforts to highlight the implications of race for casework has not aged well (Walcott 1968), and it can be judged to have been a less than useful exemplar for engagement with the issue. With the benefit of hindsight, its approach can be seen to be an individualised one in which the 'poorer and less educated West Indian' is perceived as having problems with authority and marital problems that need a 'fatherly' response. It is very much a question of how the probation officer can react to the particular problems presented by the individual, rather than deal with the problems encountered by a Black person in a racist society. Placed in its historical context, however, it at least represents an honest and constructive attempt to address the issue of difference without the benefit of knowledge subsequently to emerge from research. It was written eight years before what Denney identifies as possibly the first study (undertaken in Merseyside in 1976) revealing fewer non-custodial recommendations for Black offenders in social enquiry reports, and before Voakes and Fowler (1989) had revealed a higher number of reports on Black offenders with no recommendations (and the heightened risk of custody that followed). What Walcott's piece failed to do, though, was accelerate progress in anti-discriminatory practice. Carrington and Denney's 1981 study of the attitudes of probation officers to Rastafarians, Whitehouse's 1983 study of social enquiry reports and Tipler's (1989) study of juvenile justice in Hackney (revealing as they did the classification of Rastafarians as a problem group, the articulation of racism as the psychological problem of the victim, and at best inadvertent bias and a colour blind approach) are evidence of this failure.

Notwithstanding these findings, piecemeal progress did take place. For example, Hardiker and Curnock, in their description of the assessment process used with the Doshi family, stated that the probation officer involved had viewed the subject of the report in her family and social context and had 'identified needs in her persistent pursuit of understanding' (1984: 43). Walker and Beaumont (1981), in their socialist critique of the criminal justice system, raised awareness of oppression of Black women and men; the West Midlands Probation Service supported the Handsworth Alternative Scheme, a probation

9

linked project that specifically liaised with training and employment projects run by Black people (Denney 1992); and in response to the unrest in the St. Pauls area of Bristol, the local team engaged in detached work in the community and created a presence on the streets (Lawson 1984). (In fact, the latter is an example of practice a little nearer the empowerment model advocated by Jeffers and de Gale.) In addition, training began to be used to draw racism into 'the centre of the professional map' (Clare and Crawley 1987); and by the beginning of the 1990s (aided, perhaps, by research such as Chigwada's small study of imprisoned Black women (1989: 104) which argued that 'social work practice and social enquiry reports are deeply influenced by the values of the dominant culture') NAPO began to recognise their needs in particular (NAPO 1990), and acknowledge that 'racism is [...] deeply and subtly entrenched in the "world view" of white staff within the probation service' (NAPO 1991: 1).

Developments in policy and understanding

As Calverley *et al.* (2004) have asserted, the development of probation policy has been uneven, inconsistent and, despite Home Office Circulars 113/1977 and 75/88,[5] slow and diverse (Holdaway and Allaker 1990). The first of those circulars recognised the growing importance of work with minority ethnic groups and headlined it as 'an urgent priority'; but it was undermined by the failure to recognise Rastafarianism as a religious denomination and, as Denney (1992: 141) explains, was underpinned by 'a pre-occupation with the "immigrant" [as] deprived and lacking when measured against an imaginary white standard of normality'. The second issued a statement of intent, and set out to help Services implement policy; moreover, it proposed a permanent system of ethnic monitoring (eventually put in place in 1992). Their effect appears to have been minimal. In 1987 Dholakia asserted that the Probation Service was predominantly white and that recruitment of minority ethnic staff was 'dismal' (a mere two per cent of 6,784 members of NAPO being Black), and as late as 1999, although probation had been the second criminal justice agency to introduce monitoring in 1992, data quality deficiencies meant no information on people supervised by probation could be included in the Statistics on the Criminal Justice System S95 publication (Home Office 1999)[7] – a problem confirmed by the thematic inspection referred to previously (HMIP 2000).

During the 1990s, equal opportunities and the goal of treating all people fairly and with respect went up and down the priority ladder in National Standards (Home Office 1992, 1995, 2000b), and although equal opportunities policy was given space in the Three Year Plans covering the period 1993 to 1995, it was missing for those covering the period 1996 to 2000. Although the 1988 circular linked the issue to the Statement of National Objectives and Priorities (SNOP), it had not actually featured as an issue in SNOP (Home Office 1984). Nor did it figure as a priority issue in the various directional and discussion papers of the late 1980s and early 1990s (Home Office 1990a, 1990b, 1990c), including the plans to restructure committees. This was despite the fact that in 1987 NAPO had drawn attention to the significance of the role of committees in the recruitment of Black staff and other commentators had commented on the slow pace of change (Mantle 1990); all of which needs to be seen in the light of Nellis' (1995) argument that the managerialism with which it came imposed definite limits on the degree to which implementation of such policy could be sustained. As Robinson (2001) asserts, managerialism has been a consistent feature of the governance of the Probation Service, and it is reasonable to speculate therefore that within a managerialist organisation, the agenda of the powerful dominates and it is difficult to sustain a robust value base. In fact, a genuine commitment to anti-racism and anti-oppression can only come from cultural values that recognise oppression as the problem of dominant elites, and although progress in the direction of race equality in the criminal justice system can be discerned in the post-Macpherson period, the process remains piecemeal and is characterised by a faltering assimilation of such values by both government and Service. While progress has been made in recruitment and retention of minority ethnic staff (Flynn 1995), as Hylton (1995: 238) attests, wider progress 'has been pursued so slowly and reluctantly that its relevance to ensuring that justice is done *and seen to be done* [italics in the original] is also effectively delayed'.

The same kind of analysis can be applied to NAPO's contribution. As it acknowledges, its involvement began in the 1970s with 'some pious statements at the AGM's [*sic*]', expressions of opposition to 'racialism', urging of members to report 'breaches of the Race Relations Act' and condemnation of the National Front (NAPO 1989: 3). As early as 1980 a call was issued for probation officers to fight racism, and for NAPO to fight the cause of those imprisoned under the 1971 Immigration Act (Wyatt 1980). This was followed by what it describes as a 'flurry of activity' in the early 1980s, which included a

Social Policy Committee Report, calls to recruit minority ethnic staff, a forum on racial issues, the setting up of an Equal Opportunities Working Party, and involvement in the creation of the Race Concern organisation in conjunction with, among others, the Commission for Racial Equality (CRE), the National Council for Civil Liberties (NCCL) and the Joint Campaign for the Welfare of Immigrants (NAPO 1989: 3). In 1982 the Association of Black Probation Officers (ABPO) was founded and a few years later Asian officers formed their own group. Both began to make their presence felt. As de Gale (1992) has explained, ABPO determined to influence the nature of the services delivered and support Black staff and students. In 1985, challenged by ABPO, a National Executive Committee working party produced a self-critical report; in 1988 a report from an Assistant General Secretary exposed overt racism by white officers against Black officers; in 1987 the Probation Practice Committee produced its 'Manifesto for Action: Developing an Anti-racist Probation Practice'; the Probation Training Committee produced its report on the 'Training, Recruitment, Selection and Employment of Black Staff'; and the Association set up a conference to examine race, class and gender. All this activity culminated in the publication of a definitive policy statement covering its trade union activities, its role in the criminal justice system and social policy, probation practice, training, the workplace, conditions of service, and its functions as an employer. It recommended positive action in relation to recruitment, induction into the life of the union, representation on committees, the establishment of a Black section, and monitoring of elections (NAPO 1989). NAPO's work did not stop with this policy statement, but it did set the tone for its action during the remainder of the century and did ensure that the issue remained to the fore of union activity. The development of a value base at the end of the 1980s that included a commitment to anti-racist and anti-oppressive practice was partly the result of Marxism and the 'anti-humanist critique, as reformulated by CCETSW, NISW and NAPO' (Nellis 1995: 26). However, as Nellis has pointed out, the managerialism that put constraints on 'ethical debates and action' can be discerned in NAPO's monitoring (or 'surveillance of speech') at conferences and branches in as much as it created a 'culture of fear and obedience' (1995: 30) – an activity that has not necessarily had anything to do with 'the democratic advancement of women or ethnic minorities' (1995: 30).

Predictably, policy development from within the Service came primarily from areas with high minority ethnic populations. For example, following the Lozells and Handsworth disturbances of

1985, the West Midlands Probation Service set up a working party to 'consider what sort of response the Probation Service should make to what had happened' and find 'a new "normality" ... qualitatively different from the old' (WMPS 1986: 1). While proclaiming some progress, such as a 'more emphatic and continuing focus on racism' replacing the earlier concern with 'cultural familiarisation' (1986: 6), it owned up to unequal power relationships and ineffectiveness in empowerment through traditional probation practice; and among other things, it recommended higher visibility in public relations on the issue (and related matters), support for Black self-help groups, two-year team plans in areas with a high ethnic minority population, a Black perspective in practice, monitoring of, for example, social enquiry reports, increased recruitment of Black and Asian staff, the inclusion of a race awareness component in pre-qualifying training, and mandatory anti-racism training for all staff. Four years earlier, in co-operation with the CRE, it had published the clearest, most self-critical (and one of the earliest) attempts to review and make sense of the Probation Service's position in relation to minority ethnic clients. This included a complete survey of staff views, and its recommendations included the further development of projects, a review of resource allocation, improvements in training, increased recruitment, local registers of interpreters, recruitment of Black volunteers, reappraisal of social work methods and an ethnic consultancy agency (CRE 1981).

The Home Office, NAPO and the Service itself had less excuse for inconsistency during the 1990s as a clearer picture of both the gaps in research and the perspectives of minority ethnic service users began to emerge. In a project designed to examine ways in which the Inner London Probation Service (ILPS) might improve its work with Black offenders, Lawrence *et al.* (1992) interviewed a sample of Black offenders, Black and white workers, and staff from interested agencies, and scrutinised 59 social enquiry reports. They discerned that most clients wanted special provision that created opportunities to 'share their views and life difficulties with other black offenders', stimulated moves towards their resolution, and provided 'a means of combating their sense of social isolation within the criminal justice system' (1992: 9). In addition, the researchers concluded that popular perception of this client group was 'wide of the mark'. Indeed, the survey showed that in many respects, both with regard to the social characteristics of the Black client group seen by ILPS and patterns of offending, 'Black clients do not differ appreciably from white clients' (1992: 7).

Jeffers (1995) interviewed 44 offenders (28 Black and ethnic and 16 white men and women) and observed contact between officers and offenders. Again, he highlights the complexity of the picture:

The idea that there is a specific or distinctive Black experience of probation relies to some extent on the proposition that there is a Black or minority ethnic identity which they share and which conditions their experience of racial or ethnic discrimination. (1995: 7)

Jeffers confirms that Black and white offenders share common themes such as the desire for respect, trust and credibility and practical assistance, but exposes a difference around dealing with racial issues. Tellingly, he observes that Black offenders' perception of probation 'may be as much to do with its symbolic location, relative to the criminal justice system as a whole and the degree to which this wider system is seen as racially discriminating' (1995: 33).

Sheikh et al. (1997), in a small exploratory study of young Asian sex offenders, conclude that there is 'virtually no previous research undertaken with regard to the specific issues of sexual offending related to Asian sex offenders' (1997: 33). Moreover, Webster et al. (2004), in their examination of the impact of the Prison Service Sex Offender Treatment Programme (SOTP) on minority ethnic offenders, raise concerns about the fact that SOTP is not equally accessible to minority ethnic offenders.[8] Among those who did gain access, the treatment effects were broadly similar to white offenders. Before treatment, 'higher levels of denial of premeditation, offence, and responsibility, and greater overall minimisation of their offence' (2004: 14) were evidenced among Black offenders, but after treatment, they were the same. The researchers recognised that cultural factors might well explain this difference, levels of shame, for example, being much higher in some minority ethnic cultures.

In a more recent study Clancy and Hough (2001) found that the difference in the views of Black and white offenders on the functioning of the criminal justice system is small but that Black people's satisfaction with probation is higher than whites. In contrast, Ahmed et al. (1998) found that young Bengali men in Tower Hamlets had low expectations of the Probation Service, and recommended that the Service focused on issues of identity and personal development, employment, family work and the perceptions of probation officers themselves.

Developments in practice

Despite evidence of early individualistic and enterprising attempts to respond to diversity – for example, in the early 1980s Martin Austwick in Leeds set up an informal reporting session for Black probationers to promote among other things discussion of the National Front and prejudice (Pinder 1982) – positive development in practice has been relatively late. In their survey, Holdaway and Allaker (1990) found that only ten probation areas had a strategic approach to supervision. Furthermore, a recent inspection of the Probation Service expressed concerns about quality of supervision, and exposed some pre-sentence reports (albeit a minority) as confirming stereotypical racial beliefs (HMIP 2000). Nevertheless, there have been some good examples of attempts to refine practice so that it caters for the needs of minority ethnic offenders, and training has played a significant part in this. Initially race awareness training, it shifted to a more action based approach as anti-racist training; moreover, as mentioned earlier, attempts were made to position anti-racism at the heart of good practice. In this sense, trainers had the dilemma of how to take responsibility for the provision of training in a crucial area while not taking the responsibility for anti-racism itself. This is exactly the point Clare and Crawley (1987) make – that the existence of training courses in any Service's curriculum might be mere tokenism.

So, a number of people recognised that inculcating or reinforcing the values of anti-racism and anti-oppression needed to begin in qualifying training and not be left to post qualification. For example, in Merseyside, Collett *et al.* (1990) contended that improvement in knowledge and skill in anti-racism was essential if there was to be any significant impact on the culture of an agency, but added that selection and training were fundamental areas for change. Three years later, de Gale (at one time information officer for ABPO) and colleagues produced a training manual for the Northern Curriculum Development Project on how to improve practice (de Gale *et al.* 1993). As well as being practical aids to practitioners and managers alike, initiatives like these provided powerful reminders to the Service that it needed to be continuously reflective and self-critical as well as proactive, and that anti-racism went to the heart of what it means to be effective – a point reinforced by Kemshall's (1994) assertion that a competency approach should be applied to anti-discriminatory practice teaching.

It is impossible in a short chapter of this kind to do full justice to the efforts of both Black and white probation staff in furthering good practice in work with minority ethnic clients, nor is it intended to cover recent progress in work with racially motivated offenders, which is focused on in the next chapter: instead, some examples will be examined in order to illustrate the general trend. Awareness of the unmet needs of Black probationers stimulated a project set up by the North Thames Resource Unit (Jenkins and Lawrence 1993). The research referred to earlier into the needs and experiences of Black probation clients on which it was based (Lawrence *et al.* 1992) identified the need for the testing out of a provision exclusive to Black probationers. The programme was designed and formulated by the unit with the help of Black probation staff and training for approximately 30 Black officers followed. The goal of fulfilling the aims of the eight-week programme was pursued through a written, structured programme pack designed to empower Black clients and create the opportunity for them to explore their experiences, and examine their offending. Not only is this an interesting example of work involving an evaluative structure and agency–college co-operation, but it also shows the Probation Service responding in a considered way to the needs of a disadvantaged group.

Similar, equally innovative work was undertaken in the West Midlands' Black people and offending groups. In Merseyside Probation Service, Kett *et al.* (1992) drew from that Service's anti-racism policy to produce a resource pack for both managers and practitioners, and Wade and Macpherson (1992) reported on attempts to address race issues in the groupwork at Sherbourne House in Inner London through challenging racist clients and holding 'Being Black' sessions run by Black workers for Black probationers. As a result of concern about the 'absence and isolation' of Black offenders in offending behaviour groups and a lack of a Black perspective, Johnson *et al.* (1996) set up a group that provided Black offenders with 'an arena to examine their offending in its past and present context' (1996: 4), and in its evaluation concluded that 'a specific resource aimed at the needs of Black offenders is not only achievable but can be successful' (1996: 11). Finally in this catalogue of examples, following the Manningham disturbances in Bradford in 1995 the UMMID project was set up specifically to further good practice with Asian offenders (Butt 2001). Its primary objective was to supervise offenders in the local community on behalf of the West Yorkshire Probation Service, and the work involved supervision, dissemination of information, developing partnerships, giving advice pre-court, and crime prevention involving street counselling, drama work and anti-bullying interventions.

The role of ethnic minority staff

Significant as these initiatives are, there is a sense in which they fit a traditional pattern of probation practice development. Innovative work has often been the result of the energy, commitment and enthusiasm of a few staff or a charismatic figure, only to drop out of sight when the believers moved on (Hudson 1988). This phenomenon applies equally to the Service's policy and practice on race. The point is well made by Hylton when he asserts that 'exclusively white institutions in a multi-racial society are less likely to provide an anti-discriminatory service to the black community' (Hylton 1995: 241). In Chapter 3, Rod Morgan chronicles the progress the Service has made in the recruitment of minority ethnic staff, and while acknowledging that management grades remain overwhelmingly white, points to the fact that the proportion of minority ethnic staff is higher than the general population. In point of fact, the critical thematic inspection (HMIP 2000) accedes to this aspect of Service performance. It is doubtful whether without the voice of those members of staff the Service would have made the same amount of progress in tackling discrimination within the criminal justice system and within its own ranks (Hylton 1995).

In fact, in taking the issues forward, minority ethnic members of staff have had to draw attention to their own experience of discrimination and unfair treatment. At the end of the 1980s the West Midlands Probation Service invited David Divine to investigate the experiences of Black probation officers in the process of confirmation, and he recommended, among other things, moving away from reliance on the subjective assessments of senior probation officers, allowing Black staff the opportunity to meet, the introduction of practice supervisors in the confirmation year, clarification of role expectations, and reaching agreement over the meaning of the term 'Black' (Divine 1989).

While the fact that the West Midlands Service invited this critical scrutiny and the subsequent report pointed a way forward in itself suggests progress, some Black staff had perceived aspects of their experience as being unfair. Even five years later Raynor *et al.* (1994: 67), in their study of confirmation procedures in England and Wales, found that 'over one quarter of all black officers surveyed reported that they had experienced racial discrimination'. Moreover, in 1992 'The Black Students' Voice' conference was organised by among other organisations ABPO, 'in response to the misery and confusion experienced by black social work students, both in academic institutions and practice placements' (Burgess *et al.* 1992: 4). The existence of ABPO and the National Association of Asian Probation Staff (NAAPS), therefore, has been crucial, and as Hylton (1995: 247) argues, perhaps more than anything else has stimulated an increase in minority ethnic staff, enhanced their participation in management and practice, and furthered the confidence of the Probation Service in 'recognising the need to tackle racism in the Criminal Justice System'.

Conclusion

Although the points about innovative work and the role of Black staff generalise a much more complex picture, it remains an uncomfortable fact that at the end of the twentieth century Powis and Walmsley (2002) attributed the same pattern to work with minority ethnic offenders. The sound of their voice, however, may be less likely to be heard above the noisy wind of change that has swept over the Service in recent years. Interestingly, one of the criticisms of What Works has been its limitations in terms of sensitivity to diversity, and Durrance and Williams (2003) have argued that the principles and much of the methodology of evidence based practice may not necessarily apply to minority ethnic groups, and that an empowerment approach is what is required. Empowerment might help increase the volume of minority ethnic voices, but that said, the Service should not allow the lack of obvious attention to the issue by What Works people to result in over-hasty rejection of evidence based approaches. Effectively helping minority ethnic people with whom the Probation Service is involved to lead non-offending lives must remain the over-arching purpose of that involvement.

In summation, then, it has to be admitted that the history of the Probation Service on anti-racism is not a glorious one, but it is at least characterised by a propensity for self-scrutiny not always so evident in other government agencies and the private sector. That self-scrutiny has been confined largely to the last quarter of the twentieth century, and it has been directly influenced by the presence of minority ethnic staff: during the period when their numbers were low policy and practice initiatives reflected a dominant white perspective, and only when those numbers increased did the voice of Black and Asian staff begin to be heard. That change came primarily from the formation of representative bodies and the emergence of Black and Asian commentators from within and without the Service. Together, these intensified the focus on issues relevant to Black and Asian people, but despite their contribution inconsistency has remained the most pertinent characterisation of the Probation Service's performance. It might even be argued that the preoccupation of both the government and the Service with evidence based practice, appropriate as it has been, has deflected both managers and practitioners away from consideration of race and ethnicity and stalled a momentum that had built up in the early 1990s; and this has occurred at a time of growing authoritarianism within criminal justice policy. The Service begins the twenty-first century, therefore, with the need to place anti-racism at the heart of policy and practice as pressing as ever.

Notes

1 It is important to remember that this paper was written at a time when a report in *The Times* reporting on the Cardiff Race Riots could refer in a matter-of-fact way to the dockland area of Cardiff as 'nigger town' (*The Times* 1919).
2 This site is now inaccessible, but was originally part of the Eugenics Watch site.
3 This is most commonly referred to as casework, although sometimes it is subsumed under broader descriptions such as the treatment and medical model.
4 A publication (and loose organisation) established in 1970 at the time of the Seebohm reorganisation of social services and in opposition to the Tory government.
5 Probation Service Policies on Race.
6 It resulted from the appointment of a race relations adviser and two seminars involving senior management representatives from five Services plus two regional staff development unit representatives.
7 The inability of the Home Office (2002) to include any ethnic data on those supervised by probation in its presentation of statistics on race and the criminal justice system hindered the planning of recent research on Black and Asian probationers (Calverley *et al.* 2004).
8 An aspect of the treatment programme previously highlighted by Beech *et al.* (1999) in their evaluation.

References

Agozino, B. (1997) *Black Women and the Criminal Justice System*. Aldershot: Ashgate.

Ahmed, S. H., Webster, R. and Cheston, L. (1998) 'Bengali Young Men on Supervision in Tower Hamlets', *Probation Journal*, 45: 2, 78–81.

Beech, A., Fisher, D. and Beckett, R. (1999) *STEP 3: An Evaluation of the Prison Sex Offender Treatment Programme.* London: Home Office.

Bowling, B. and Phillips, C. (2002) *Racism, Crime and Justice.* London: Longman.

Brown, I. and Hullin, R. (1992) 'A Study of Sentencing in the Leeds Magistrates Courts', *British Journal of Criminology*, 32: 1, 41–53.

Burgess, R. M., Crosskill, D. and LaRose-Jones, L. (1992) *'The Black Students' Voice': Report of the Black Students' Conference 1992.* Inner London Probation Service.

Butt, T. (2001) *UMMID PROJECT (1995–2001).* Wakefield: West Yorkshire Probation Service.

Calverley, A., Cole, B., Kaur, G., Lewis, S., Raynor, P., Sadeghi, S., Smith, D., Vanstone, M. and Wardak, A. (2004) *Black and Asian Offenders on Probation*, Home Office Research Study 277. London: Home Office.

Carrington, B. and Denney, D. (1981) 'Young Rastafarians and the Probation Service', *Probation Journal*, 28: 4, 111–7.

Case Con (1970) *Special on Racism.* Winter, Issue 24.

Chesney-Lind, M. (1997) *The Female Offender: Girls, Women and Crime.* London: Sage.

Chigwada, R. (1989) 'The Criminalisation and Imprisonment of Black Women', *Probation Journal*, 36: 3, 100–5.

Chigwada-Bailey, R. (1997) *Black Women's Experiences of the Criminal Justice System.* Winchester: Waterside Press.

Church of England Temperance Chronicle (1873) Canon Ellison's Sermon at St Pauls, 1st May.

Clancy, A. and Hough, M. (2001) *Crime, Policing and Justice: The Experience of Ethnic Minorities. Findings of the 2000 British Crime Survey.* Home Office Research Study 223. London: Home Office.

Clare, R. and Crawley, C. (1987) 'Anti-Racist Training: Staying with the Task', *Probation Journal*, 34: 3, 85–7.

Collett, S., Evans, M. and Simpson, P. (1990) 'Practice Teaching: Developing and Anti-Racist Perspective', *Probation Journal*, 37: 3, 112–18.

CRE (1981) *Probation and After-Care in a Multi-Racial Society.* London: Commission for Racial Equality and West Midlands Probation and After-Care Service.

Crowe, I. (1987) 'Black People and the Criminal Justice System in the UK', *Howard Journal*, 26: 4, 303–14.

Crowe, I. and Cove, J. (1984) 'Ethnic Minorities and the Courts', *Criminal Law Review*, 413–17.

de Gale, H. (1992) 'Political Justice', *Social Work Today*, 3rd September, 17–18.

de Gale, H., Hanlon, P., Hubbard, M., Morgan, S. and Denney, D. (1993) *Improving Practice in the Criminal Justice System: A Training Manual*, (Northern Curriculum Development Project. Leeds: CCETSW.

Denney, D. (1992) *Racism and Anti-racism in Probation*. London: Routledge.

Dholakia, N. (1987) 'Black People and the Criminal Justice System', in *Access to Justice: Race, Class and Gender. Proceedings of a Professional Conference held between July 1st and 3rd 1987 at the University of York*. London: National Association of Probation Officers.

Divine, D. (1989) *Unpublished Report on the Experiences of First Year Probation Officers during their Confirmation Year in the West Midlands Probation Service*. Commissioned by the West Midlands Probation Service.

Durrance, P. and Williams, P. (2003) 'Broadening the Agenda Around What Works for Black and Asian Offenders', *Probation Journal*, 50: 3, 211–24.

Fitzgerald, M. (1993) *Ethnic Minorities in the Criminal Justice System*, Home Office Research Study 20, Royal Commission on Criminal Justice. London: Home Office.

Flynn, N. (1995) 'Equality in the Probation Service', in D. Ward and M. Lacey (eds) *Probation: Working for Justice*. London: Whiting and Birch.

Fryer, P. (1984) *Staying Power: The History of Black People in Britain*. London: Pluto Press.

Hardiker, P. and Curnock, K. (1984) 'Social Work Assessment Processes in Work with Ethnic Minorities – The Doshi Family', *British Journal of Social Work*, 14, 23–47.

HMIP (Her Majesty's Inspectorate of Probation) (2000) *Towards Race Equality: A Thematic Inspection*. London: HMIP.

Hodson, C. B. S. (1932) 'Biological Aspects of Crime', *Probation*, 10, 151–2.

Holdaway, S. and Allaker, J. (1990) *Race Issues in the Probation Service: A Review of Policy*. Wakefield: Association of Chief Officers of Probation.

Holmes, T. (1900) *Pictures and Problems from London Police Courts*. London: Thomas Nelson & Sons.

Home Office (1977) *Probation and After-care Service and Ethnic Minorities*, Home Office Circular 113/1977. London: Home Office.

Home Office (1984) *Probation Service in England and Wales: Statement of National Objectives and Priorities*. London: Home Office.

Home Office (1988) *Probation Service Policies on Race*, Home Office Circular 75/88. London: Home Office.

Home Office (1990a) *Crime, Justice and Protecting the Public: The Government's Proposals for Legislation*. Cm 965 White Paper. London: HMSO.

Home Office (1990b) *Supervision and Punishment in the Community: A Framework for Action*. Cm 966. London: HMSO.

Home Office (1990c) *Partnership in Dealing with Offenders in the Community: A Discussion Paper*. London: Home Office.

Home Office (1992) *National Standards for the Supervision of Offenders in the Community*. London: Home Office.

Home Office (1994) *Statistics on Race and the Criminal Justice System*. London: Home Office.

Home Office (1995) *National Standards for the Supervision of Offenders in the Community*. London: Home Office.

Home Office (1998) *Statistics on Race and the Criminal Justice System*. London: Home Office.

Home Office (1999) *Statistics on Race and the Criminal Justice System*. London: Home Office.

Home Office (2000a) *Statistics on Race and the Criminal Justice System 2000*. London: Home Office.

Home Office (2000b) *National Standards for the Supervision of Offenders in the Community*. London: Home Office.

Home Office (2002) *Statistics on Race and the Criminal Justice System 2001*. London: Home Office.

Hood, R. (1992) *Race and Sentencing*. Oxford: Clarendon Press.

Hood, R., Shute, S. and Seemungal, F. (2003) *Ethnic Minorities in the Criminal Courts: Perceptions of Fairness and Equality of Treatment*, Research Series 2/03. University of Oxford in association with the University of Birmingham School of Law.

Howard Association (1878) *Annual Report*.

Hudson, B. (1988) 'Social Skills Training in Practice', *Probation Journal*. 35: 3, 85–91.

Hylton, B. (1995) 'Black Professionals in Search of Race Equality: The Proactive Role of Black Professionals', in D. Ward and M. Lacey (eds) *Probation: Working for Justice*. London: Whiting and Birch.

Jeffers, S. (1995) *'Black' and Ethnic Minority Offenders' Experience of Probation*. Report to the School for Advanced Urban Studies, University of Bristol.

Jenkins, J. and Lawrence, D. (1993) 'Inner London's Black Groups Initiative', *Probation Journal*, 40: 2, 82–4.

Johnson, E., Lotay, S., Stephens, W. and Davies, H. (1996) *Black People and Offending Group. Pilot Programme, January–March 1996*. Birmingham: West Midlands Probation Service.

Kalunta-Crumpton, A. (1999) *Race and Drug Trials*. Aldershot: Ashgate.

Kemshall, H. (1994) 'Anti-Racist Practice Teaching', *Probation Journal*, 41: 1, 8–13.

Kett, J., Collett, S., Barron, C., Hill, I. and Metherell, D. (1992) *Managing and Developing Anti-racist Practice within Probation: A Resource Pack for Action*. Liverpool: Merseyside Probation Service.

Lawrence, D., Pearson, G. and Aina, C. (1992) *Black Offenders Project*, Report to the Inner London Probation Service and the Islington Safer Cities Project. London: Department of Community Studies, Goldsmiths' College.

Lawson, J. (1984) 'Probation in St Paul's. Teamwork in a Multi-racial, Inner City Area', *Probation Journal*, 31: 3, 93–5.

Mair, G. (1986) 'Ethnic Minorities, Police and the Magistrates Court', *British Journal of Criminology*, 46: 2, 147–55.

Mantle, G. (1990) 'Increasing Black Membership of Probation Committees: Slow Progress and Uncertain Rationale', *Probation Journal*, 37: 2, 68–71.

McConville, M. and Baldwin, J. (1982) 'The Influence of Race on Sentencing in England', *Criminal Law Review*, 652–8.

McCulloch, J. W., Smith, N. J. and Balta, I. D. (1974) 'A Comparative Study of Adult Crime amongst Asians and their Host Population', *Probation Journal*, 21: 1, 16–21.

Mirrlees-Black, C. (2001) *Confidence in the Criminal Justice System: Findings from the 2000 British Crime Survey*, Home Office Research Findings 137, London: Home Office.

Moxon, D. (1988) *Sentencing Practice in the Crown Court*. Home Office Research Study 102. London: Home Office.

NAPO (National Association of Probation Officers) (1987) *Training, Recruitment , Selection and Employment of Black Staff*, Training Committee Report. London: NAPO.

NAPO (1989) *Draft Policy Document*. London: NAPO.

NAPO (1990) *Black Women in the Criminal Justice System*, Criminal Justice Committee Discussion Paper. London: NAPO.

NAPO (1991) *Anti-Racism Training for White Staff: Post Qualification*. Policy Document. London: NAPO.

Nellis, M. (1995) 'Probation Values for the 1990s', *Howard Journal*, 34, 19–44.

Phillips, C. and Bowling, B. (2003) 'Racism, Ethnicity and Criminology: Developing Minority Perspectives', *British Journal of Criminology*, 43: 2, 269–90.

Phillips, C. and Brown, D. (1998) *Entry into the Criminal Justice System: A Study of Police Arrests and their Outcomes*, Home Office Research Study 185. London: Home Office.

Pinder, R. (1982) 'On What Grounds? Negotiating Justice with Black Clients', *Probation Journal*, 29: 1, 19–23.

Powis, B. and Walmsley, R. K. (2002) *Programmes for Black and Asian Offenders on Probation: Lessons for Developing Practice,* Home Office Research Study 250. London: Home Office.

Raynor, P., Roberts, S., Thomas, L. and Vanstone, M. (1994) *Confirmation of Probation Officers: Equitable Evaluation or Lottery?* Sheffield: Pavic Publications.

Robinson, G. (2001) 'Power, Knowledge and "What Works" in Probation', *Howard Journal*, 40: 3, 235–54.

Shallice, A. and Gordon, P. (1990) *Black People, White Justice? Race and the Criminal Justice System*. London: Runnymede Trust.

Sheikh, B. A. (1997) *Sexual Crimes and Young Asian Offenders: An Exploratory Study*. Department of Applied Social Studies, University of Bradford.

Smith, D. J. (1997) 'Ethnic Origins, Crime, and Criminal Justice', in M. Maguire, R. Morgan and R. Reiner (eds) *The Oxford Handbook of Criminology*, 2nd edn. Oxford: Clarendon Press.

Smith, N. J., Balta, I. D. and McCulloch, J. W. (1975a) 'A Comparison by Colour of Boys in a Classifying School', *Probation Journal*, 22: 3, 87–91.

Smith, N. J., Balta, I. D. and McCulloch, J. W. (1975b) 'A comparison by Colour of Boys in a Classifying School', *Probation Journal*, 22: 4, 116–21.

Taylor, H. (1921) 'The Study of the Nature of the Child', *National Association of Probation Officers*, 15, p. 298.

The Times (1919) 'Cardiff Race Riots', Saturday 14 June.

23

Tipler, J. (1989) 'Is Justice Colour Blind? Race and Juvenile Justice', *Research, Policy and Planning*, 7: 1, 18–23.

Vanstone, M. (2004) *Supervising Offenders in the Community: A History of Probation Theory and Practice*. Aldershot: Ashgate.

Voakes, R. and Fowler, Q. (1989) Sentencing and Social Enquiry Reports. West Yorkshire Probation Service.

Wade, A. and Macpherson, M. (1992) 'Addressing Race Issues in Groupwork', *Probation Journal*, 39: 3, 129–32.

Walcott, R. (1968) 'The West Indian in the British Casework Setting', *Probation Journal*, 14: 2, 45–7.

Walker, M. and Beaumont, B. (1981) *Probation Work: Critical Theory and Socialist Practice*. Oxford: Blackwell.

Walker, M. A. (1988) 'The Court Disposal of Young Males, by Race, in London in 1983', *British Journal of Criminology*, 28: 4, 441–60.

Waters, R. (1988) 'Race and Criminal Justice Process', *British Journal of Criminology*, 28: 1, 82–94.

Webster, S. D., Akhtar, S., Bowers, L. E., Mann, R. E., Rallings, M. and Marshall, W. L. (2004) 'The Impact of the Prison Service Sex Offender Treatment Programme on Ethnic Minority Offenders: A Preliminary Study', *Psychology, Crime and Law*, 10: 2, 113–24.

Whitehouse, P. (1983) 'Race, Bias and Social Enquiry Reports', *Probation Journal*, 30: 2, 43–9.

Willis, C. (1983) *The Use, Effectiveness and Impact of Police Stop and Search Powers*. Home Office Research and Planning Unit Paper 15. London: Home Office.

WMPS (West Midlands Probation Service) (1986) *After the Disturbance: NOT BACK TO NORMAL. A Report to the West Midlands Probation Service following Lozells and Handsworth Disturbances of 1985*. Birmingham: West Midlands Probation Service.

Wyatt, R. (1980) 'Immigration Law and Probation Practice', *Probation Journal*, 27: (2), 56–7.

Chapter 2

Racially motivated offenders and the Probation Service

David Smith

As was shown in Chapter 1, the Probation Service began to explore the implications of a commitment to anti-racist and anti-discriminatory practice in the last quarter of the twentieth century. What might be regarded as the corollary of work with minority ethnic people, however – work with the perpetrators of racially motivated offending – has developed slowly and unevenly. There is even evidence that some probation staff have tended to avoid contact with racist offenders. In this chapter, possible reasons for such avoidance are explored, as are the ideas of probation staff who have sought to confront rather than evade the issue. The chapter draws on research on the perpetrators of racist violence who were contacted through the Probation Service in Greater Manchester (Ray *et al.* 2002, 2003a, 2003b), and discusses recent attempts to develop resources intended to help practitioners working with this category of offenders.

On not finding racially motivated offenders in probation offices

Sibbitt (1997) discussed the Probation Service's response to racially motivated offenders in two London boroughs, which she called Elmore and Burnaston. In neither area was she able to contact a single perpetrator of racist violence or harassment through the Probation Service. This was before the introduction under the 1998 Crime and Disorder Act of the new category of 'racially aggravated' offences, the first clear case of 'hate crime' legislation in Britain (Ray and Smith 2001; Burney and Rose 2002), and therefore offences could not reach probation officers already labelled as having a racist motivation. While racist motivation could in principle be detected at the stage of writing a pre-sentence report, Sibbitt (1997: 43) found that offenders 'identified in this way ... appeared to be few and far between'. Racist motivation was more likely to emerge in the course of supervision, but 'the potential for tackling racist attitudes during supervision was rarely exploited' by probation officers in either borough. This was the case even though staff at a probation centre in Elmore recognised that offending with a racist motive was a problem locally, which led them to incorporate an element of anti-racist work into a programme for young male offenders. This involved splitting the group on ethnic lines, which appeared to cause resentment among both black and white members, the former because they felt they were 'being treated as if they were unaware of their own ethnicity', the latter because they felt labelled as racists, while black offenders were treated as 'victims of the system' (Sibbitt 1997: 43).

This initiative had developed in the absence of any local policy on racially motivated offenders. The service in Burnaston, however, was developing such a policy at the time of Sibbitt's research. This distinguished – although it did not say how officers should distinguish – between 'racially motivated offenders' (in whom the motive might be wholly or partly 'racial') and 'racist offenders', whose behaviour or attitudes were overtly racist. The document noted that offenders in both categories could pose a risk to black staff, but argued that members of racist organisations should be regarded as racially rather than politically motivated (Sibbitt 1997: 66–7). This seems to have been a reference to the policy being developed at the time by the National Association of Probation Officers (NAPO 1995), which also distinguished between the 'racially motivated' and the 'racist', and argued that while probation officers should challenge racist attitudes they should refuse to work with offenders who were members of racist organisations. Sibbitt found that in practice it was rare for probation officers to find themselves working with anyone whose offending had been identified as racially motivated, although they often worked with people whom they regarded as having the same racist views and attitudes as many members of their local communities. According to Sibbitt (1997: 68), 'the very culture of the probation service discouraged' offenders from being open and truthful about these views and attitudes: notices on the walls of offices and waiting areas made it clear 'that the use of racist language or behaviour (by anyone) was unacceptable on Probation premises and would "not be tolerated" '.

Sibbitt concluded that the result was that racist attitudes tended to remain hidden, and that this was not unwelcome to probation officers, since if an offender did use racist language or behaviour they would not know what to do about it, apart from taking action under the Service's equal opportunities policies. There were associated problems, such as what to do if an offender refused to be supervised by a minority ethnic officer; given that there was some support for the idea that a black or Asian offender might reasonably prefer a black or Asian supervisor, how could a racist offender consistently be refused the same choice? It would also be harder to sustain a view of the offender as 'needy' and disadvantaged if overt racism entered the relationship. For such reasons, 'ordinary' racism went unchallenged, while some officers 'almost demonised racist offenders as extremely violent political extremists' (Sibbitt 1997: 94), caricaturing them (without having any real contact with them) as members of far right political organisations. This anxiety about dangerous and violent racists was, Sibbitt argues, out of all proportion to the likelihood that probation officers would ever have to deal with them. To put it mildly, Sibbitt's account does not cast a very positive light on the Probation Service's work with racially motivated offenders. At the time of her research, however, some probation practitioners – as well as NAPO on their behalf – had already been considering relevant issues of practice, and this literature, and its development since Sibbitt's research, sheds light on the problems identified by practitioners who did not simply try to evade them.

Trying to make sense of practice

In the early 1990s, Wade and Macpherson (1992: 129) could already write: 'Racism within clients of the Probation Service is notoriously difficult to work with effectively and it can be stressful to deal with.' Describing their experiences in a day centre for young adults, they noted that there could be dangers in challenging implicit racism in a groupwork setting, 'where racist statements can feed and escalate further racism within the group'. As part of their programme they ran a session on prejudice, which all group members were expected to attend, and then two sessions, for black clients with black staff, on 'Being Black', and two sessions on 'Being White', run by white staff for white clients. (The timing makes it unlikely that these were the sessions viewed critically by Sibbitt in Elmore.) Wade and Macpherson report that the 'Being Black' sessions were well received, but those on 'Being White' were not. They sometimes felt they 'had opened a "Pandora's Box" of vile abuse' that they could not control (an anxiety also felt by some officers in the late 1990s (see Ray *et al.* 2002). They found it difficult to convey an understanding of racism in which all white people are powerful relative to minority ethnic people, since most of their white clients could not 'see themselves as powerful in any context'. At the centre they often felt intimidated by the greater solidarity of black clients, and at home could experience an even greater 'sense of powerlessness'. 'As a result they see themselves as victims', and become angry when presented with an account of racism that portrays them as inherently more powerful than black – and more specifically than Asian – people (Wade and Macpherson 1992: 130). Wade and Macpherson explain how they developed a way of working that was less directly confrontational and accusatory and therefore less liable to provoke defiance and resistance. Their perceptive analysis of the ways in which whites 'invert' racism by claiming that they, not minority ethnic people, are in fact the victims of oppression and disadvantage has been echoed by subsequent commentators (Webster 1997; Ray *et al.* 2003a, 2004), and it is likely that any effective work with racist offenders will need to be based on a recognition that racism often emerges from feelings not of power and superiority, as in the standard accounts of racist ideologies, but from a sense of weakness and subordination (see Chapter 11 for further discussion of this issue).

Some of the problems for probation practice identified by Sibbitt appear in the brief account by Khan (1991) of taking breach action against a client who refused to co-operate with a probation order on the grounds that no Asian should be a probation officer. Khan suggests that this case may have been the first of its kind, but the experience described is exactly what led NAPO to its position that minority ethnic staff needed to be protected from abuse and hostility on the part of overtly racist white offenders. Racism as overt as that reported by Khan is, however, rare compared with the 'covert' or only intermittently expressed racism that is covered by the 'racially motivated' category that Sibbitt found was used in Burnaston. Gill and Marshall (1993) recognise this, and discuss reasons why 'covert' racism in clients often remains unchallenged by probation officers, and indeed unacknowledged at any stage in the criminal justice process. They argue (1993: 56) that some 'white officers are debilitated by their own feelings and angst concerning their ability to deal with racism', while others, in the absence of resources and organisational support, are liable to collude with clients' racism. Since racist motivation is rarely the sole impulse behind an offence (an insight in line with the later findings of Ray *et al.* (2002, 2003a, 2003b) and of Burney and Rose (2002), it is tempting for officers to avoid the potential difficulties and deny or ignore the racist element in the offending. According to Gill and Marshall (1993: 56), some 'workers have developed ways of working with racist offenders', but their experience has not become part of a generally available pool of knowledge. Gill and Marshall (1993: 58–9) go on to describe their own 'structured model' of intervention, which consisted of three stages: race awareness, challenging myths, and empowerment. The use of 'empowerment' is interesting in this context, because it shows that Gill and Marshall were fully aware that it would be counter-productive to leave clients 'with a set of negative feelings', such as they might experience after being exposed and denounced as racists. The intervention used exercises and questionnaires that the authors presented at the 'What Works' conference in 1992, so they did receive a wider airing (and were referenced by Gast and Kay 1998), without, apparently, entering into general use.

The writing of all these practitioners reveals an awareness of the complexities of working on racist attitudes and motivations: of the need to recognise that many racists feel themselves to be weak, not powerful, of the risk of promoting defiance, of the need to convey the unacceptability of racism without rejecting clients with racist views as also unacceptable, and of the dangers of leaving clients feeling worse about themselves than they did before the intervention. Apart from the local initiatives of practitioners, the other main source of ideas on working with racism was the probation officers' trades union and professional association, NAPO. It is clear from Gill and Marshall (1993) that the question of whether probation officers should be working with racist offenders at all was at that time a matter of debate. Gill and Marshall treat the answer as something to be decided by individual conscience, but note that probation officers routinely work with other offenders whose ideas and attitudes they deplore, and argue that many white offenders are in any case racist, so that in practice there is no option but to work with them.

As noted above, NAPO produced a policy statement on working with racist offenders in 1995. This represented an effort to balance a recognition that many (or perhaps all) white clients were to some degree racist with NAPO's long-standing position that its members should be wary of working with offenders whose motivation was primarily political, and its argument – criticised by Sibbitt (1997) – that racist offenders posed unique risks to health and safety. Hence NAPO's (1995) distinction between 'racist offenders and those whose offences are motivated by racism', which by 1999 seemed untenable to some practitioners. Edwards (1999: 38) argued that the policy was confusing, and that it was not clear why 'active committed racists' should be excluded from the attention of probation officers who might be continuing to work with murderers and rapists. In support of Edwards' position, Dixon and Okitikpi argued (1999: 157) that 'there exists a clear public mandate to engage in work with racially motivated offenders', and that NAPO's policy was therefore untenable. Writing in response to Edwards and Dixon and Okitikpi, Ledger (1999: 288), who was at the time vice-chair of NAPO, explained that the 1995 policy was explicitly designed to address the safety of staff working with politically motivated racist offenders, and that it had never been intended to exclude 'challenging and confrontative work' with racist clients.

Developing resources for practice

Like earlier writers, Dixon and Okitikpi recognised that staff might be anxious and apprehensive about working on issues of racism, but, unlike their predecessors, they were able to point to the existence of training and educational materials on which practitioners could draw. The most important of these was *From Murmur to Murder* (Gast and Kay 1998), introduced by its editors as follows: 'This handbook for Probation officers has taken a long time to reach production. For a number of years the need for such a resource has been recognised but resources to finance the work have not been available.' Published just before the implementation of the parts of the 1998 Crime and Disorder Act that introduced racial aggravation of offences as a new legal category, the handbook was the result of an initiative by the Midlands group of chief probation officers, for which they obtained support from the Probation Unit in the Home Office.

While some aspects of the handbook could be criticised for careless editing (on page 8 the reader is told that the 1998 Act will 'minimise' the number of racially motivated offenders coming to the attention of the Probation Service), it is a substantial and serious effort to meet the long identified lack of resources for probation staff that would enable them to work with racist offenders with reasonable assurance and a sense that such work is justified by the Service's overall purposes and values. It argues (1998: 20) that 'changing racist attitudes is a central part of the public protection responsibilities of the Probation Service', and is critical (1998: 36), as was Sibbitt (1997), of the 'political correctness' that encouraged a 'zero tolerance' policy on the expression of racist attitudes. Using what was then up-to-date research, including Sibbitt's, Gast and Kay (1998) bring a wide range of sources together to establish a knowledge base before suggesting elements of good practice in pre-sentence report preparation and risk assessment, including ideas – adapted from experience of work with sex offenders – on how to elicit racist attitudes and motives in a non-confrontational way. A specimen programme and exercises for use in practice take up the second half of the handbook. According to Linda Gast's website (www.lindagast. fsbusiness.co.uk/publications.htm, accessed on 15 March 2005), the handbook received wide acclaim and was used in agencies other than the Probation Service, selling over 1,000 copies.

A practitioner account of how *From Murmur to Murder* could engender the confidence needed to engage with racism as a motive for offending was provided by McDonald (2000), who describes intensive individual work with a prisoner who had pleaded guilty to racist murders eight years previously. McDonald found *From Murmur to Murder* in an office where it had been 'gathering dust' (2000: 207) for six months and supplemented it with other material, including academic and documentary sources and a dramatic representation of racial conflict in the context of an industrial dispute. While sensitive to the issue of worker safety, McDonald's account suggests that he quickly shed any initial doubts about the value of this intervention. He had the advantage, of course, that the prisoner sought help and did not deny his racist motivation, so the problems identified by other practitioners, of identifying racist motives and overcoming offenders' tendencies to deny them, did not apply.

Work with racially motivated offenders was a relatively minor theme of the thematic inspection report by Her Majesty's Inspectorate of Probation (HMIP 2000), *Towards Race Equality*. The theme of racial equality was selected in the wake of the publication of the Macpherson Report (1999) on the killing of the black teenager Stephen Lawrence and the failure of the police investigation to identify suspects who could be successfully prosecuted. A main recommendation of the Inspectorate report was that the Macpherson definition of a 'racist incident' should be universally adopted by probation as well as police services. (This required the police to record a racist element in all incidents reported to them in which any party believed that racism formed a part or all of the motivation.)

The part of the report that dealt with work with racially motivated offenders – Chapter 7 – also noted the relevance of the Crime and Disorder Act's provisions and cited Sibbitt's (1997) criticisms of probation practice as indicating the need for a 'cultural shift' if the Service was to work effectively with these offenders (HMIP 2000: 96). The Inspectorate found that despite the Act there was no common definition of a racist incident; most of the ten services inspected had no definition at all. Management responsibility for developing work with racially motivated offenders was defined in five areas, including Inner London, but in most a formal commitment to the importance of the work was not reflected in training or practice development, and the use of *From Murmur to Murder* was uneven.

The Inspectorate found, as others had, that racist motivation was very rarely identified at the court stage (it appeared in only three out of 484 pre-sentence reports (PSRs) examined, and only one of the defendants concerned was identified as white), and had been raised as an issue in supervision of white offenders in only 15 of 183 probation cases examined (and appeared in none of the risk assessments). In four areas the case files suggested that racism had not been discussed with any of the offenders, but it had been raised in one third of the cases in Inner London. The inspectors detected evidence of racism in ten cases where it had not been raised in supervision. Recognising that progress had been made in two services, Merseyside and the West Midlands, the inspectors recommended that the management of all Probation Services should produce new policy and practice guidance to support and develop work with racially motivated offenders.

Generalist or specialist provision

Subsequent developments – or the lack of them – are discussed by Dixon (2002), who was a member of a national sub-group set up at the request of the Joint Accreditation Panel to produce a programme specifically for racially motivated offenders. The 'theory manual' that resulted from this proposed that different groupwork programmes should be piloted, but by that time the position of the National Probation Directorate was – and apparently remains – that racially motivated offenders should generally be allocated to one-to-one programmes. According to Dixon, the intense pressure on the Probation Service to be seen to be taking action on racist offending that followed the publication of the Macpherson Report in 1999 had dissipated by 2002; the government's response to the riots in towns in the north of England in 2001 emphasised the need to build community cohesion as a protection against racial conflict, rather than focusing on the motives and meanings of racist violence. By that time, too, the work of Ray *et al.* (2002) had strongly suggested that perpetrators of racist violence in touch with the Probation Service were much more likely to be 'generalists' than 'specialists', casting doubt on the need for a distinct programme specifically for racially motivated offenders. This work also showed, however, that racist attitudes were widespread in the areas – typically poor outlying estates with high levels of unemployment and nearly all-white populations – that produced the greatest concentrations of racist offenders, with the implication that programmes for offenders from such areas might include some work on racism as a matter of routine.

Dixon (2002), while agnostic on the need for specialist programmes (and on the question of whether group or individual work should be preferred), was concerned that racist offending should remain on the Probation Service's agenda for change, and that the Service should not retreat into denial and avoidance of the issue. She noted the development on Merseyside of a specialist programme, 'Against Human Dignity', and the piloting of a programme in south-west London, the Diversity Awareness Programme. This included a module on racial violence that, according to Dixon (2002: 212), was 'perhaps the most complex as the motivation and level of premeditation varies with different offenders'. Dixon's account reflects a perception of racist offending that is much more nuanced and empirically grounded than the stereotypical view of extreme politically motivated violence found by Sibbitt (1997), and Dixon is also clear (like Wade and Macpherson 1992) that a simple denunciation of racist attitudes is likely to be counter-productive, since 'offenders have to develop a respect for their own culture in order to start respecting others ... and promoting a positive cultural identity is a crucial objective' of the programme (Dixon 2002: 213). Responding to Dixon from the National Probation Directorate perspective, Perry (2002: 307) summarised 'three potential pathways', based on recommendations from the Joint Accreditation Panel and presumably not mutually exclusive: to test the impact of general offending programmes on racially motivated offenders, to develop relevant modules within existing programmes, and to develop a one-to-one programme specifically for racist offenders. The path represented by the programmes in Merseyside and London was therefore not to be followed nationally, on the grounds of insufficient evidence of effectiveness and the fact that numbers of readily identifiable racist offenders remained low, despite the provisions of the 1998 Act.

Towards more sensitive practice

Reports on the development of practice and understanding in the course of the piloting of the London programme were given by Court (2003) and Dixon and Court (2003). Court's article also provides some illumination of the processes of attrition that produce a much smaller number of racially motivated offenders accessible to probation intervention than might be expected from the number of locally reported racist incidents. Court was appointed to a specialist developmental post in Greenwich, the area in which Stephen Lawrence – among other young minority ethnic men – had been killed. Relevant groups of offenders were whites convicted of a racially aggravated offence, 'downgraded' cases of whites originally charged with such offences but convicted of the basic offence, and offenders already under supervision who were identified as having some racial motivation. The third category, whose racism had not been identified prior to their conviction, produced only two cases in the year Court was in post, and Court found many probation officers reluctant to identify clients as racist, on the grounds that this would be to attach a negatively stigmatising label or that they were in any case not really racist (for example, they were drunk at the time of the offence, or had black friends or relatives). This reluctance to engage with the issue of racism, and the reasons for the reluctance, are very close to those identified earlier by Ray *et al.* (2002, 2003b).

Court (2003) identified 114 cases of offenders initially charged with racially aggravated offences; 35 were convicted of such offences, and 18 were convicted after the charges against them had been downgraded to remove the 'racially aggravated' element. Eleven were given orders requiring them to attend the one-to-one Diversity Awareness Programme, another four received community penalties with an element of individual supervision, and in four cases where offenders were imprisoned the court suggested that attendance at the programme should be part of their post-release supervision. These numbers – coming from an area in which racist violence was a recognised and widely publicised problem – suggest that at the scale of a London borough a specialist programme would struggle to find a sufficient number of offenders to appear cost-effective (at least in the continued absence of any significant number of referrals from outside the court process). Court describes the use of a 'Racial Attitudes Screening Tool' as a standard assessment device, but what was useful about this was its capacity to open out areas for discussion, rather than its detection of racist attitudes: not surprisingly, offenders gave the 'right', pro-social answers to its specific questions. As also reported by Ray *et al.* (2002), offenders are fully aware that racism is widely regarded as morally unacceptable; in the Greater Manchester research, offenders rarely seemed inhibited in discussing their use of violence, but were usually reluctant to acknowledge that it had any racist motivation.

Dixon and Court (2003) describe the piloting of the Diversity Awareness Programme in other areas of London, and show that as experience develops so too does a sense of the complexity of racist motivation. They stress the importance of considering dynamic as well as static risk factors, and among the dynamic factors they stress the importance of locality. This is another theme that has resonances with the Greater Manchester research, which found not only that racist offenders were concentrated in particular neighbourhoods (Ray *et al.* 2003a) but that the nature of the problem was defined in specific local ways: in Oldham, for example, the police and the local newspaper constructed an image of racist violence in which the main perpetrators were young Asian men, and the main victims vulnerable white people (Ray and Smith 2004). Dixon and Court give the example of repeated vandalism of the stone erected in memory of Stephen Lawrence, for which the stated motive was resentment at the negative portrayal of the area in the media. Noting the inability of generalist programmes to address such issues, and the neglect in cognitive-behavioural approaches of the emotions, Dixon and Court (2003: 150) argue that racist motivation is 'frequently sub-conscious', and will only be uncovered by 'very specific and informed intervention' based on an understanding of 'the futility and counter-productiveness of labelling offenders as "racist" '. The approach advocated by Dixon and Court is a long way from the 'challenging and confrontative work' proposed by Ledger four years earlier (1999), and indicates a positive capacity to attend to the messages of both research and experience.

The Inspectors' view

Despite this growing sense of the specificity of racially motivated offending, the National Probation Directorate came to the view that the best approach was to use the already accredited Priestley One-to-One programme, on the basis of advice from the accreditation panel that the criminogenic needs of racially motivated offenders were substantially the same as those of general offenders (HMIP

2005: 8). The possibility that the programme could be adapted for racially motivated offenders was kept open, however, and work was under way at the end of 2004 to develop a practical guide for the use of the programme with them (HMIP 2005: 39). The Inspectorate found, however, that staff in some areas continued to believe that a dedicated programme would be helpful, and noted – in its follow-up report *Towards Race Equality* – the use of a programme based on *From Murmur to Murder* in West Yorkshire (HMIP 2004). In its thematic report on work with racially motivated offenders, the Inspectorate found that a smaller than expected number of offenders identified as belonging to this category were in contact with the Service, and that good systems for their identification and monitoring were still generally lacking (HMIP 2005); the systems some areas had introduced remained fallible. The Merseyside programme Against Human Dignity was the only dedicated programme found in the areas covered by the inspection, though the report noted that programmes were also running in a minority of other areas, without the backing of the National Probation Directorate. Elsewhere the main resource where any work was being undertaken on racist motivation was *From Murmur to Murder*; often, however, racially motivated offenders (RMOs) were seen as unsuitable for general offending programmes until work had been done on their racism – and this work was usually not done.

The Inspectors found that practitioners faced some familiar problems in working with racially motivated offenders. Despite having access to 'relatively good' training, 'many staff interviewed expressed a lack of confidence in working with RMOs ... In many cases, staff had left unchallenged the racially aggravated/motivated dimension and had colluded with offenders' minimisation' (HMIP 2005: 15). The confidence of the case managers responsible for Against Human Dignity was exceptional. Initial assessments and pre-sentence reports sometimes identified a racist motive that was later redefined by the case manager as not really racist (for example, the offender was drunk at the time or had acted out of character); as the Inspectors comment (2005: 19), this 'seemed at odds with the Macpherson definition of a racist incident', to which all areas officially subscribed. Even when staff planned to address issues of racism, it often took months before they got round to doing so. Identifying 'emerging issues', the Inspectors note that although most staff had been trained in anti-discriminatory practice and could articulate its importance, 'when it came to confronting offenders about their racist attitudes and behaviour the resolve of case managers often weakened' (2005: 35). They concluded the present state of practice with racially motivated offenders was unsatisfactory, in that in most cases the issue of racism was not directly addressed:

> The lack of meaningful engagement with many RMOs was a concern because the failure to confront and engage with these offenders does not present a pro-social message about the role of the NPS and its responsibility to promote social justice in the communities it serves. (HMIP 2005: 37)

The Inspectors considered that practitioners who had access to Against Human Dignity were able to tackle issues of racism more confidently and directly than most of those who did not, but the report makes no recommendation about the future use of the programme, which seems to have remained confined to Merseyside. This arguably represents a waste of resources, since the programme is clearly based on substantial research and development. It consists of 15 weekly sessions, intended for groupwork, of which 11 constitute the core of the programme, the first and last two being concerned respectively with information-giving and assessment, and with evaluation and feedback. In between, the programme provides information on minority ethnic people and the history of racism, with a stress on distinguishing fact from opinion; encourages positive thinking about minority ethnic people; aims to help offenders understand the connection between negative attitudes and behaviour; encourages offenders to think about the consequences for themselves of racist offending; aims to promote victim empathy and positive thinking about victims of racism; and encourages planning to prevent relapse. The material provided, drawn from a wide range of sources, is impressively clear, detailed and thorough, and avoids moralising and condemnation. It could be adapted to one-to-one working, and could be a useful source of ideas and information even for practitioners who were not in a position to deliver the full programme. It is easy to believe that those able to use it would feel a confidence and clarity about the purpose of their work, and about the methods appropriate to achieving it, which are evidently lacking in most probation interventions with racist offenders.

Conclusion

The story so far of the Probation Service's involvement with racially motivated offenders is one of words rather than action, of good intentions not realised in practice, and of promising local initiatives that have remained local rather than becoming nationally available resources. There is plentiful evidence that even since the 1998 Crime and Disorder Act much racially motivated offending goes unrecognised, and if recognised ignored by practitioners who feel anxious, disempowered and uncertain how to proceed in the face of attitudes and emotions they are likely to find repellent and may therefore judge too dangerous to bring into the open. Nevertheless, the work reviewed here, much of it by pioneering practitioners, represents a potentially valuable source of guidance to practitioners, in the continuing absence of an accredited and widely available programme for racially motivated offenders. There is no doubt that there has been a genuine increase in knowledge and understanding of the problems that such offenders pose for effective intervention; the problem, as always, is what to do with this knowledge, and how to make it widely available in a form that practitioners can turn to practical use.

Probation officers' stereotyping and fear of racist offenders, as described by Sibbitt (1997), is no longer defensible, if it ever was: there were accounts by practitioners from the early 1990s that could have been used to construct a more positive and realistic account. It is possible, on the basis of work since then, to make a number of reasonably confident generalisations. First, racial motivation will rarely be the only motivation of offenders with whom the Probation Service comes into contact; typically, racism will be embedded in motives derived from feelings of dispossession and victimhood, resentment, shame and rage (Ray et al. 2004). Second, it follows that the classic image of racist violence as 'hate crime', in which a victim who is unknown to the offender is selected because of his or her perceived membership of a hated social group, will usually be unhelpful; typically, racially motivated offenders know their victims (though they rarely know them well). Third, very few racially motivated offenders regard themselves as racists, or at least are willing to declare themselves as such to probation officers; they know that racism is regarded as morally unacceptable, and minimisation or denial of the racist element in their offending is to be expected. Fourth, it follows that didactic moralising about the evils of racism is more likely to do harm than good, by promoting defiance rather than repentance; offenders will have heard condemnations of racism – and celebrations of multi-culturalism and difference – before; these did not turn them into anti-racists when they first heard them, and are unlikely to do so when they hear them again. Fifth and finally, racist offending – at least at the more serious end – is usually the product not of rational thought but of intense and complex emotions that, given the right combination of immediate circumstances, find expression in violence, and unless interventions take account of the 'irrational' element in racist offending they are likely to fail. Chapter 11 explores the implications of these conclusions for practice.

References

Burney, E. and Rose, G. (2002) *Racist Offences – How is the Law Working? The Implementation of the Legislation on Racially Aggravated Offences in the Crime and Disorder Act 1998*, Home Office Research Study 244. London: Home Office.

Court, D. (2003) 'Direct Work with Racially Motivated Offenders', *Probation Journal*, 50: 1, 52–8.

Dixon, L. (2002) 'Tackling Racist Offending: A Generalized or Targeted Approach?', *Probation Journal*, 49: 3, 205–16.

Dixon, L. and Court, D. (2003) 'Developing Good Practice with Racially Motivated Offenders', *Probation Journal*, 50: 2, 149–53.

Dixon, L. and Okitikpi, T. (1999) 'Working with Racially Motivated Offenders: Practice Issues', *Probation Journal*, 46: 3, 157–63.

Edwards, R. (1999) 'Working with Racially Motivated Offenders', *Probation Journal*, 46: 1, 37–9.

Gast, L. and Kay, J. (eds) (1998) *From Murmur to Murder: Working with Racist Offenders*. Birmingham: West Midlands Training Consortium.

Gill, A. and Marshall, T. (1993) 'Working with Racist Offenders: An Anti-Racist Response', *Probation Journal*, 40: 2, 54–9.

HMIP (Her Majesty's Inspectorate of Probation) (2000) *Towards Race Equality: A Thematic Inspection.* London: HMIP.

HMIP (2004) *Towards Race Equality: Follow-up Inspection Report.* London: HMIP.

HMIP (2005) *'I'm Not a Racist but …'.* London: HMIP.

Khan, S. (1991) 'Breach of a Racist Client', *Probation Journal*, 38: 3, 140.

Ledger, J. (1999) 'Misunderstanding of Racially Motivated Offenders Policy', letter, *Probation Journal*, 46: 4, 288.

McDonald, C. (2000) 'Some Relevant Questions for Work with Racist and Racially Motivated Offenders, *Probation Journal*, 47: 3, 206–9.

Macpherson, W. (1999) *The Stephen Lawrence Inquiry: Report of an Inquiry by Sir William Macpherson of Cluny.* Cm 4262. London: The Stationery Office.

NAPO (National Association of Probation Officers) (1995) *Probation Work with Racist Offenders and Those Whose Offences are Motivated by Racism*, Policy Document PD3-95. London: NAPO.

Perry, D. (2002) 'Racially Motivated Offenders: The Way Forward', *Probation Journal*, 49: 4, 305–9.

Ray, L. and Smith, D. (2001) 'Racist Offenders and the Politics of "Hate Crime" ', *Law and Critique*, 12, 203–21.

Ray, L. and Smith, D. (2004) 'Racist Offending, Policing and Community Conflict', *Sociology*, 38: 4, 681–99.

Ray, L., Smith, D. and Wastell, L. (2002) 'Racist Violence and Probation Practice', *Probation Journal*, 49: 1, 3–9.

Ray, L., Smith, D. and Wastell, L. (2003a) 'Understanding Racist Violence', in E. A. Stanko (ed.) *The Meanings of Violence*. London and New York: Routledge, 112–29.

Ray, L., Smith, D. and Wastell, L. (2003b) 'Racist Violence from a Probation Service Perspective: Now You See it, Now You Don't', in: R. M. Lee and E. A. Stanko (eds) *Researching Violence: Essays on Methodology and Measurement*. London and New York: Routledge, 217–31.

Ray, L., Smith, D. and Wastell, L. (2004) 'Shame, Rage and Racist Violence', *British Journal of Criminology*, 44: 3, 350–68.

Sibbitt, R. (1997) *The Perpetrators of Racial Harassment and Racial Violence*, Home Office Research Study 176. London: Home Office.

Wade, A. and Macpherson, M. (1992) 'Addressing Race Issues in Groupwork', *Probation Journal*, 39: 3, 129–32.

Webster, C. (1997) 'Inverting Racism', paper to the British Criminology Conference, Liverpool.

Chapter 3

Race, Probation and Inspections

Rod Morgan

Introduction

It is a British conceit that the British are a tolerant, motley crew. That British character, identity and institutions are the product, over centuries, of waves of immigration and assimilation and this has produced our peculiarly resilient and open-minded character. That, ironically, our self-proclaimed bulldog yet tolerant virtues have mongrel origins. The study of race and crime poses a particular challenge to such complacent self-assessments.

It is historically true that the British Isles have been so occupied. Further, as Norman Davies (1999: 870–1) has found it necessary to remind us, the United Kingdom is not, and never has been, a nation state and its inhabitants, particularly the English (as opposed to the Welsh, the Scots and the Irish), are peculiarly confused about their identity. British tolerance is a conceit inasmuch as we have had a tendency to argue that there is nothing new or different about recent immigration patterns and thus no great need to make special provision in response to them. New immigrants, it was argued, must learn to accept our ways, which are themselves the product of previous accommodations. Yet, as Gilroy (1987) emphasises, 'there ain't no black in the Union Jack' (Gilroy 1987), and this much vaunted tolerance was grounded on an imperial tradition of racial domination about which the British have often displayed great complacency, if not pride.

The latest (2001) Census of England and Wales reveals that 2.8 per cent of the resident population is black, 4.7 per cent is of Asian origin and 1.2 per cent comprises some other minority ethnic group. That is, approaching one in ten residents, a substantial increase on the 1991 Census figures, are members of visibly distinctive, minority ethnic groups, most of whom came to Britain in the second half of the twentieth century. These minority ethnic populations are very different from each other in their origins, cultures, living patterns, demographic characteristics and socio-economic circumstances. Yet, taken as a whole, their profile is in several respects distinctively different from the white population. The largest groups, for example, include a significantly higher proportion of young people in the age range generally responsible for crime than is the case for the white population. Second, a high proportion of the minority ethnic groups are distinctly socio-economically disadvantaged, are disproportionately in low income occupations and live overwhelmingly in the poorest neighbourhoods of our major metropolitan cities. This is not invariably the case: some minority ethnic groups are relatively wealthy and have an educational profile superior to that of the majority white population. But they are exceptions. Members of the minority ethnic populations are conspicuous by their absence from rural and small town Britain and the affluent stretches of commuting suburbia.

Both before and after the Race Relations Act 1968, which first made it unlawful to discriminate on grounds of race, colour, or ethnic or national origins in the provision of goods, facilities and services, research showed that the minority ethnic groups were widely discriminated against. Perceived 'colour' was the major determinant (Daniel 1968; Smith 1977; Brown 1984; Brown and Gay 1986). Thus Asians and Afro-Caribbeans were equally discriminated against when it came to employment recruitment and provision of accommodation and other services compared, for example, to more light-skinned groups such as the Turkish Cypriots or Chinese communities. But the Afro-Caribbean and Indian subcontinent communities did not initially perceive the discrimination in the same way. The Afro-Caribbeans, a relatively homogeneous group who came to Britain speaking English, had relatively high expectations and were disproportionately employed as skilled manual workers, were more conscious of their unequal treatment. By contrast the highly differentiated Asian communities were differently situated and reacted differently. The Pakistani and Bangladeshi communities were particularly disadvantaged linguistically and educationally, but tended to look for support within their own communities. The Indian and African-Asian communities already possessed an educational profile similar to the white population and were better placed to circumvent the obstacles put in their way (Jones 1993). These differences were, and are, reflected in the manner in which the different minority ethnic groups experience the police and criminal justice system.

The evidence of racial discrimination in the criminal justice system

Ever since the Criminal Justice Act 1991 (Section 95) the Home Office has annually produced Statistics on Race and the Criminal Justice System. The 2004 report (Home Office 2004a) shows that black citizens aged ten years or over (the age of criminal responsibility) are significantly more likely than one would expect from their presence in the general population to be stopped and searched by the police, arrested, cautioned, defined as young offenders, received into prison and making up the average daily prison population. Members of the Asian population, by contrast, are under-represented among defined young offenders and in the prison population, though they are marginally more likely to be stopped and searched by the police than are whites (see Table 3.1). The latter distinction may have been exacerbated among the Muslim population since the 9/11 attack on the World Trade Center in New York in 2001 and British participation in the invasion of Iraq in 2003.

The question inevitably arises as to whether this is because black people are engaged in more crime or because, by reason of discrimination, they are subject to greater surveillance and, if found to have committed an offence, criminalised. These possibilities are of course not discrete. The law does not bear equally on different sections of the population. As Anatole France (1894) observed, the poor 'have to labour in the face of the majestic equality of the law, which forbids the rich as well as the poor to sleep under bridges, to beg in the streets, and to steal bread'. Further, the law is both a reflection and a source of prejudice. It suggests bias and enforces it. And, as Smith (1994) has emphasised, there are interactive effects. Bias that is enforced may serve to alienate and shape behaviour, which may then be acted against in a self-fulfilling or self-perpetuating manner. Determining the relative weight to be attached to one or another factor is complex and difficult but not inherently more difficult than in any other field of human behaviour.

Research evidence of increasing sophistication (for overall reviews see Smith 1997; Phillips and Bowling 2002; Bowling and Phillips 2002) has shown that:

- In self-report studies, black and white respondents report very similar offending rates, whereas Asian respondents report significantly lower ones (Bowling *et al.* 1994; Graham and Bowling 1995; Flood-Page *et al.* 2000). Roughly the same pattern emerges from self-report studies of drug use.

- Victims, however, are more likely to report crimes to the police where offenders are from a discernibly minority ethnic group (Shah and Pease 1992; Fitzgerald and Hale 1996).

- Furthermore, street robberies (or muggings) do appear, according to victim survey data collected from white and minority ethnic respondents, to be disproportionately committed by black offenders (McConville and Shepherd 1992; Kershaw *et al.* 2000; Povey *et al.* 2001).

Table 3.1: Proportion (%) of ethnic groups at different stages of the criminal justice process, England and Wales, 2003/04

	Ethnicity					
	White	Black	Asian	Other	Unknown/ not recorded	Total
General population (aged 10 & over) @ 2001 Census	91.3	2.8	4.7	1.2	0.0	100
Stops and searches (1)	74.3	14.7	7.3	1.5	2.3	100
Arrests (2)	84.3	8.8	4.8	1.4	0.7	100
Cautions (2)	84.2	6.7	4.7	1.2	3.2	100
Youth offences	83.5	6.3	3.1	2.9	4.3	100
Crown Court (3)	76.8	12.2	7.4	3.6	*	100
Prison receptions (4) (5)	80.5	9.7	4.8	2.9	2.1	100
Prison population (5)	77.1	15.5	3.1	4.1	0.1	100

Note: Figures may not add to 100% due to rounding.

(1) Stops and searches recorded by the police under Section 1 of the Police and Criminal Evidence Act 1984 and other legislation.
(2) Notifiable offences.
(3) Information on ethnicity is missing in 35% of cases; therefore, percentages are based on known ethnicity.
(4) 'Other' includes those prisoners who classified their ethnicity as 'Mixed'.
(5) Sentenced.

- Black people are more likely to be subject to proactive policing, particularly stop and search (Modood and Berthoud 1997; Fitzgerald 1999; Home Office 2004a).

- Black people are disproportionately arrested, are more likely to have their cases terminated (Mhlanga 1997, 1999) and, if charged with an offence, are more likely to be remanded in custody (Walker 1989; Hood 1992; Brown and Hullin 1992).

- If convicted, black offenders are more likely, when all legally relevant factors have been taken into account, to receive a custodial sentence and if imprisoned both black and Asian offenders are more likely to receive a longer sentence than whites (Hood 1992).

Most commentators have concluded that the weight of empirical evidence supports the conclusion that there is cumulative discrimination – the product of selective reporting of offences and discretionary law enforcement – against minority, especially black minority, groups. They disagree, however, about whether this accounts for the level of over-representation of blacks in the prison system (see, for example, Smith 1994, 1997; Bowling and Phillips 2002; Phillips and Bowling 2002). What is the evidence that the Probation Service contributes to this discrimination?

The Probation Service and race

As far as decision-making is concerned, the Probation Service's key influence in criminal careers lies in its preparation of court reports and, in particular, the proposals, implicit or explicit, as to an appropriate sentence. Not surprisingly, therefore, this topic has been the principal focus of race-related probation research. Relationships between probation supervisors or case managers (they are not necessarily the same thing) and their enforcement decisions have, somewhat surprisingly, received remarkably little research attention from a race standpoint. Before considering the findings from this slim body of work we should first sketch the race profile of the profession itself and the Service's approach to the minority ethnic composition of its clientele.

The Probation Service, like other criminal justice agencies, was until relatively recently an overwhelmingly white service. But in recent years it has recruited and retained a higher proportion of minority ethnic staff than any of the other agencies. According to the National Association of Probation Officers (NAPO 1987) the first minority ethnic officer, an Afro-Caribbean, was not appointed until 1961. Over the next two decades the recruitment of black and Asian staff remained modest. In 1987 there were still only 127 (1.9 per cent) minority ethnic probation officers (HMIP 2000: 32, footnote 12). However, by 2003 11.2 per cent of probation officers were drawn from the ethnic minorities and at 10.5 per cent, almost as high a proportion of other probation staff, both administrative support and front-line staff (probation officers now constitute just under half of all National Probation Service staff). As in other agencies, the senior grades within the Service remain overwhelmingly white. Nevertheless the proportion of minority ethnic probation staff exceeds that in the population generally and the Service has exceeded its recruitment target in this respect (Home Office 2004b: Tables 8.8–8.12). In two parts of the country – London and the West Midlands – more than one quarter of Probation Service staff are from the minority ethnic communities. This has not been an easy achievement: in the late 1980s there were reports, particularly from the West Midlands, that black staff were disproportionately likely to be refused confirmation of their appointments after their first year in post. A number of attitudes and procedures had to be re-examined as a result (Divine 1989; Raynor *et al.* 1994; see also Chapter 1 in this volume).

In the 1970s the recruitment of specialists, ideally members of the minority ethnic communities, was judged an adequate response to the fact that an increasing proportion of supervised offenders was black. The specialists, Home Office circulars suggested, would serve to mediate or avoid cultural misunderstandings. The Service prided itself on being colour blind and, as in Northern Ireland with respect to the Troubles and the sectarian context of offending behaviour (McEvoy 2001), it largely ignored in its work with offenders the racial and racist dimensions of offenders' lives. That changed following the disorders in Brixton and elsewhere in 1981. Lord Scarman (1981: 45) found that the disturbances represented 'an outburst of anger and resentment by young black people against the police', and shortly after his report most of the then 54 local, more or less autonomous Probation Services introduced some form of anti-racism training (HMIP 2000: 31–2). Various policy statements were issued by the Home Office, the Central Council of Probation Committees (CCPC) and NAPO and these led, the Inspectorate found, most local services to adopt equal opportunities policies in staff recruitment, training, development and monitoring policies, most of which, apart from the number of minority ethnic staff in post, did not generate codes of practice capable of measurement (HMIP 2000: 32).

Race and pre-sentence reports (PSRs)

During the 1980s a clutch of studies looked at the preparation and content of PSRs as one possible driver for the over-representation of black offenders in the prison population. Given that a significant proportion of offenders sentenced to immediate imprisonment were not the beneficiaries (insofar as it is a benefit) of PSRs (this proportion has reduced but remains significant: it is currently estimated to be 17 per cent – see HMIPP 2001: para 4.6), a key question was whether black defendants were less likely to have had a PSR requested and prepared than white defendants. PSRs have ideally always comprised an account of the offence and the factors underlying it (there is now a focus on the risk or harm and reoffending), a description of the offender's history and circumstances and a proposal as to how the offender might appropriately be dealt with. Since PSRs seldom propose a custodial sentence (see Home Office 2002: Table 6.4) and overwhelmingly concentrate on community based options, the absence of a PSR might disadvantage a defendant (this hypothesis, given the contemporary emphasis on risk assessment, may no longer apply to the same extent. Risk assessment is heavily weighted towards prior convictions, a factor which, by virtue of cumulative discrimination, may disadvantage black defendants). The research revealed an inconsistent picture, some investigators concluding that black defendants were more likely than whites to have had a PSR prepared (Mair 1986; Shallice and Gordon 1990), others finding a lower rate (Hudson 1989) or the same rate (Crowe and Cove 1984).

As far as the contents of PSRs were concerned a similarly mixed picture of findings emerged. Whereas Whitehouse (1983) found a number of negative references in PSRs prepared on black defendants to aspects of Afro-Caribbean culture, family life and economic circumstances, which were likely to have influenced sentence proposals, Gelsthorpe (1992) found no such pattern. Likewise several investigators (Crowe and Cove 1984; Mair 1986; Shallice and Gordon 1990) found no difference in PSRs prepared on black and white defendants with regards to sentence proposals. It was also found, however, that black and Asian defendants were more likely to have been the subject of court reports lacking any sentence proposal (Voakes and Fowler 1989; Gelsthorpe 1992; Home Office 1996). It is a commonplace in research on court reports that 'no recommendation' often implicitly means, or is taken to mean, that no alternative to custody is considered feasible. Certainly a failure to provide a community based proposal leaves the door open to a more severe, custodial sentence. It was nevertheless concluded by several researchers that the proportionate use of custody for like defendants was broadly the same for blacks as for whites (Jefferson and Walker 1992; Home Office 2000). There was no evidence of discrimination: cases tended to be dealt with in a routine, bureaucratic fashion.

The piece of research that was taken most seriously by the Probation Service was Hood's (1992) study of sentencing in the Crown Court in the West Midlands. This study was seminal because Hood matched his census of Afro-Caribbean, Asian and other minority ethnic defendants found guilty and sentenced in the Crown Court in 1989 with an equivalent random sample of white defendants and because he undertook a complex (logistic regression) analysis of the resulting data. Though rates varied according to judge and court, he found that 48 per cent of whites, 57 per cent of Afro-Caribbeans and 40 per cent of Asians received a custodial sentence. He identified the many legal factors – offence seriousness, mode of trial, bail status, number of charges, previous offences and compliance history, etc. – that best predicted the probability of a custodial outcome, and on this basis worked out the degree to which Afro-Caribbeans were more likely to be committed to custody than their Probability of Custody Score predicted. He concluded that Afro-Caribbeans were five per cent more likely to receive a custodial sentence than were whites when all these legal factors were accounted for, and that when custody was imposed Afro-Caribbeans and Asians received sentences three and nine months longer than whites respectively. Relating his findings to the over-representation of blacks within the prison population, Hood concluded that 70 per cent of the over-representation was attributable to the greater number of blacks appearing for sentence, ten per cent to legal case factors (the greater seriousness of offences or the number of previous convictions, for example) and 20 per cent to other non-legitimate factors. The greater length of sentences on black and Asian offenders was tied to their greater propensity to plead not guilty and be tried in the Crown Court where, if found guilty, they received no sentence discount for an early guilty plea.

Hood also tied the greater likelihood of blacks receiving a custodial sentence to court reports. A significantly higher proportion of Afro-Caribbeans and Asians (42 and 43 per cent respectively) than whites (28 per cent) had not had a court report prepared and of these, whether or not they pleaded guilty, a significantly higher proportion received a custodial sentence. Whereas 26 and 31 per cent of young black and Asian defendants sentenced to custody had not had a court report prepared, only 13 per cent of whites were in the same position.

For adults, 47 and 40 per cent of the black and Asian defendants sentenced to custody had no court report compared to 30 per cent of whites. The proportions of blacks and whites sentenced to custody for whom court reports had been prepared was almost identical.

As far as sentencing proposals in those court reports that were prepared was concerned, Hood found that whites were much more likely than blacks and Asians to have probation proposed and even where this outcome was recommended, blacks were more likely to receive a suspended sentence or a community service order than probation. Asians, by contrast, were more likely to be fined or conditionally discharged.

It has been argued (Bowling and Phillips 2002: 184) that Hood's analysis provides a conservative estimate of the impact of 'race effects' within the criminal justice system. The legal factors for which Hood controlled are almost certainly not all race neutral. In addition, he could not, by definition, assess the impact of cumulative, criminal career considerations. He found, for example, that black defendants were more likely than whites to have been arrested as a result of proactive police action. Further, black defendants' propensity to plead not guilty might, quite apart from reflecting distrust on their part of the process, lead to indirect discrimination against them going beyond loss of sentencing discount. What is clear, however, is that Hood's research provided the Probation Service with unequivocal statistical evidence that the absence of court reports, and to some extent the content of court reports, contributed to a process the outcome of which was racially discriminating. As Hood summed up his study:

Being already in custody [on remand], pleading not guilty, and not having a report were all associated with a higher probability of receiving a custodial sentence or with a lengthier sentence. And all of them, of course, limit the possibilities for effective pleas in mitigation. Those who have been in custody have less opportunity to show that they have been of exemplary behaviour or have sought to make amends by, say, entering regular employment since they were charged with the offence. Those who deny the offence cannot suddenly, on being found guilty, convincingly express remorse. For those without social inquiry reports there is often insufficient information on hand to put the offence in its social context and no opportunity to take advantage of a specific proposal from a probation officer for an alternative sentence to custody. (Hood 1992: 181)

It all added up to a pattern of 'indirect discrimination' of which the Probation Service was a part. Hood recommended that close attention be paid to the manner in which the courts in future exercised their discretion to sentence in the absence of a pre-sentence report (1992: 191).

The Probation Inspectorate race thematic reports

The Probation Service – in its statements of purpose, in the development of National Standards, and so on – has long made reference to delivering an *equal* service, treating offenders *fairly* and taking action to prevent *discrimination*. But it has tended to assume that merely intoning these values in training sessions and key documents is sufficient. This is reflected in the annual reports of the Probation Inspectorate throughout the 1980s and 1990s. There was virtually no reference to race until the shock waves from the Macpherson Report into events following the murder of Stephen Lawrence rippled through the Home Office in 1999. Macpherson famously pronounced that the investigation by the police of the murder of Stephen Lawrence was characterised by both incompetence and *institutional racism*, which he defined as 'the collective failure of an organisation to provide an appropriate and professional service to people because of their colour, culture or ethnic origin', and which could be seen or detected in 'processes, attitudes and behaviour which amount to discrimination through unwitting prejudice, ignorance, thoughtlessness and racist stereotyping which disadvantage minority ethnic people' (Macpherson 1999: 28). This definition, relatively easily owned up to – 'unwitting' behaviour is arguably less culpable morally than witting behaviour – was rapidly accepted by the Home Secretary as characterising not merely the police but other criminal justice agencies (Bowling and Phillips 2002: 160). Within the Home Office there was a rapid response and in May 1999 the Chief Inspector of Probation, Sir Graham Smith, announced that he would undertake a thematic inspection, the aim of which would be 'to determine the extent to which probation services promote and achieve race equality in its employment practices and its work with offenders' (HMIP 2000: 11).

The Inspectorate is not a research unit and its resources and methodology for the race review were limited. This had knock-on consequences for the approach adopted in a follow-up review undertaken in 2003: there was naturally a desire to collect data that could be compared to those collected earlier. During visits in

1999/2000 to ten of the then 54 local Probation Services, a total of 484 pre-sentence reports were read. They related to defendants 37 per cent of whom were black, 37 per cent white, ten per cent Asian and 13 per cent 'other' minority ethnic groups. A significantly higher proportion of the black offenders had been remanded in custody (28 compared to 16 per cent of the white defendants) and a higher proportion of white than black defendants had court reports prepared for them: this appeared to confirm Hood's findings, though may largely have been explained by the more serious offences of which many black defendants stood convicted (HMIP 2000: paras 4.8–9). The review failed to examine the relationship between the content of those who had court reports prepared and subsequent sentencing decisions. Rather, the focus was on the content and quality of PSRs. Significant differences relating to the ethnicity of subjects emerged. In particular:

- The proportion of reports in which sources for the information drawn on was cited was significantly lower for black than white, Asian and 'other' defendants.

- The proportion of reports where there was an adequate assessment of the context of the offence and the culpability of the defendant was significantly lower for black than white defendants. This difference was not explained by the degree to which prosecution papers were available.

- Reports in which previous convictions or disposals were cited were in roughly the same proportion for all groups, but the degree to which information was included that enhanced the readers' understanding of these facts was not: 71 per cent of reports on white defendants contained such material compared to 57 per cent for black.

- It was found that 56 per cent of reports on black and Asian defendants contained material on defendants' financial position compared to 69 per cent for whites.

- Where risk of reoffending or harm to the public was identified, reports differed in the degree to which the question as to how that risk might be managed was addressed: 52 and 70 per cent respectively of the reports on white and Asian defendants addressed that issue, but only 38 per cent of those on black defendants did so.

- The proportion of reports containing sentence proposals (and the extent to which those proposals were logical and convincing) was found not to differ between ethnic groups, but the language and quality of presentation of reports was different: the presentation of reports was generally considered better for white and Asian defendants than black, and 16 and 11 per cent of reports on black and Asian defendants respectively were judged to reinforce stereotypical attitudes about race and ethnic origin.

The overall assessment was that PSRs prepared for black defendants (49 per cent) were significantly less likely to be satisfactory in quality than reports on 'other', white and Asian defendants (59, 60 and 63 per cent respectively). These 'worrying' findings (HMIP 2000: para 4.47) went unexplained, neither the reports' authors or their subjects having been interviewed. What the findings suggest, however, is that, for whatever reason, probation officers tend not to engage as well with black as with other offenders and this is reflected in the depth and quality of the reports they write about them. Further, the differential persists, albeit to a lesser degree and in the context of a significant overall improvement in the quality of reports prepared. The Inspectorate's 2004 follow-up report found that the proportion of PSRs prepared on white defendants continued to be more satisfactory than those on minority ethnic defendants (83 compared to 75 per cent). For this and other reasons the Inspectorate's original recommendation, of measures to be taken to improve the overall quality of PSRs prepared on minority ethnic offenders, was judged to have been only 'partially met' (HMIP 2004: para 4.12).

In 2000 the Inspectorate also assessed the supervision of offenders, an issue almost entirely neglected by academic researchers up to that time. They did so, however, by file reading alone, a method with severe limitations if the quality of engagement and depth of interaction is appraised. The exercise revealed few significant differences between minority ethnic groups, an unsurprising outcome given the small sample sizes and the thinness of the paper traces.

If, according to the court report analyses, probation staff generally fail to engage as well with black as with white offenders, how does the Service treat its minority ethnic staff? The Inspectorate assessed this question in 2000, and again in 2004. However, only minority ethnic staff were contacted and of those identified only 29 per cent returned questionnaires in 2000, falling to 18 per cent in 2004. Since many of the issues about which staff were questioned were of a general nature – the extent and quality of induction, supervision and support, for example – it is difficult to interpret the results in specifically racial terms. Those staff who returned questionnaires may have been unrepresentative and their white colleagues might, had they been asked, have been even more negative in relation to some of the questions gone into. Nevertheless some issues were relatively race specific.

Despite the increasing numbers of minority ethnic staff, a significant minority of respondents said they felt isolated at work and did not perceive their race had been taken into account when allocating them to posts. A good many had not been appraised as required by Home Office guidelines and only one third of respondents said that they considered the level of supervision received satisfactory. Further, though the management of all the Probation Services surveyed said they gave active support to members wishing to participate in Association of Black Probation Officers (ABPO) and National Association of Asian Probation Staff (NAAPS) activities, the staff survey revealed that this was not reportedly converted into practical support in terms of expenses, workload allowance and time off in a significant number of cases. When it came to promotion, minority ethnic staff 'consistently remarked on their perception of being excluded from the informal networks to which they believed white staff had access' (HMIP 2000: para 12.14). However, as the Inspectorate concluded, the validity of this perception was difficult to assess. Any minority group poorly represented within senior grades suffers the self-fulfilling prophecy of having few role models available to emulate. The Inspectorate pointed to the need for positive action measures (the provision of support groups, etc.) with a view to increasing the level of minority ethnic group representation at middle and senior management level.

Most disturbing was the reported experience of racism from offenders, colleagues or members of related services. The majority of staff reported experiencing this. Though a high proportion of these incidents were reported to managers, levels of satisfaction with the results were low. Staff interviewed spoke of their lack of confidence in managers' willingness to challenge and deal effectively with such behaviour and their fear of victimisation. The Inspectorate concluded that 'the climate in many teams appeared to militate against open discussion between white and minority ethnic staff' on this topic (HMIP 2000: para 13.21). There was need, the Inspectorate recommended, for a separate complaints system to be instituted to deal with such issues. By 2004, according to the follow-up report, there had been a significant decline in staff experience of racism from offenders but only a modest drop in their experience of racism from other sources and no separate complaints procedure had been instituted. There was a 'continuing sense of disadvantage experienced by some minority ethnic members of staff' (HMIP 2004: Foreword).

Conclusion

The evidence shows unequivocally that members of the minority ethnic communities are disproportionately drawn into the criminal justice system and are significantly over-represented in the deeper end of the system – Crown Court proceedings and the prison system. The degree to which this is true varies according to the particular minority ethnic group but in Britain being distinctively black is manifestly a key factor. In this regard the British experience mirrors that in other jurisdictions (see Tonry 1997). There is clearly an interactive, inter-generational effect in which racial discrimination, socio-economic disadvantage and institutional racism all play a part. A high proportion of the principal minority ethnic groups are young, reside in relatively high crime inner-city zones, and suffer discrimination, all of which exacerbates their relative disadvantage; they are subject to proactive policing, much of which is targeted at street crimes, for which black youths are disproportionately responsible. A mistrust of the system and a tendency to plead not guilty means they are further disadvantaged because those defendants and offenders who are non-compliant reap none of the available rewards.

The Probation Service figures in this reinforcing sequence. Black defendants, because they tend to plead not guilty and are more often tried in the Crown Court, are less often the subject of court reports prepared by the Probation Service. Defendants without court reports are more likely to receive custodial sentences. It is not clear that this relationship is causal nor how important it is that black defendants *with* court reports tend to have less satisfactory reports – the latter appear no more likely to receive custodial sentences though they *are* less likely to receive community sentences involving Probation Service supervision.

The proportion of probation staff drawn from the minority ethnic groups – particularly from the Afro-Caribbean communities – has greatly increased in recent years and now exceeds the proportion in the population generally. Even so, and despite much good practice, there remains disquieting evidence that many minority ethnic staff do not feel well supported within the Service and that minority ethnic offenders are not engaged with by staff as well as are white offenders. Whether black staff generally engage better with black offenders is an interesting issue on which there is, as far as I am aware, no real evidence, although some information about black and Asian probationers' preferences in relation to the ethnicity of their supervisors can be found in the recent Home office study (Calverley *et al.* 2004; see also Chapter 10 in this volume).

References

Bowling, B., Graham, J. and Ross, A. (1994) 'Self-reported Offending Among Young People in England and Wales', in: J. Junger-Tas, J-G. Terlouw, and M. Klein (eds) *Delinquent Behaviour Among Young People in the Western World.* Amsterdam: Kugler.

Bowling, B. and Phillips, C. (2002) *Racism, Crime and Justice.* London: Longman.

Brown, C. (1984) *Black and White Britain: The Third PSI Survey.* London: Heinemann.

Brown, C. and Gay, P. (1986) *Racial Discrimination: 17 Years after the Act.* London: Policy Studies Institute.

Brown, I. and Hullin, R. (1992) 'A Study of Sentencing in the Leeds Magistrates' Court', *British Journal of Criminology*, 32: 1, 41–53.

Calverley, A., Cole, B., Kaur, G., Lewis, S., Raynor, P., Sadeghi, S., Smith, D., Vanstone, M. and Wardak, A. (2004) *Black and Asian Offenders on Probation*, Home Office Research Study 277. London: Home Office.

Crowe, I. and Cove, J. (1984) 'Ethnic Minorities in the Courts', *Criminal Law Review*, July, 413–17.

Daniel, W. W. (1968) *Racial Discrimination in England.* Harmondsworth: Penguin.

Davies, N. (1999) *The Isles: A History.* London: Macmillan.

Divine, D. (1989) *Towards Real Communication*, Report to the West Midlands Probation Service.

Fitzgerald, M. (1999) *Searches Under Section 1 of the Police and Criminal Evidence Act.* London: Metropolitan Police.

Fitzgerald, M. and Hale, C. (1996) *Ethnic Minorities, Victimisation and Racial Harassment: Findings from the 1988 and 1992 British Crime Surveys, Home Office Research Study 154.* London: Home Office.

Flood-Page, C., Campbell, C., Harrington, V. and Miller, J. (2000) *Youth Crime Findings from the 1998/9 Youth Lifestyle Survey*, Home Office Research Study 209. London: Home Office.

France, A. (1894) *Le Lys Rouge.* Paris.

Gelsthorpe, L. (1992) *Social Inquiry Reports: Race and Gender Considerations*, Home Office Research Bulletin 32, 17–23. London: Home Office.

Gilroy, P. (1987) *There Ain't No Black in the Union Jack: The Cultural Politics of Race and Nation.* London: Hutchinson.

Graham, J. and Bowling, B. (1995) *Young People and Crime*, Home Office Research Study 145. London: Home Office.

HMIP (Her Majesty's Inspectorate of Probation) (2000) *Towards Race Equality: A Thematic Report*. London: HMIP.

HMIP (2004) *Towards Race Equality: Follow-Up Inspection Report*. London: HMIP.

HMIPP (Her Majesty's Inspectorates of Prisons and Probation) (2001) *Through the Prison Gate: A Joint Thematic Review by HM Inspectorates of Prisons and Probation*. London: Home Office.

Home Office (1996) *Probation Statistics*. London: Home Office.

Home Office (2000) *Statistics on Race and the Criminal Justice System 2000*. London: Home Office.

Home Office (2002) *Probation Statistics England and Wales 2001*. London: Home Office.

Home Office (2004a) *Statistics on Race and the Criminal Justice System 2003*. London: Home Office.

Home Office (2004b) *Probation Statistics England and Wales 2002*. London: Home Office.

Hood, R. (1992) *Race and Sentencing*. Oxford: Clarendon Press.

Hudson, B. (1989) 'Discrimination and Disparity: The Influence of Race on Sentencing', *New Community*, 16: 1, 23–34.

Jefferson, T. and Walker, M. A. (1992) 'Ethnic Minorities in the Criminal Justice System', *Criminal Law Review*, February, 83–95.

Jones, T. (1993) *Britain's Ethnic Minorities*. London: Policy Studies Institute.

Kershaw, C., Budd, T., Kinshott, G., Mattinson, J., Mayhew, P. and Myhill, A. (2000) The British Crime Survey, Home Office Statistical Bulletin 18/00. London: Home Office.

Macpherson, W. (1999) *The Stephen Lawrence Inquiry: Report of an Inquiry by Sir William Macpherson of Cluny*. Cm 4262-1. London: The Stationery Office.

Mair, G. (1986) 'Ethnic Minorities, Probation and the Magistrates' Courts', *British Journal of Criminology*, 26: 2 147–55.

McConville, M. and Shepherd, D. (1992) *Watching Police Watching Communities*. London: Routledge.

McEvoy, K. (2001) *Paramilitary Imprisonment in Northern Ireland: Resistance, Management and Release*. Oxford: Oxford University Press.

Mhlanga, B. (1997) *The Colour of English Justice: A Multivariate Analysis*. Aldershot: Avebury.

Mhlanga, B. (1999) *Race and Crown Prosecution Service Decisions*. London: The Stationery Office.

Modood, T. and Berthoud, R. (1997) *Ethnic Minorities in Britain: Diversity and Disadvantage*. London: Policy Studies Institute.

NAPO (National Association of Probation Officers) (1987) *The Recruitment, Selection, Training and Employment of Black Staff: An Agenda for Action*. London: NAPO.

Phillips, C. and Bowling, B. (2002) 'Racism, Ethnicity, Crime and Criminal Justice', in M. Maguire, R. Morgan and R. Reiner (eds) *The Oxford Handbook of Criminology*, 3rd edn. Oxford: Oxford University Press.

Povey, D., Cotton, J. and Sisson, S. (2000) *Recorded Crime Statistics of those Born between 1953 and 1978*, Home Office Statistical Bulletin 12/00. London: Home Office.

Raynor, P., Roberts, S., Thomas, L. and Vanstone, M. (1994) *Confirming Probation Officers in Appointment: Equitable Evaluation or Lottery?* Sheffield: Pavic Publications.

Scarman, Lord (1981) *The Brixton Disorders 10–12 April 1981*. Cmnd. 8427. London: HMSO.

Shah, R. and Pease, K. (1992) 'Crime, Race and Reporting to the Police', *Howard Journal*, 31: 3, 192–9.

Shallice, A. and Gordon, P. (1990) *Black People, White Justice? Race and the Criminal Justice System*. London: Runnymede Trust.

Smith, D. J. (1977) *Racial Disadvantage in Britain*. Harmondsworth: Penguin.

Smith, D. J. (1994) 'Race, Crime and Criminal Justice', in M. Maguire, R. Morgan, and R. Reiner (eds) *The Oxford Handbook of Criminology*, 1st edn. Oxford: Oxford University Press.

Smith, D. J. (1997) 'Ethnic Origins, Crime and Criminal Justice', in M. Maguire, R. Morgan and R. Reiner (eds) *The Oxford Handbook of Criminology*, 2nd edn. Oxford: Oxford University Press.

Tonry, M. (ed.) (1997) *Ethnicity, Crime and Immigration: Comparative and Cross-National Perspectives*. Chicago: University of Chicago Press.

Voakes, R. and Fowler, Q. (1989) *Sentencing, Race and Social Inquiry Reports*. Bradford: West Yorkshire Probation Service.

Walker, M. A. (1989) 'The Court Disposal and Remands of White, Afro-Caribbean and Asian Men (London 1983)', *British Journal of Criminology*, 29: 4, 353–67.

Whitehouse, P. (1983) 'Race, Bias and Social Inquiry Reports', *Probation Journal*, 30: 2, 43–9.

Part Two

Black and Minority Ethnic offenders: their needs and experiences

Chapter 4

Black and Asian men on probation: who are they, and what are their criminogenic needs?

Peter Raynor and Sam Lewis

Introduction

This chapter is based on interviews with 483 male minority ethnic offenders under supervision by the National Probation Service in 2001–2. The interviews were carried out as part of a Home Office funded study of the 'criminogenic needs' of Black and Asian probationers (Calverley *et al.* 2004). This chapter discusses what we learned from these interviews about the characteristics of these offenders, about their attitudes and beliefs, and about how these compared with what was known about similar white offenders. (Other material about how they saw their experiences in society, and particularly in the criminal justice system, can be found in Chapter 5, and their opinions about probation supervision and programmes are covered in Chapter 10.) First, however, it is necessary to say something about how the purposes of this study were understood by the Home Office, and how the sometimes controversial concept of 'criminogenic need' was understood and used by the research team.

Thinking about criminogenic need

The original thinking about this research project within the Home Office was carried out in the context of the intensive development effort within the Probation Service which was known as 'What Works'. This was financed as part of the government's Crime Reduction Programme and focused largely on the development, accreditation and roll-out of structured programmes designed around social learning principles, which offenders were to undertake as part of their community sentences. (For critical retrospective appraisals of the Crime Reduction Programme as a whole, see Hough 2004 and Homel *et al.* 2005; for discussion of its particular impact in Probation Services, see Raynor 2004a, 2004b). The somewhat simplistic assumption that came to drive some of these developments was that for each group of offenders it should be possible to identify a particular set of 'criminogenic needs' and to design a programme to meet them; however, there was not a clear consensus about either needs or interventions where Black and Asian offenders were concerned (see Chapters 1, 8 and 9 in this volume). As the invitation to tender for the study put it, 'in order for interventions to be effective, the criminogenic needs of black and Asian offenders must be identified and addressed … The objective of this research is to identify what needs to be done in order to develop programmes that work for black and Asian offenders' (Home Office 2001a: 1; see also Probation Circular PC 76/2001 (Home Office 2001b) for a similar public announcement of aims). It seemed to the research team that these matters were not quite so straightforward as this confident statement implied, and this was reflected in the eventual design.

The concept of 'criminogenic need' as used in the What Works literature (see, for example, Andrews and Bonta 1998) is equivalent to the concept of a 'dynamic risk factor', that is, a characteristic of a person or his or her environment that increases the probability of reconviction and which, in principle, is capable of being changed (unlike 'static risk factors' such as age and sex). The idea is that the risk of reconviction can be reduced by addressing these needs, which can be assessed through the use of well-designed assessment instruments and methods (Bonta 1996). Against this it has been argued that instruments used in the assessment of needs can underplay cultural or gender differences; that professional assessments may not be immune from stereotypical assumptions, and that risk factors identified in research on white male offenders cannot straightforwardly be translated to other groups (Shaw and Hannah-Moffatt 2000, 2004). Others have argued that a focus on dynamic risk factors tends to redefine social disadvantages as individual deficits or shortcomings: as Garland puts it, 'rehabilitation … is thereby being re-inscribed in a risk-management regime rather than the other way around' (Garland 1997: 6). In the context of research on disadvantaged groups, we also need to remember that assessment is generally a process applied by the powerful to the less powerful, and that conviction rates are an imperfect measure of actual offending behaviour. On the other hand, criminogenic need theory has the advantage, in an era of 'toughness', that it is designed to guide rehabilitative efforts rather than more punitive approaches (recently this has been recognised by one of its long-standing critics: see Hannah-Moffat 2005). Much recent research suggests that some risk factors have broad applicability across social divisions (Simourd and Andrews 1994; Andrews *et al*. 2004), as one might expect from concepts that derive largely from social learning theory.

Certainly criminogenic need assessments are social constructs and the products of social practices, as are criminal convictions, but neither are normally constructed at random or out of nothing. Provided that they are used with due regard for their limitations and possible biases, they can help us to understand how individual characteristics or social positions influence people's behaviour. It is, of course, possible to develop an anti-empiricist critique of almost any attempt to measure needs or evaluate intervention (Raynor 1984; Smith 2004), but an exaggerated emphasis on this critique runs the risk of disengaging social science from the real world of social action – a deconstructing spectator rather than an active source of advice. Research on issues of racial justice is *necessarily* engaged research, and a critical realist approach encourages the use of forms of measurement that are properly understood.

The initial Home Office plan for this research made a number of assumptions that were contested by the research team as part of the tendering process. For example, it was originally envisaged that all the assessments of criminogenic need would be made using the Home Office's own risk/need assessment instrument, the Offender Assessment System (OASys), and training in its use was offered to the researchers. However, OASys was not fully validated at that time (Raynor forthcoming 2006), and some members of the research team had concerns about its feasibility as a research instrument as a result of using it in other studies (Lewis *et al*. 2003). Not only was it designed for use by trained criminal justice personnel rather than social researchers, practitioners were finding that it took so long to administer that it was unlikely to be accommodated within a voluntary research interview of reasonable length.

Instead, the research team decided to design an interview schedule to elicit self-reports (rather than potentially biased professional assessments) and to use interviewers from a variety of ethnic backgrounds. The necessary element of comparability with studies of white probationers was provided by incorporating the CRIME-PICS II questionnaire (Frude *et al.* 1994) as part of the interviews. CRIME-PICS is a well-established research instrument known to be related to risk of reconviction (Raynor 1998), and designed to measure beliefs, attitudes and self-reported problems likely to contribute to an increased risk of offending. It had already been widely used in probation research, including Pathfinder evaluations, and was part of the standard 'psychometric battery' of assessments used in the National Probation Service's accredited programmes; in addition, information was available from its use with groups of white offenders. Of course, like all such instruments, the original development and validation samples had been predominantly white, and we were conscious that it might fail to cover issues of importance to our Black and Asian respondents: for example, it did not include questions about experiences of racism. Consequently it was used only as part of our interview schedule, and other parts concentrated on information about experiences of the criminal justice system and of society in general, and about perceived fair or unfair treatment.

It was normal practice in the Home Office Research, Development and Statistics Directorate to determine the basic methodology of a study before inviting tenders, in order to help in calculating the notional budget and assessing the tenders received. It was also open to tendering research teams to suggest variations (as our team did), but some options were effectively closed off by budget decisions: for example, the study was limited by the original Home Office specification to male offenders only, and funds were available to cover interviews with the target group only, so that data on comparable white offenders had to be derived from other studies. Future research in this area would probably benefit from a more robust comparative design, such as that used successfully by Hood *et al.* (2003) in their study of perceived fairness and equality in the criminal courts (funded by the Lord Chancellor's Department). In addition, no provision could be made for direct comparison with Black and Asian non-offenders, which would have been needed in order to explore the important question of whether experience of racism could itself be regarded as a criminogenic need. In spite of these limitations, the study was able to provide a large amount of new information about the needs, experiences and opinions of Black and Asian probationers.

Who they were: characteristics of the sample

In order to arrive at a sample that could be reasonably representative of minority ethnic male offenders supervised by the Probation Service, appropriate cases were sought in a total of 17 probation areas, which were selected to include areas having high, medium and low proportions of minority ethnic probationers. In order to ensure adequate representation of the 'lower density' areas these were over-sampled, since a simple proportionate sample of all areas would have resulted in the vast majority of interviewees being drawn from 'high density' areas. The resulting figures were then weighted to approximate as closely as possible to the actual distribution of minority ethnic probationers in England and Wales. Readers interested in the technical detail of the sampling strategy and the weighting factors used will find these in the Home Office report (Calverley *et al.* 2004). In this chapter, all figures in the tables are weighted except where otherwise stated.

Ethnicity was classified under four general headings: Black, Asian, mixed heritage, and Other. The terms 'Black' and 'Asian' were used in accordance with the 1991 Census of Population codes where Black is defined as African, Caribbean and Black other, and Asian is defined as Pakistani, Bangladeshi, Indian and Asian other. In addition, a number of interviewees defined themselves as of mixed heritage or mixed race, and it appeared useful to count these as a category in their own right. Interviewees described as being of mixed heritage tended to have one white parent and one minority ethnic parent.[1] Table 4.1 shows the ethnic breakdown of the sample.

The 'Other' category includes people such as one interviewee who described his ethnic origin as 'international', one who said he was an Arab, and another who, when asked how he would describe his ethnic background, said it was 'kind of confused. I've got Irish and Scottish blood in me, because of [my] parents I'm half Somalian and Jamaican. I've been around Black Americans all my life.'

The mean age of respondents at interview was 29.7 years, with slight variations in mean age by ethnic group. The age distribution of the survey sample was broadly similar to that found for male probationers generally, although more survey respondents were in the 21 to 29 age band, and fewer in the lower age bands, than in the general probation population. Patterns of offending tend to differ according to age (see Mair and May 1997: Table 3.14), and the survey respondents proved to be no exception. Interviewees aged 18 to 20 were more likely to have been convicted of robbery, burglary,

Table 4.1 Ethnic composition of the (unweighted and weighted) sample

Ethnicity	Frequency (unweighted)	Per cent (unweighted)	Frequency (weighted)	Per cent (weighted)
Black African	60	12.4	77	16.0
Black Caribbean	146	30.2	187	38.7
Black other	35	7.2	45	9.2
All Black	*241*	*49.9*	*309*	*63.9*
Pakistani	74	15.3	36	7.4
Bangladeshi	12	2.5	6	1.3
Indian	62	12.8	31	6.5
Asian other	24	5.0	13	2.6
All Asian	*172*	*35.6*	*86*	*17.8*
Mixed heritage	57	11.8	72	15.0
Other	13	2.7	16	3.3
TOTAL	483	100	483	100

criminal damage and/or motoring offences than those in other age groups. Respondents aged 21 to 29 were more likely to have been convicted of theft and handling, fraud, forgery and deception and/or drug offences than their older and younger counterparts. Interviewees aged 30 and over were more likely to have been convicted of violent and/or sexual offences than younger respondents.

The majority of interviewees (83 per cent) said that they were British. Christianity (45 per cent) and Islam (16 per cent) were the religions most commonly professed by respondents. A further 27 per cent of respondents said that they did not follow any religion. Christian respondents were usually Black, while Muslim respondents tended to be Asian.

Offences, disposals and orders

Table 4.2 shows which offence(s) led to the interviewees being placed on probation.[2] (Percentages do not add to 100 because some offenders had been convicted of multiple offences).

The index offence varied according to ethnicity. Black interviewees were more likely to have been convicted of criminal damage than

Table 4.2 The index offence

Offence category	Frequency	Per cent
Violence against the person	84	17.5
Sexual offences	11	2.3
Burglary	31	6.4
Robbery	24	5.0
Theft and handling	104	21.6
Fraud, forgery and deception	35	7.1
Criminal damage	18	3.7
Drug offences	45	9.2
Other offences	51	10.6
Motoring offences	142	29.5

Asian or mixed heritage interviewees. Asian interviewees were more likely to have been convicted of sexual offences, fraud, forgery and deception, drug offences and motoring offences, than their Black and mixed heritage counterparts. Mixed heritage respondents were more likely to have been convicted of violence against the person, burglary, robbery and theft and handling, than the Black and Asian people in the sample. Of all men starting probation orders in 2001, theft and handling (25 per cent), violence against the person (ten per cent) and burglary (six per cent) represented the largest specific offence groups[3] (Home Office, 2002b: Table 3.4).

Eighty-nine per cent of interviewees were or had been on a probation (or community rehabilitation) order (n = 430). The remaining respondents discussed the probation supervision and in some cases attendance at a probation programme that they had experienced as part of another order (n = 53), such as a community punishment and rehabilitation order. Almost half of the interviewees (49 per cent) were or had been on a probation (or community rehabilitation) order that included an additional requirement to attend a probation-led programme. The remainder were or had been on an 'ordinary' probation order with no such stipulation. Tables 4.3 and 4.4 show the breakdown of interviewees by type and stage of order.

Less than half of the respondents (44 per cent) said that this was their first experience of probation supervision. Of those who had had previous experience (56 per cent), 45 per cent reported having done community service, 45 per cent had received a probation order, 31 per cent had been given a supervision order, and 30 per cent had had a detention and training order, young offender licence, or a borstal or youth custody licence.

Table 4.3 Number and percentage of interviewees at different stages of a 'programme order'

Stage of programme order	Frequency	Per cent of those on a programme order	Per cent of total sample
Current	91	38.6	18.8
Completed programme but still on order	78	33.1	16.1
Failed to complete/breached	30	12.7	6.2
Had yet to start	37	15.7	7.7
TOTAL	236	100	48.9

Table 4.4 Number and percentage of interviewees at different stages of a non-programme order

Stage of ordinary order	Frequency	Per cent of those on an ordinary order	Per cent of total sample
Early	87	35.2	18.0
Mid	57	23.1	11.8
Late	77	31.2	15.9
Failed to complete/breached	26	10.5	5.4
TOTAL	247	100	51.1

Length of probation order

As Table 4.5 shows, survey respondents had, on average, been given longer sentences than the probation population as a whole, with just 52 per cent receiving orders of 12 months or less, compared with 66 per cent of the general probation population. (Here, as in some other tables, n is less than 483 as not all interviewees answered or were able to answer the question). A breakdown of the average length of order by ethnicity showed that the difference was even more marked for some minority ethnic groups.[5]

Table 4.5 The length of orders given to probationers in 2001, and to the interviewees

Length of probation order	Persons starting probation order in 2001[4]		Survey respondents	
	Frequency	%	Frequency	Valid %
Under 12 months	6657	12.2	29	6.1
12 months	29094	53.4	216	45.9
13–24 months	17572	32.3	208	44.2
25–36 months	1147	2.1	18	3.8
All lengths (Total)	54470	100.0	470	100.0
Average length of order (months)	15.9		16.8	

Criminogenic needs

As explained in the introduction to this chapter, a central aim of this study was to attempt some quantitative assessment of the major criminogenic needs of minority ethnic offenders on probation, to inform decisions about what kind of services should be developed for or offered to them. In this chapter we concentrate on needs that can be assessed in a standardised way and therefore compared with studies of other groups. Other needs not covered in this chapter, such as experiences of social exclusion or discrimination, are discussed further in Chapter 5.

The CRIME-PICS II questionnaire used as part of the interview schedule for this study concentrates particularly on attitudes and beliefs that are conducive to offending and on self-reported life problems, producing scores on five scales known as G, A, V, E and P. (These stand for General attitude to offending, Anticipation of reoffending, Victim hurt denial, Evaluation of crime as worthwhile, and Problems.) Both raw and scaled (standardised) scores are produced for G, A, V, E and P, and a separate score for each of the 15 problem areas covered by P.

A number of studies that have used CRIME-PICS II were examined to identify possible comparison groups for this study. Some of them were unsuitable because of the way in which findings were reported (for example, mean scores with no standard deviations,[6] or no information about ethnicity), or because they were drawn from very different sentences or parts of the penal system where different scores might be expected anyway. Many studies omitted general risk measures such as OGRS (the Offender Group Reconviction Scale) or OGRS 2 (a later version of OGRS)[7] that might help to establish comparability. For example, Wilkinson (1998) gave results for 205 probationers, but without standard deviations or ethnic breakdown, although about one-third of his sample was Black. Harper (1998) covered 65 probationers, but again with no standard deviation or ethnic breakdown. McGuire *et al.* (1995) provided only problem scores, and Surrey Probation Service (1996) provided change information but no scores, and had a low number of offenders. The research report on resettlement Pathfinders (Lewis *et al.* 2003) gave full CRIME-PICS II data on 843 offenders, but comparability is limited as the offenders were short-term prisoners (some ethnic comparisons from this study are mentioned below). Other studies (Maguire *et al.* 1996, on Automatic Conditional Release prisoners; Richards 1996, on the Cambridgeshire Intensive Probation Centre; Jones 1996, on another probation centre in Dyfed) involved small numbers and in some cases different kinds of offender.

Other promising studies included a study of a probation centre in the Midlands (Davies 1995) which involved 117 offenders known to be 87 per cent white and 81 per cent male; a study by Hatcher and McGuire (2001) of the early pilots of the 'Think First' programme, which provided data on 357 offenders, clearly mainly white and 94 per cent male; the data kindly supplied by the Cambridge team evaluating community punishment Pathfinders (see Rex *et al.* 2003), which enabled us to extract scores for 1,341 white male offenders; and, most usefully, the original validation sample for CRIME-PICS II in Mid Glamorgan (Frude *et al.* 1994). This covered 422 offenders supervised by the Mid Glamorgan Service between 1991 and 1993 (including the STOP evaluation cohort – Raynor 1998), almost entirely male, at a time when the Mid Glamorgan caseload was 99.5 per cent white (Home Office 1994). OGRS scores were not available for all these groups, but the average OGRS score for the community punishment study is reported as 47 per cent, and the average risk of reconviction for probationers in 1993 is given by May (1999) as 53 per cent, which is consistent with other information suggesting that the Mid Glamorgan sample would score well below 55 per cent. All the CRIME-PICS II comparisons in this report are either within the survey sample or with these four groups, and particularly with the original validation sample. Although none of these comparison groups was weighted to improve its representativeness of offenders under supervision in general, the general characteristics of the validation sample resemble those of probationers at the time, including May's sample (1999) which was selected to represent a range of areas. Overall the available CRIME-PICS II studies represent the best available comparison information on the criminogenic needs of white offenders until large volumes of OASys data become available in the future.

It was also hoped that a number of offenders in the sample would have been assessed using the assessment instruments LSI-R (Level of Service Inventory Revised) or ACE (Assessment, Case Management and Evaluation) that could then be compared to norms established in previous studies (Raynor *et al.* 2000). Some OASys assessments might also have been carried out. However, so few examples of such assessments were made available that no meaningful analysis could be attempted. In 90 cases (equivalent to a weighted 78 cases) OGRS scores were provided, which were of some value in comparing static risk levels. The latest national information available at the time of the study indicated that the average OGRS score for offenders on community rehabilitation orders in the first quarter of 1999 was 52.8 (Home Office, 2003), which is close to the survey sample's weighted average of 51.8.

CRIME-PICS II scores in the sample and the comparison groups

Table 4.6 and Figure 4.1 show the weighted raw G, A, V, E and P scores for the survey sample compared to the CRIME-PICS II validation sample ('White comparison'). The scores showed little variation between high, medium and low density areas.[8] Table 4.6 also shows scores for each of the main ethnic groups (omitting the 13 members of the heterogeneous 'other' group). Scores are not available for one of the 483 respondents, so n = 482. OGRS scores are included, and significant differences (derived from t-tests) are indicated in the CRIME-PICS II scores. For the identified ethnic groups, the indicated probabilities refer to the significance of differences between the particular ethnic group and the remainder of the full survey sample. In the final column they refer to the significance of differences between the full survey sample and the CRIME-PICS II validation sample. In both cases * = p<0.05, ** = p<0.01.

It is immediately clear that the survey sample shows lower scores than the white comparison group on all scales, apart from Asian offenders on the V scale. Within the survey sample there are also a number of differences between ethnic groups: Black offenders were slightly but not significantly higher than the sample as a whole on all scales except the P scale; Asian offenders were significantly lower on G, A and E but higher on V; and offenders of mixed heritage were significantly high on G and A but low on V. All group scores, even those that were high for the sample, were lower than for the white comparison group. The only problem areas in which the survey subjects reported greater difficulties than the white comparison sample were relationships, housing (particularly among Black offenders), health (particularly among Asian offenders) and not feeling good about oneself (particularly among offenders of mixed heritage).

Table 4.7 compares the survey sample with the other studies identified above. Scaled scores are used here as some studies only provided these. Differences are in the expected directions: the Think First and Probation Centre groups score higher than the survey sample, and the community punishment group scores lower, reflecting the known tendency for people on community punishment orders to have fewer problems than those on probation/community rehabilitation orders (Raynor 1998).

Table 4.7 also compares those members of the survey sample who were involved in programmes with those who were supervised

Table 4.6 Raw CRIME-PICS II scores compared

Scale	Full weighted sample	Black	Asian	Mixed heritage	White comparison
Weighted N	482	308	86	72	
(Unweighted)	(482)	(240)	(172)	(57)	(422)
G	38.28	38.48	35.66 **	40.61 *	44.84 **
A	12.20	12.27	11.15 **	13.16 *	13.89 **
V	8.04	8.09	8.74 *	6.79 **	8.58 **
E	10.50	10.59	9.73 **	11.14	12.03 **
P	26.62	26.33	26.86	27.36	28.62 **
OGRS	51.8	49.7	44.6	62.6	53.0[9]
(No. of OGRS scores available)	(n=90)	(n=36)	(n=38)	(n=14)	

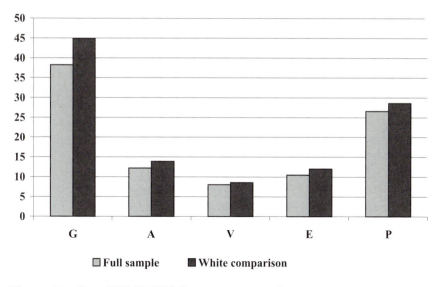

□ Full sample   ■ White comparison

Figure 4.1 Raw CRIME-PICS II scores compared

Table 4.7 Other CRIME-PICS II comparisons

Scale	Full weighted sample	Probation Centre (Davies 1995)	Think First (Hatcher and McGuire 2001)	Com- munity Punish- ment (Rex *et al.* 2002)	Pro- gramme sub- sample (weighted)	Non- pro- gramme sub- sample (weighted)
N	482	117	357	1341	250	247
G	2.5	4.1	4.6	2.0	2.5	2.6
A	3.8	4.5	5.4	3.1	3.8	3.8
V	4.0	4.3	3.5	4.1	3.8	4.2
E	3.7	4.5	5.0	2.8	3.6	3.7
P	4.1	4.6	5.3	3.1	3.8	4.3
OGRS	51.8				55.0	44.8
	(n=90)				(n=60)	(n=30)

without programmes. It is interesting that offenders on programmes had a higher risk of reconviction (as indicated by their higher average OGRS score), but fewer crime-prone attitudes and beliefs and self-reported problems (as indicated by their lower CRIME-PICS II scores) than those not on programmes, although the differences in CRIME-PICS II scores were only statistically significant on the P scale.[10] There was no evidence that these differences were due to a programme effect, since the CRIME-PICS II scores for those who had completed a programme were not significantly lower than for those who were part-way through a programme, and were not lower than scores for those who had yet to start. There were statistically significant differences[11] in the proportion of different ethnic groups who were on programmes (51.5 per cent of Black offenders, 39.5 per cent of Asian offenders and 66 per cent of mixed heritage offenders were on programmes). This may have been at least partly due to differences in OGRS scores.

Other comparative studies

These findings can be compared with those of some other studies that have included direct comparisons between minority ethnic offenders and white offenders within the British penal system. The numbers of Black and Asian offenders in these studies are lower than in the present study, but the parallels are interesting.

The second pilot study undertaken for the OASys instrument in 1999–2000 covered 2,031 offenders of whom 180 are described as Black and 83 as 'south Asian' (Clark *et al.* 2002). Both Black and Asian offenders had lower average OASys scores than white offenders, indicating a lower level of criminogenic need and probably a lower risk of reoffending. In particular, Black offenders showed significantly lower scores on lifestyle and associates, alcohol misuse, drug misuse and emotional problems. Asian offenders scored significantly lower on criminal history, accommodation problems, educational need, financial problems, lifestyle, drug misuse, 'interpersonal problems' and thinking skills. Among offenders located in the community rather than in prison, the proportion of Black and particularly Asian offenders who showed the appropriate level and profile of needs to be assessed as well 'fitted' to an offending behaviour programme was lower than the corresponding proportion of white offenders. This is a further indication of lower assessed need.

A study reported by Merrington (2001) of assessments carried out by probation officers in Greater Manchester using the ACE assessment system (see Roberts *et al.* 1996) covered 3,746 offenders, of whom 365 were Black or Asian. The analysis did not separate Black from Asian offenders, but it showed that Black/Asian offenders had lower 'offending-related' scores (the ACE measure of criminogenic need) and were less likely than white offenders to be assessed as having problems with accommodation, alcohol and drugs, mental health, emotional stability and self-esteem. There were 'no areas in which ethnic minorities are judged to have more criminogenic problems than whites' (Merrington 2001: 8).

Finally, direct comparisons of CRIME-PICS II scores between ethnic groups were possible in the first phase of the 'Pathfinder' evaluation of resettlement projects for short-term prisoners (Lewis *et al.* 2003). Initial scores were available for 730 white, 67 Black and 25 Asian prisoners. Minority ethnic offenders showed lower criminogenic needs and problem scores, though the differences were not statistically significant. Overall, the convergence between these other studies and the current study is quite striking, particularly as some of them (those using OASys and ACE) were based on assessments by professionals and others (using CRIME-PICS II) were based on offenders' own statements.

Implications of the CRIME-PICS II findings

Analysis of the CRIME-PICS II scores within the survey sample showed lower levels of crime-prone attitudes and beliefs than other studies have found in white offenders subject to probation/ community rehabilitation orders. This is true of both Black and Asian offenders in the sample, with the largest difference found among Asian offenders. Offenders of mixed ethnic origin scored closest to white probationers, but still had slightly lower scores. Levels of self-reported problems showed less difference between Black, Asian and mixed heritage offenders and were closer to (but still in most problem areas lower than) those recorded for white probationers. These findings are important when considered alongside the known over-representation of minority ethnic people in the criminal justice system (Home Office 2002a) and the fact that the survey respondents were serving probation orders of greater than average length (see Table 4.5 above).

The finding that the criminogenic needs of minority ethnic probationers were, on average, lower than those of their white counterparts suggests that minority ethnic offenders were tending to receive the same community sentences as white offenders who had higher levels of criminogenic need. This finding, based on small but significant differences in levels of criminogenic need, may have a number of explanations; however, one possibility that deserves consideration is that it was at least partly a result of differential sentencing. In other words, it raises the possibility that at least some comparable white offenders were receiving less serious sentences, and that some minority ethnic offenders were more likely than comparable white offenders to receive sentences above the community sentence range. When the editor of the *Probation Journal* summarised this study for his readers, he pointed out that this 'does suggest a need to maintain a critical focus on possible biases in both sentencing and the content of pre-sentence reports' (Bhui 2004).

There were no significant differences in CRIME-PICS II scores between those on programmes and those not on programmes, except that those not on programmes reported slightly but significantly more problems.[12] There was no evidence that this was due to any effect of the programmes on those who attended them. The average OGRS score was higher for those on programmes, suggesting that allocation to programmes had reflected differences in static risk factors rather than differences in criminogenic needs (in theory, allocation to programmes should have been based on criminogenic need, but the absence of reliable assessment methods in general use would have made this difficult at the time of the study). Asian offenders (who, as a group, had the lowest mean OGRS scores) were less likely to have been allocated to a programme than other offenders in the sample (the difference was statistically significant), and mixed heritage offenders (who had higher OGRS scores) were significantly more likely to have been allocated to a programme.

The findings concerning attitudes, beliefs and self-reported problems suggest that a balance needs to be struck between two kinds of provision: services designed to address attitudes and beliefs, and services designed to address problems and social disadvantages. The appropriate balance between these should reflect assessed needs, and the evidence in this study suggests that for many minority ethnic offenders a focus on opportunities to address problems and disadvantages would be helpful.

Notes

1 Of the 40 mixed heritage interviewees who gave details of their parents' ethnic origin, 33 (82.5 per cent) said that one parent (usually their father) fell into one of the 'Black' categories, while the other parent was white. It is not possible to say whether the same applies to the 17 mixed heritage interviewees who did not provide these details. However, there

was no indication that this group differed in any major respect from the 40 who did provide this information.

2 Lists of the offences that fall within each offence category can be found in the Home Office (2000) *OASys Manual: Version 5*, pp. 146–51.

3 The offence group sizes in Table 4.2 and the Home Office figures are not directly comparable. The Home Office figures include indictable offences only, while Table 4.2 includes summary *and* indictable offences.

4 Home Office 2002b: Table 3.14.

5 Average length of orders in months by ethnicity: Black African 15.7, Black Caribbean 16.5, Black other 18.1, Pakistani 17.5, Bangladeshi 12.4, Indian 15.6, Asian other 17.2, mixed heritage 16.9, other 22.6.

6 The standard deviation is the normal statistical measure of the dispersion of scores in a sample. It is required to calculate the significance of differences between means.

7 It is likely that the scores in some of the reports discussed below were calculated using OGRS while others were calculated using OGRS 2, because of the different times at which offenders were assessed. For simplicity we refer to OGRS throughout the rest of the chapter.

8 The average unweighted scores in high (H) and medium and low (ML) density areas were: G (H = 37.85, ML = 37.07), A (H = 12.04, ML=11.63), V (H = 8.22, ML = 8.10), E (H = 10.33, ML = 10.44), and P (H = 26.72, ML = 26.43).

9 This is an estimate based on the data collected for the STOP study (Raynor and Vanstone 1997).

10 $p<0.05$.

11 $p<0.01$.

12 $p<0.05$.

References

Andrews, D. A. and Bonta, J. (1998) *The Psychology of Criminal Conduct*. Cincinnati: Anderson.

Andrews, D. A., Bonta, J. and Wormith, J. S. (2004) *LS/CMI: Level of Service/ Case Management Inventory: An Offender Assessment System, User's Manual*. Toronto: Multi-Health Systems.

Bhui, H. (2004) 'Black and Asian perspectives on Probation', *Probation Journal*, 51(3): 264–5.

Bonta, J. (1996). 'Risk-needs Assessment and Treatment,' in A. Harland (ed.) *Choosing Correctional Options that Work*. London: Sage.

Calverley, A., Cole, B., Kaur, G., Lewis, S., Raynor, P., Sadeghi, S., Smith, D., Vanstone, M. and Wardak, A. (2004) *Black and Asian Offenders on Probation*, Home Office Research Study 277. London: Home Office.

Clark, D., Garnham, N. and Howard, P. (2002) *An Evaluation and Validation of the Offender Assessment System (OASys)*. Draft report to the Home Office.

Davies, H. (1995) *Evaluation of Probation Centres*. Birmingham: West Midlands Probation Service.

Frude, N., Honess, T. and Maguire, M. (1994) *CRIME-PICS II Manual*. Cardiff: Michael and Associates.

Garland, D. (1997) 'Probation and the Reconfiguration of Crime Control', in R. Burnett (ed.) *The Probation Service: Responding to Change*, Proceedings of the Probation Studies Unit First Colloquium: Probation Studies Unit Report No. 3. Oxford: University of Oxford Centre for Criminological Research.

Hannah-Moffatt, K. (2005) 'Criminogenic Needs and the Transformative Risk Subject', *Punishment and Society*, 7(1): 29–51.

Harper, R. (1998) *An Evaluation of Motivational Interviewing*. London: Middlesex Probation Service.

Harper, R. (2000) *Quality of Service Survey*. London: Middlesex Probation Service.

Hatcher, R. and McGuire, J. (2001) *Report on the Psychometric Evaluation of the Think-First Programme in Community Settings*. Liverpool: University of Liverpool Department of Clinical Psychology.

Home Office (1994) *Probation Statistics England and Wales 1993*. London: Home Office.

Home Office (2000) *OASys Manual: Version 5*. London: Home Office.

Home Office (2001a) *Invitation to Tender for a Survey of Black and Asian Offenders – Their Criminogenic Needs and Experiences of Probation Service Programmes in England and Wales: Schedule 1: Specification for Research*. London: Home Office.

Home Office (2001b) *What Works Diversity Issues and Race*, Probation Circular PC76/2001. London: National Probation Directorate.

Home Office (2002a) *Statistics on Race and the Criminal Justice System 2001*. London: Home Office.

Home Office (2002b) *Probation Statistics England and Wales 2001*. London: Home Office.

Home Office (2003) Personal communication.

Homel, P., Nutley, S., Webb, B. and Tilley, N. (2005) *Investing to Deliver: Reviewing the Implementation of the UK Crime Reduction Programme*, Home Office Research Study 281. London: Home Office.

Hood, R., Shute, S. and Seemungal, F. (2003) *Ethnic Minorities in the Criminal Courts: Perceptions of Fairness and Equality*. London: Lord Chancellor's Department.

Hough, M. (ed.) (2004) *Criminal Justice* 4:3. Special Issue: *Evaluating the Crime Reduction Programme in England and Wales*.

Jones, C. (1996) *A Probation Centre and Attitude Change: An Empirical Investigation*, unpublished dissertation. Swansea: University of Wales, Swansea.

Lewis, S., Vennard, J., Maguire, M., Raynor, P., Vanstone, M., Raybould, S. and Rix, A. (2003) *The Resettlement of Short-term Prisoners: An Evaluation of seven Pathfinders*, RDS Occasional Paper 83. London: Home Office.

Maguire, M., Perroud, B. and Raynor, P. (1996) *Automatic Conditional Release: The First Two Years*, Home Office Research Study 156. London: Home Office.

Mair, G. and May, C. (1997). *Offenders on Probation*, Home Office Research Study 167. London: Home Office.

May, C. (1999) *Explaining Reconviction Following a Community Sentence: The Role of Social Factors*, Home Office Research Study 192. London: Home Office.

McGuire, J., Broomfield, D., Robinson, C. and Rowson, B. (1995) 'Short-term Impact of Probation Programs: An Evaluative Study', *International Journal of Offender Therapy and Comparative Criminology*, 39: 23–42.

Merrington, S. (2001) *ACE Profiles for Female, Ethnic Minority and Young Offenders: A Sub-group Analysis of the Data used in ACE Practitioner Bulletin 4*, unpublished.

Raynor, P. (1984) 'Evaluation with One Eye Closed: The Empiricist Agenda in Social Work Research', *British Journal of Social Work*, 14(1): 1–10.

Raynor, P. (1998) 'Attitudes, Social Problems and Reconvictions in the STOP Probation Experiment', *Howard Journal*, 37: 1–15.

Raynor, P. (2004a) 'The Probation Service "pathfinders": Finding the Path and Losing the Way?', *Criminal Justice*, 4(3): 309–25.

Raynor, P. (2004b) 'Rehabilitative and Reintegrative Approaches', in A. Bottoms, S. Rex and G. Robinson (eds) *Alternatives to Prison*. Cullompton: Willan.

Raynor, P. (forthcoming 2006) 'Risk and Need Assessment in British Probation: The Contribution of LSI-R', *Psychology, Crime and Law*.

Raynor, P., Kynch, J., Roberts, C. and Merrington, M. (2000) *Risk and Need Assessment in Probation Services: An Evaluation*, Home Office Research Study 211. London: Home Office.

Rex, S., Gelsthorpe, L., Roberts, C. and Jordan, P. (2003) *Crime Reduction Programme: An Evaluation of Community Service Pathfinder Projects*, RDS Occasional Paper 87. London: Home Office.

Richards, M. (1996) *Evaluation of the Intensive Probation Centre*. Cambridge: Cambridgeshire Probation Service.

Roberts, C., Burnett, R., Kirby, A. and Hamill, H. (1996) *A System for Evaluating Probation Practice*, Probation Studies Unit Report 1. Oxford: Centre for Criminological Research.

Shaw, M. and Hannah-Moffatt, K. (2000) 'Gender, Diversity and Risk Assessment in Canadian Corrections', *Probation Journal*, 47: 163–72.

Shaw, M. and Hannah-Moffatt, K. (2004) 'How Cognitive Skills Forgot about Gender and Diversity', in G. Mair (ed.) *What Matters In Probation*. Cullompton: Willan.

Simourd, L. and Andrews, D. (1994) 'Correlates of Delinquency: A Look at Gender Differences', *Forum on Corrections Research*, 6: 26–31.

Smith, D. (2004) 'The Uses and Abuses of Positivism', in G. Mair (ed.) *What Matters In Probation*. Cullompton: Willan.

Surrey Probation Service (1996) *The Day Centre: CRIME-PICS II*. Godalming: Surrey Probation Service Information and Inspection Team.

Wilkinson, J. (1998) *Developing the Evidence-base for Probation Programmes*, PhD thesis, University of Surrey.

Chapter 5

Black and Asian men on probation: Social exclusion, discrimination and experiences of criminal justice

Bankole Cole and Ali Wardak

This chapter examines the extent of the social exclusion experienced by Black and Asian offenders on probation. It is based on findings from the national survey of 483 Black and Asian male offenders on probation (hereinafter referred to as the national survey or Calverley *et al.* 2004). We also examine these 483 offenders' experiences of the criminal justice system as a whole. The chapter is divided into two parts. The first examines the nature and extent of the exclusion of the 483 Black and Asian offenders based on three categories of exclusion – economic, educational, and geographical or environmental. In the second part, the views of these offenders of criminal justice agencies and their treatment within the system are examined. We conclude with a theoretical debate on how the social exclusion of these offenders, combined with their experience of the criminal justice system, can be used to explain why Black and minority ethnic people have low confidence in the criminal justice system and may question its legitimacy.

Introduction

Inspired by social and political theorising in France in the 1950s, the concept of social exclusion has become central to the analysis of social and economic deprivation and its consequences or correlates in Europe (Silver 1994; Levitas 1996). Within this conceptual context, the emphasis of social analysts and policy-makers is not merely on poverty and material deprivation, but on the extent to which the poor experience certain structural and cultural obstacles in the process of their participation in the wider society as citizens. According to Room (1995), these structural and cultural obstacles experienced by specific segments of society, and their prejudicial treatment in key spheres of social and public life, deny them the rights of full citizenship. This has consequently resulted in the lack of integration of the socially excluded into the wider society and its economic, political and cultural life.

Thus, unlike the more conservative Anglo-Saxon understanding of 'poverty' and Charles Murray's thesis of the 'underclass' (1990), which tend to blame the poor for their poverty, the lack of integration of the socially excluded into the wider society is seen mainly as the failure of society. It is therefore the responsibility of society (the state) to create social, economic and cultural conditions that enable the socially excluded to participate in society as full citizens, and to become involved in its social, cultural, economic and political institutions.

However, despite its roots in the fertile land of social and political theory and the enthusiasm of many politicians and policy-makers, the term 'social exclusion' has never been clearly defined. The existing body of literature indicates that there is little agreement among scholars and social analysts on what constitutes social exclusion and who exactly the socially excluded are. As Atkinson (1998) has pointed out, the main point of agreement is that it is not possible to define social exclusion by reference to any single and unique criterion. It is partly because of this profound confusion about the definition of social exclusion that the New Labour government describes it in very general terms:

> [Social exclusion] is a shorthand label for what can happen when individuals or areas suffer from a combination of linked problems such as unemployment, poor skills, low incomes, poor housing, high crime environments, bad health and family breakdown. (SEU 1998a)

This empirically oriented description is in line with what was said earlier: social exclusion is a multi-dimensional phrase that generally refers to certain structural and cultural conditions that prevent some segments of society from participating fully in the wider society as citizens. It is this general description of the term that guides the presentation of these findings.

There is well-documented evidence that shows that Britain's

minority ethnic populations have, in general, experienced various forms of social exclusion since their arrival in Great Britain. They have particularly experienced exclusionary practices in the areas of employment (Carter 2001), housing, education and sports (Wardak 2000). The following analysis of the responses from the 483 Black and Asian probationers who took part in the national survey (Calverley *et al.* 2004) confirms that many of them experienced all the three categories of exclusion described at the beginning of this chapter, namely economic, educational and geographical.

Economic exclusion

Economic exclusion is generally related to an individual or family's socio-economic status in terms of employment or lack of it, house ownership or quality of housing, and general standard of living. Those who are likely to be categorised as excluded would be those who are unemployed, on benefits, have low-paid jobs, live in sub-standard housing or are generally poor.

Table 5.1 shows that about two-thirds of the interviewees in the survey were unemployed. Just 17 per cent of the sample was in full-time employment and nine per cent was unavailable for work. The last category included those on incapacity benefit, in full-time study or retired. (All figures in this chapter are weighted to reflect the actual distribution of minority ethnic probationers in England and Wales, as explained in Chapter 4).

Altogether, 69.2 per cent of respondents were on state benefits and 3.6 per cent had no source of income. Less than a quarter of the interviewees (22.7 per cent) said that their own wages were their main source of income. Other available statistics indicate that the

Table 5.1 Work situation or employment status

Employment status	Number (valid per cent)
Full-time	80 (16.6)
Part-time	26 (5.3)
Temporary/casual	15 (3.0)
Unemployed	318 (65.9)
Unavailable for work	45 (9.2)
TOTAL	483 (100)

extent of unemployment among offenders in the United Kingdom is high: a survey undertaken by the National Association of Probation Officers (NAPO) in 1993, involving a sample of 1,331 people under probation supervision, found that 55 per cent of the probationers had been unemployed for more than a year. The percentage of long-term unemployment rose depending on where the supervision was undertaken. For example, the percentage of those classed as long term unemployed rose to 80 per cent in Newcastle, Birmingham and Liverpool (NAPO 1993). In the national survey, Black Caribbean, Black Other, mixed heritage and Bangladeshi respondents had the highest levels of unemployment (71.1 per cent, 77.3 per cent, 70.8 per cent and 66.7 per cent respectively) and the lowest levels of full-time employment. Conversely, the unemployment rates for Indian and Pakistani interviewees were more than ten per cent lower than the sample average, while their full and part-time employment rates were approximately ten per cent higher than the sample average.

This general pattern was repeated for the question 'What is your main source of income?', with Asian respondents less likely than all the Black groups to be on state benefits (55.3 per cent compared to 71.0 per cent) and more likely to be supported by their own wages (35.3 per cent compared to 19.2 per cent). Of all the ethnic groups, interviewees of mixed heritage were the most economically excluded from the labour market, with 80.8 per cent of interviewees from this group saying that state benefits were their main source of income and only 16.4 per cent supported by their own wages.

Lack of educational qualifications or low educational attainment and poor skills are major causes of unemployment for offenders. The interviewees were asked if they had any educational qualifications. Nearly two-thirds (63.3 per cent) of all respondents reported having educational qualifications (see Table 5.2).

The majority of these qualifications were GCSE, O level or similar certificates. Many also claimed to have vocational qualifications such

Table 5.2 Educational qualifications

Qualifications?	Number (valid per cent)
Yes	304 (63.3)
No	177 (36.7)
TOTAL	481 (100)

as NVQs, City and Guilds, BTEC National Diplomas, HNCs and HNDs. The other reported qualifications included training or trade certificates. Degrees or postgraduate and equivalent qualifications were reported by 3.1 per cent (see Table 5.3).

It is interesting to note that whereas 63.3 per cent of the sample said that they had some educational qualifications, about the same proportion (65.9 per cent) was unemployed. This indicates that, for many of the offenders, having qualifications did little for them in terms of employment.

Many of the interviewees blamed racial discrimination in the job market for their employment status and unemployment. The following statements are some of the views expressed by the offenders:

> In this country I think colour is part of the reason why Black and Asian people don't get the same opportunities. I've been to jobs where I've been more qualified than white people have but I haven't got the job 'cause of racism.

> Loads of my Black friends, like me, don't have jobs. It's very hard to get a job if you're Black and even worse if you've been in prison. And another thing, even if you do get a job it's nearly always a shit job that doesn't pay well or is boring.

Table 5.3 Nature and level of educational qualifications

Qualifications	Number (per cent)
Basic vocational qualifications: NVQ 123, HNC, City and Guilds, CLAIT, BTEC National Diploma	168 (34.7)
Higher vocational or professional qualifications: NVQ42, HND, nursing, accountancy	21 (4.3)
CSE/GCSE/O level	174 (35.9)
OA or AS level	1 (0.1)
A level or equivalent	30 (6.1)
Degree, postgraduate or equivalent	15 (3.1)
Other qualifications: access, bodyguard training, first aid, health and safety, modelling, Prince's Trust certificate, Pitman Typing qualifications, ESOL	31 (6.3)

I've applied for so many jobs [and] sent CVs, but it's really hard getting a job if you're a young Black man. I applied to McDonald's but they said that they couldn't give me a job 'cause of my haircut, but that's my ethnic identity, it's my culture. What would you think if I told you to cut your hair to do what you're doing? It's ridiculous innit?

Over one-fifth (23.7 per cent) of the interviewees cited problems with employment, while 40.4 per cent mentioned problems with money as reasons for them getting into trouble. Ex-offender unemployment is positively linked to reoffending (SEU 2002). There is also evidence of a link between ex-offenders gaining employment and desistance from reoffending (Goldblatt and Lewis 1998). Apart from ex-prisoners, ex-probationers are also more likely to reoffend if they are not in regular employment (ACOP 1994; Davis *et al.* 1997). Low income and unemployment are key drivers of social exclusion and future criminality. For example, the Cambridge Study in Delinquent Development has shown that offenders who have had a reasonably stable record of employment are less likely to reoffend than those who have not (Farrington 1995).

Educational exclusion

One of the main reasons why the interviewees did not have higher or more useful qualifications could be linked to their experience of schooling. Almost half (40.8 per cent) of the respondents gave negative accounts of schooling, compared with 35.3 per cent who gave positive accounts. Twenty-two per cent gave mixed accounts of school while 1.5 per cent gave no opinions because they did not have any experience of schooling (see Table 5.4).

Table 5.4 Experience of school

Opinions of school	Number (valid per cent)
Positive	165 (35.3)
Negative	191 (40.8)
Mixed	105 (22.4)
Didn't go to school	7 (1.5)
TOTAL	468 (100)

Table 5.5 shows differences in terms of ethnicity. It can be seen that while many respondents had poor experiences of school, this was particularly true for the Black and mixed heritage groups.

There are also marked differences within these ethnic categories (n = 469). Black African respondents were significantly (p<0.01) more likely to give positive accounts of school than all other ethnic groups. While a majority of Black African offenders described their feelings about school as generally positive (56.0 per cent), only a quarter of Black Caribbean (26.7 per cent) and Black Other (24.4 per cent) offenders and a third of mixed heritage offenders (30.6 per cent) did likewise. Black African offenders were also less likely than Black Caribbean offenders to report that they truanted or were suspended. They were also more favourable in their responses to their teachers: two-thirds (69.2 per cent) gave positive accounts of their teachers compared to one-third (35.2 per cent) of Black Caribbean responses. Finally, Black Africans were less likely to report experiencing racism at school (11.7 per cent) than the Black Caribbean (19.3 per cent), Pakistani (13.9 per cent), Bangladeshi (33.3 per cent), Indian (22.6 per cent) and mixed heritage (23.6 per cent) interviewees.

These negative experiences of education are important. In particular, evidence suggests that truants are more than three times more likely to offend than non-truants and that there is a link between time lost from education and crime in later life, with a third of all prisoners having been regular truants from school and half of all male prisoners having been excluded from classes (SEU 1998b; Berridge *et al.* 2001). More importantly, it is reasonable to assume that truancy and permanent school exclusion can lead to low educational achievement, which could lead to unemployment, social exclusion and possible future offending or reoffending.

Table 5.5 School experiences by ethnicity

Ethnicity	Positive n (%)	Negative n (%)	Mixed response n (%)	No comment (didn't go to school) n (%)
Black	101 (33.7)	125 (41.7)	72 (24.0)	2 (0.7)
Asian	34 (43.0)	27 (34.2)	18 (22.8)	
Mixed heritage	22 (30.6)	34 (47.2)	13 (18.1)	3 (4.2)
Other	8 (47.1)	5 (29.4)	2 (11.8)	2 (11.8)
TOTAL	165 (35.3)	191 (40.8)	105 (22.4)	7 (1.5)

Research already shows that African-Caribbean children are six times more likely to be excluded from school (SEU 1998b). While the causes of school exclusion are complex, experience of racism or racist bullying while in school, and the lack of an inclusive and more culturally aware school curriculum that would make children of Black and minority ethnic backgrounds feel more respected and valued, and thereby feel more willing to attend school, are likely causes in relation to many Black and minority ethnic children (see Cooper 2002). Research has shown that some white teachers' perceptions and expectations of African-Caribbean pupils 'played an active though unintended role in the creation of conflict with African-Caribbean pupils, thereby reducing black young people's opportunity to achieve' (Sparkes 1999; Sparkes and Glennerster 2002).

Geographical and environmental exclusion

Geographical exclusion in the context of the present study is measured in terms of housing (or lack of it) and geographical area or community. First, we discuss what our interviewees told us about their housing conditions. Being socially excluded in terms of housing could involve a wide range of circumstances, such as living in property that is unfit or in serious disrepair, being trapped in run-down housing estates, living in communities with crime and disorder problems, or being homeless (see Bradshaw *et al.* 2004). Table 5.6 shows that two-thirds of the offenders in the national survey said they lived in rented or supported housing (for example, sheltered accommodation), less than a quarter said that they lived in their own houses and the remainder lived in 'other' types of accommodation (including with relatives or friends) or had 'no fixed abode'.

Table 5.6 The types of housing in which the offenders lived

Type of housing	Number (valid per cent)	
Own	88	(18.6)
Rented or supported	305	(64.4)
No fixed abode	20	(4.3)
Other	60	(12.7)
TOTAL	**473**	**(100)**

The low number of those with no fixed abode (homeless) conceals the nature and extent of the problems of housing faced by these offenders. The 'Other' category typically included people with transitional housing arrangements such as living with friends or in supported or temporary accommodation like hostels for ex-offenders, who may well be considered as being homeless. Studies have shown that people from Black and ethnic minority groups are disproportionately more likely to be homeless. Whereas Black and minority ethnic groups were under-represented among rough sleepers, they are over-represented among those in hostels (Burrows 1997). Research has also shown that there is a possible link between lack of housing and offending or reoffending by ex-offenders (Carlisle 1996; NACRO 1999; National Housing Federation 2000; Wardhaugh 2000). The risks are high among offenders who live in temporary accommodation, as indicated by one interviewee:

> I left home when I was 17. Since then I've been in hostels. [I am] 25 now – that's a long time. Because I've been moving from hostel to hostel I've been meeting new people who are into stealing and crime. You've nothing to do in [a] hostel, no money, and as you're living with them you need to 'stay in with them'. If I had my own flat I wouldn't be doing any stealing or getting into trouble.

A further dimension of housing is its social location, or the nature and characteristics of the surrounding community. Many of our interviewees did not describe the areas where they lived. For those who did, the most common descriptions were: 'an inner city area' (13.1 per cent), a poor area with lots of crime (20.0 per cent), or a predominantly non-white or mixed area (14.7 per cent). One interviewee described his area in these words:

> Dirty, smells, crack heads. [I] dislike living on the estate – [it] makes it harder to stay out of trouble. [I] would like to move to [the] country [and] start again. [I] would not bring up [my] family here if I had a choice. All my choices are closed off.

Indeed, those members of Britain's ethnic minority population who are subject to exclusionary practices in the housing market have little or no opportunity to live in more desirable areas. This has led to the creation of ethnic enclaves (see Wardak 2000 for an account of 'closed' Asian communities in Scotland). The Social Exclusion Unit's definition of social exclusion refers to both people and places: to individuals and to the areas where they live. People who are poor and live in a deprived neighbourhood are presumed to be worse off than poor people who live in other areas. The geographical area may also affect outcomes such as education and employment (Atkinson and Kintrea 2001; Buck 2001). For example, it has been found that neighbourhoods do influence educational outcomes irrespective of family resources, albeit to a small degree. According to Gibbons (2002), 'a child brought up in a neighbourhood ranked at the bottom of the educational hierarchy would need parents educated to something like degree level to give him or her the same educational opportunities as another from an average background' (cited in Bradshaw *et al.* 2004: 88). Research appears also to indicate that there is an association between living in deprived neighbourhoods and a variety of social problems, including crime, which cannot be explained by individual factors alone (see Ellen and Turner 1997).

Experiences of the criminal justice system

The Black and Asian probationers were asked about their experiences of the criminal justice system as a whole and of different criminal justice agencies in particular. They expressed their views about the police, probation officers, lawyers, magistrates, judges, court staff and prison officers (Calverley *et al.* 2004: 49–51). The interviews revealed a common feeling that treatment by criminal justice agencies was generally fair, with the exception of the police, where the majority felt that their treatment was unfair. The offenders were then asked to mention what they regarded as 'unfair treatment'. Examples of unfair treatment included being treated differently compared with their white counterparts (for example, being picked on because of their colour, and the use of racially abusive and belittling language such as nicknames), being looked down upon, being misrepresented or simply not being listened to. Others included the use of unreasonable force, being treated like a criminal, being assumed to be guilty and experiencing staff as not caring. Table 5.7 (based on Calverley *et al.* 2004) gives a list of the three most frequently occurring allegations of unfair treatment levelled against each criminal justice agency.

Several features of this table are interesting. The use of unnecessary force is mentioned in relation to the two agencies within the criminal justice system legally authorised to use force, namely the police and prison staff. In addition, some police were said to make unfair

Table 5.7 Behaviour regarded as unfair treatment: most frequently occurring responses (excluding 'other')
Percentages are of all respondents (weighted)

Professional group	Most frequent complaint	Second most frequent complaint	Third most frequent complaint
The police	Using unnecessary force (17.7 per cent)	Picked on me because of my colour (16.1 per cent)	Making unfair assumption of guilt (7.2 per cent)
Magistrates	Being excessively punitive (12.0 per cent)	Not listening (6.8 per cent)	Picked on me because of my colour (3.9 per cent)
Prison staff	Picked on me because of my colour (7.7 per cent)	Using belittling language (5.7 per cent)	Using unnecessary force (3.4 per cent)
Judges	Being excessively punitive (7.7 per cent)	Picked on me because of my colour (4.3 per cent)	Not listening (3.7 per cent)
Court staff	Using belittling language (4.2 per cent)	Picked on me because of my colour (0.7 per cent)	Treated me like a criminal (0.3 per cent)
Probation officer who wrote your report	Misrepresented me/what I did/what I will do (3.6 per cent)	Not listening (0.7 per cent)	Being excessively punitive (0.7 per cent)
Your solicitor	Didn't care about me (3.3 per cent)	Could not be bothered (3.0 per cent)	Picked on me because of my colour (0.8 per cent)
Probation officer in court	Using belittling language (0.9 per cent)	Misrepresented me (0.7 per cent)	Didn't care about me (0.6 per cent)

assumptions of guilt. Allegations of racist behaviour ('being picked on because of my colour') were levelled against some police, and, by a lower proportion of interviewees, against some solicitors, magistrates, judges, court and prison staff. Similarly, some solicitors were accused of not caring or simply 'couldn't be bothered', while some judges and magistrates were seen as excessively punitive, and some court staff and prison staff were described as using belittling language.

Although probation officers emerged relatively well from this part of the survey (and were hardly ever believed to have 'picked on me because of my colour'), the most frequent complaint against them concerned misrepresentation in pre-sentence reports. Overall, while there are obvious possibilities of subjectivity and bias in complaints of this kind, there are issues raised here which all criminal justice agencies will need to consider in their attempts to deliver equal justice.

Several studies on the experiences of Black and minority ethnic people within the criminal justice system have grappled with the question of whether the disproportionate representation of these offenders in official crime and victimisation figures is due to differential offending, discriminatory practices within the criminal justice system or other factors (see Bowling and Phillips 2002). While many studies of police stop and search, arrest, detention and court sentencing claim to have identified elements of prejudice, discrimination or injustice in the treatment of Black and minority offenders in the British criminal justice system, conceptual and methodological problems make it difficult to reach general conclusions. Most studies have settled for various definitions of 'indirect' racism, while only a few have alleged direct racism (see Hood 1992; FitzGerald 1993). In recent years, the debates have moved swiftly towards the position that these discriminatory practices may indeed be institutionalised (Macpherson 1999). The responses of the interviewees in this study suggest that they believed some of their treatment to be racially motivated. Other experiences such as 'belittling language', being misrepresented, unnecessary force and unfair assumptions of guilt could also imply racism, but in addition raise questions about procedural fairness and unprofessional conduct.

Experiences as victims

Questions were also asked about the offenders' experiences as victims of crime. The majority of the offenders in the survey (64.6 per cent) claimed that they had been victims of crime. Property crime, robbery (including mugging) and violent (non-racist) crimes were the most frequently experienced crimes.

British Crime Survey figures since the 1980s have persistently shown minority ethnic people to have higher levels of victimisation than whites. Findings from the 2001/02 and 2003/04 British Crime Surveys show that people from Black and minority ethnic backgrounds were at greater risk of experiencing crime overall (including racially motivated crime) than the white majority (see Home Office 2004, 1981; Maung and Mirrlees-Black 1994; Percy 1998).

The results of the national survey of probationers confirm the findings of previous studies that being a victim of crime is strongly correlated to place of abode, which is also influenced by economic status and 'race'. Studies have shown that disadvantaged communities generally have high rates of burglary and there is a tendency for people who live in such areas to be assaulted nearer their own homes (Hirschfield *et al.* 1995). Deprivation has also been found to be linked to repeat victimisation (Ellingworth *et al.* 1995; Osborne *et al.* 1996; Farrell *et al.* 1996; see also Gray 2000 on repeat victimisation in Asian communities). Communities with the highest crime rates have been found also to have a higher concentration of poor young families, an increasing concentration of children and teenagers, poor young Black and Asian families, lone parents, ex-prisoners and political asylum seekers (Osborne *et al.* 1992; Osborne and Tseloni 1995, cited in Bradshaw *et al.* 2004). With specific reference to racist crimes, Bowling (1999) argued that the risks are higher for low income Black and minority ethnic people living in poor areas.

In addition, analysis of British Crime Survey data shows that areas with high density minority populations are more likely to be places with high levels of anti-social behaviour (Budd and Sims 2001; Ellis and Fletcher 2003; Nicholas and Walker 2004). Analysis of the number of Anti-Social Behaviour Orders (ASBOs) issued in the 42 police force areas between April 1999 and September 2001 shows that the highest numbers of ASBOs were issued in police force areas with high density minority ethnic populations (Campbell 2002). Research has also shown that minority ethnic people are less likely than whites to report their victimisation to the police (Seagrave 1989; Bowling 1999; Home Office 2004; Yarrow 2005). In this national survey, only 63.2 per cent of those who were victims of crime reported their victimisation to the police. Lack of confidence that the police would do anything was the most frequently mentioned reason for not reporting the crimes to the police (32.8 per cent). Half (51.9 per cent) of those who made the effort to report the crime said that they were not treated fairly by the police. Studies have shown that police response to everyday crimes that affect minority ethnic people, and particularly racially motivated crimes, could be insensitive and sometimes racist (Bowling 1999; Macpherson 1999).

Implications for attitudes towards the criminal justice system and its legitimacy

The national survey explored the nature and extent of social disadvantage experienced by Black and Asian probationers and their views of the criminal justice system. The study revealed that these offenders have experiences of social exclusion that result, in part, from their ethnicity, geographical location, economic positions and experiences of schooling. In addition, the study shows that these offenders have also experienced what they report as discriminatory and unfair treatment from criminal justice agencies. These exclusionary and discriminatory practices, in turn, have important implications for the way in which Black and Asian offenders relate to the criminal justice system, for their confidence in the system and most importantly for their perceptions of the legitimacy of the system.

Confidence in the criminal justice system is influenced by expectations of what the system could and should deliver. Findings from the 2001 British Crime Survey show that ethnic minorities have confidence in many aspects of the criminal justice system but not as regards the treatment of suspects and witnesses (Mirrlees-Black 2001; Cole *et al.* 2005; Green *et al.* 2004; Johnson *et al.* 2005). Lack of trust or confidence affects perceptions of legitimacy. Judgements about the fairness of outcomes play an important role in shaping people's reactions to decisions made by authorities (see Tyler 1990, 2001). The less confidence people have in the criminal justice system, the less likely they are to accept the decisions of criminal justice professionals as legitimate.

Legitimacy refers to the belief that an authority is entitled to be obeyed. Theories and research on the psychology of justice suggest that people are strongly affected by their assessments of what is just or fair. The motivation underlying everyday compliance with the law is not typically the fear of punishment but is essentially because the process is perceived to be fair and unbiased and in accord with moral values. When people view legal authorities as legitimate, they voluntarily follow their directives, even if they do not think they will be caught and punished for ignoring them. In other words, people who have trust and confidence in the fairness of the procedures and feel that they are fairly treated are more likely to obey the law. People who have lost respect for the law's legitimacy are more likely to break the law themselves.

Widespread legitimacy is also essential for criminal justice professionals themselves to be able to function effectively. A reduced sense of the legitimacy of the criminal justice system emanating from biased and discriminatory practices can result in public isolation or even rejection, of criminal justice agencies or what they stand for. In an American study, Lind and Tyler found that people who feel fairly treated are more willing to accept decisions, even if those decisions are unfavourable (Lind and Tyler 1992; see also Tyler *et al.* 1997).

In the national survey, Black and Asian offenders' perceptions of fairness relate to unbiased (non-racist) behaviour, being treated with dignity and respect and having their cultural needs and concerns acknowledged. This confirms Lind and Tyler's position that people focus on ethical rather than personal gains and losses, when they are reacting to their experiences with the criminal justice system. Perceptions of fairness can also be connected with respecting the religious needs of offenders and accepting their cultural needs even where they tend to conflict with dominant legal doctrines – for example, the tradition of carrying ritual weapons in some public religious festivals.

Legitimacy can be partly restored where legal authorities build a culture within which people feel a moral responsibility to abide by the law. More importantly, confidence and legitimacy can be restored where criminal justice departments are more representative of the communities they serve. This was mentioned by a majority of offenders in the national survey. However, the issues of confidence in criminal justice and its legitimacy are also closely linked to the disadvantageous structural and cultural locations of Black and Asian people in the wider British society. Until Black and Asian people are fully included into the economic, social, cultural and political institutions of the wider British society and are treated as full citizens, they are likely to continue to question the legitimacy of the official institutions of this exclusive society.

References

ACOP (Association of Chief Officers of Probation) (1994) *Advice on Employment, Training and Education Issues.* London: ACOP.

Atkinson, A. (1998) 'Social Exclusion, Poverty and Unemployment', in A. Atkinson and J. Hills (eds) *Exclusion, Employment and Opportunity*, CASE Paper 4. London: CASE.

Atkinson, R. and Kintrea, K. (2001) 'Disentangling Area Effects: Evidence from Deprived and Non-deprived Neighbourhoods', *Urban Studies*, 38, 2277–98.

Berridge, D., Brodie, I., Pitts, J., Porteous, D. and Tarling, R. (2001) *The Independent Effects of Permanent Exclusion from School on the Offending Careers of Young People*, RDS Occasional Paper No. 71. London: Home Office.

Bowling, B. (1999) *Violent Racism: Victimisation, Policing and Social Context*, revised edn. Oxford: Oxford University Press.

Bowling, B. and Phillips, C. (2002) *Racism, Crime and Justice*. London: Longman.

Bradshaw, J., Kemp, P., Baldwin, S. and Rowe, A. (2004) *The Drivers of Social Exclusion: A Review of the Literature for the Social Exclusion Unit*. York: Social Policy Research Unit, University of York.

Buck, N. (2001) 'Identifying Neighbourhood Effects on Social Exclusion', *Urban Studies*, 38, 2251–75.

Budd, T. and Sims, L. (2001) *Antisocial Behaviour and Disorder: Findings from the 2000 British Crime Survey*. London: Home Office.

Burrows, R. (1997) 'The Social Distribution of the Experience of Homelessness', in R. Burrows, N. Pleace and D. Quilgars (eds), *Homelessness and Social Policy*. London: Routledge.

Calverley, A., Cole, B., Kaur, G., Lewis, S., Raynor, P., Sadeghi, S., Smith, D., Vanstone, M. and Wardak, A. (2004) *Black and Asian Offenders on Probation*, Home Office Research Study 277. London: Home Office.

Campbell, S. (2002) *A Review of Anti-social Behaviour Orders*, Home Office Research Study 236. London: Home Office.

Carlisle, J. (1996) *The Housing Needs of Ex-Prisoners*. York: Centre for Housing Policy.

Carter, J. (2001) *Ethnicity, Exclusion and the Workplace*. London: Palgrave Macmillan.

Cole, B., Davidson, N., Adamson, S. and Murtuja, B. (2005) *Black and Minority Ethnic People's Confidence in the Criminal Justice System in West Yorkshire*, Final Report. Hull: University of Hull.

Cooper, C. (2002) *Understanding School Exclusion: Challenging Processes of Docility*. Hull: University of Hull.

Davis, G., Caddick, B., Lyon, K., Doling, L., Hasler, J., Webster, A., Reed, M. and Ford, K. (1997) *Addressing the Literacy Needs of Offenders under Probation Supervision*, Home Office Research Study 169. London: Home Office.

Ellen, I. and Turner, M. (1997) 'Does Neighbourhood Matter? Assessing Recent Evidence', *Housing Policy Debate*, 8, 833–66.

Ellingworth, D., Osborne, D. R., Trickett, A. and Pease, K. (1995) *Prior Victimisation and Crime Risk*, Quantitative Criminology Group Report. Manchester: University of Manchester.

Ellis, C. and Fletcher, G. (2003) 'Antisocial Behaviour and Disorder', in C. Flood-Page and J. Taylor (eds) (2003) *Crime in England and Wales 2001/2002: Supplementary Volume.* London: Home Office.

Farrell, G., Ellingworth, D. and Pease, K. (1996) 'High Crime Rates, Repeat Victimisation and Routine Activities', in T. Bennett (ed.), *Preventing Crime and Disorder: Tackling Strategies and Responsibilities.* Cambridge: Institute of Criminology.

Farrington, D. P. (1995) 'The Development of Offending and Antisocial Behaviour from Childhood: Key Findings from the Cambridge Study in Delinquent Development', *Journal of Child Psychology and Psychiatry and Allied Disciplines*, 36: 6, 929–64.

FitzGerald, M. (1993) *Ethnic Minorities in the Criminal Justice System,* Home Office Research Study 20, Royal Commission on Criminal Justice. London: Home Office.

Gibbons, S. (2002) *Neighbourhood Effects on Educational Achievement: Evidence from the Census and National Child Development Study.* London: Centre for the Economics of Education.

Goldblatt, P. and Lewis, C. (eds) (1998) *Reducing Offending: An Assessment of Research Evidence on Ways of Dealing with Offending Behaviour,* Home Office Research Study 187. London: Home Office.

Gray, P. (2000) 'Repeat Victimisation in the Asian Community: A Study of Domestic Burglary', *Crime Prevention and Community Safety: An International Journal*, 2: 2, 53–65.

Green, H., Connolly, H. and Farmer, C. (2004) *2003 Home Office Citizenship Survey: People, Families and Communities,* Home Office Research Study 289. London: Home Office.

Hirschfield, A., Bowers, K., and Brown, P. J. B. (1995) 'Exploring Relations Between Crime and Disadvantage on Merseyside', *European Journal on Crime Policy and Research*, 3: 3, 93–112.

Home Office (1981) *Racial Attacks: Report of a Home Office Study.* London: Home Office.

Home Office (2004) *Ethnicity, Victimisation and Worry about Crime: Findings from the 2001/02 and 2002/03 British Crime Surveys.* London: Home Office Research, Development and Statistics Directorate.

Hood, R. (1992) *Race and Sentencing.* Oxford: Clarendon Press.

Johnson, A., Wake, R. and Hill, R. (2005) *Confidence in the Criminal Justice System: Explaining Area Variations in Public Confidence*, Home Office Research Findings No. 251. London: Home Office.

Levitas, R. (1996) 'The Concept of Social Exclusion and the New Durkheimian Hegemony', *Critical Social Policy*, 16, 5–20.

Lind, E. A., and Tyler, T. (eds) (1992) *The Social Psychology of Procedural Justice.* New York: Kluwer.

Macpherson, W. (1999) *The Stephen Lawrence Inquiry: Report of an Inquiry by Sir William Macpherson of Cluny.* Cm 4262-1. London: Home Office.

Maung, N. A. and Mirrlees-Black, C. (1994) *Racially Motivated Crime: A British Crime Survey Analysis.* Research and Planning Unit, Paper 82. London: HMSO.

Mirrlees-Black, C. (2001) *Confidence in the Criminal Justice System: Findings from the 2000 British Crime Survey.* London: Home Office.

Murray, C. (1990) *The Emerging British Underclass.* London: IEA Health and Welfare Unit.

NACRO (1999) *Going Straight Home.* London: NACRO.

NAPO (National Association of Probation Officers) (1993) *Probation Caseload: Income and Employment. A Study of the Financial Circumstances of 1331 Offenders on Probation Supervision.* London: NAPO.

National Housing Federation (2000) *All You Ever Wanted to Know about Housing.* London: National Housing Federation.

Nicholas, S. and Walker, A. (eds) (2004) *Crime in England and Wales 2002/2003: Supplementary Volume 2. Crime, Disorder and the Criminal Justice System – Public Attitudes and Perceptions.* London: Home Office.

Osborne, D. R., and Tseloni, A. (1995) *The Distribution of Household Property Crimes,* Manchester School of Economic Studies Discussion Paper No. 9530. Manchester: University of Manchester.

Osborne, D. R., Ellingworth, D., Hope, T. and Trickett, A. (1996) 'Are Repeatedly Victimised Households Different?', *Journal of Quantitative Criminology,* 12, 223–45.

Osborne, D. R., Trickett, A. and Elder, R. (1992) 'Area Characteristics and Regional Varieties as Determinants of Area Property Crime Levels', *Journal of Quantitative Criminology,* 8, 265–85.

Percy, A. (1998) *Ethnicity and Victimisation: Findings from the 1996 British Crime Survey,* Statistical Bulletin 6/1998. London: Home Office.

Room, G. (1995) 'Poverty in Europe: Competing Paradigms of Analysis', *Policy and Politics,* 23:2, 103–13.

Seagrave, J. (1989) *Racially Motivated Incidents Reported to the Police,* Research and Planning Unit Paper 54. London: HMSO.

SEU (Social Exclusion Unit) (1998a) *Bringing Britain Together: A National Strategy for Neighbourhood Renewal.* London: Office of the Deputy Prime Minister.

SEU (1998b) *Truancy and School Exclusion.* London: Office of the Deputy Prime Minister.

SEU (2002) *Reducing Re-offending by Ex-prisoners.* London: Office of the Deputy Prime Minister.

Silver, H. (1994) 'Social Exclusion and Social Solidarity: Three Paradigms', *International Labour Review,* 133: 35–6, 531–78.

Sparkes, J. (1999) *Schools Education and Social Exclusion.* London: Centre for Analysis of Social Exclusion.

Sparkes, J. and Glennerster, H. (2002) 'Preventing Social Exclusion: Education's Contribution', in: J. Hills, J. Le Grand, and D. Piachaud, (eds), *Understanding Social Exclusion.* Oxford: Oxford University Press.

Tyler, T. R., Boekmann, R. J., Smith, H. J. and Huo, Y. J. (1997) *Social Justice in a Diverse Society.* Boulder, Co.: Westview Press.

Tyler, T. R. (1990) *Why People Obey the Law.* New Haven: Yale University Press.

Tyler, T. R. (2001) 'Obeying the Law in America: Procedural Justice and the Sense of Fairness', *Issues of Democracy: An Electronic Journal of the U.S. Department of State,* 6: 1, 16–21.

Wardak, A. (2000) *Social Control and Deviance: A South Asian Community in Scotland.* Aldershot: Ashgate.

Wardhaugh, J. (2000) *Sub-City: Young People, Homelessness and Crime.* Aldershot: Ashgate.

Yarrow, S. (2005) *The Experiences of Young Black Men as Victims of Crime.* London: Home Office, Office for Criminal Justice Reform.

Chapter 6

The experiences of female minority ethnic offenders: the other 'other'

Loraine Gelsthorpe

As a forty nine year old Black lesbian feminist socialist mother of two, including one boy, and a member of an interracial couple, I usually find myself a part of some group defined as other, deviant, inferior, or just plain wrong.

(Audre Lorde, in *Age, Race, Class and Sex: Women Redefining Difference*, 1992)

Introduction

Justice is relatively easy to picture and very hard to grasp, and the delivery of justice on the ground is highly contentious. This is particularly so when we consider that we live in a gendered and multicultural society and when we consider the social inequalities in society that mean that not all are equal before the law. Race and gender issues are therefore highly pertinent to considerations of Probation Services and programmes for offenders. It is right and proper to pose questions about the way in which the Probation Service acknowledges and responds to diversity in meaningful ways.

The aim of this chapter is thus to focus on some of the issues relating to the experiences of minority ethnic group women within the probation service. The chapter is considerably hampered by a general failure to consider both race and gender issues in the same piece of research or set of statistics, and by a general failure to clarify concepts and categories of ethnicity. Essentially, within the broad realm of Criminology we find that 'race' and 'gender' have been given exclusive attention. What has been conspicuously absent from analyses is an investigation of their various intersections.[1] We might surmise that the combination of being female and being part of a minority group would lead to double problems, but this would be simplistic; it is rather that the effect may concern specific interactions of these identifying features and context. Put another way, minority women offenders may well face a 'double-whammy' of being female in a context where women are 'out of place' (Worrall 1990) and 'alien' because of their ethnicity, but we know far too little about the effect of these additive factors.

Given moves to extend the traditional criminological gaze in recent years, the neglect of a race and gender focus in research is somewhat surprising. Feminist scholarship has had a major impact on criminological thinking at both a theoretical level and in terms of criminal justice practice, for example, and therefore it is perplexing to find it so very difficult to locate relevant statistical information that cuts across the gender and ethnicity divide. Certainly feminist scholars have worked to expose the obvious but hitherto unacknowledged fact that western criminology has been the 'criminology of men' (Gelsthorpe and Morris 1990: 3). Traditional theories based on the study of only half the population were thought to have 'general' application (Gelsthorpe and Morris 1990; Heidensohn 2002). But early feminist critiques of criminology were themselves subject to criticism because of the ethnocentric approach inherent in those critiques of 'man-made' criminology.

Although not the first to address acknowledge ethnicity, Marcia Rice (1990) has forcefully taken feminists to task in this way.[2] As she writes, 'Over the past decade feminist criminologists have been challenging stereotypical representations of female offenders. Despite these advances, black women and women from developing countries have been noticeably absent from this discourse' (1990: 57). She goes on to identify that although there was (at that time) increasing recognition given to black men and crime, none of the studies included a focus on black women. Certainly, writers such as Gilroy (1987), Solomos (1993) and Bowling and Phillips (2002) have argued that social, political and economic marginalisation are relevant factors in any interpretations of the high numbers of black men in the criminal justice system, but there has been relatively little effort to locate Black and Minority Ethnic (BME) women in theoretical discussions and in the criminal justice system (cf. Lewis 1981; Hassan and Thiara 2000; SEU 2002).[3]

This chapter is divided into three sections. In the first section

I make some general observations about the BME population in England and Wales on the grounds that this is pertinent to later considerations of BME women and probation. In the second section I describe a little of what is known about ethnic minority offenders and gender differences in sentencing – since who gets what and why are questions that are critical to an understanding of experiences of a particular penalty. The review of sentencing that this necessarily entails is illustrative of key issues rather than exhaustive, however, due to the diverse nature and limited coverage of the studies drawn upon. In the final section I address what is known about female BME offenders in probation practice and make some general comments on the need to accommodate difference and diversity in probation practice.

The BME population in England and Wales

According to the most recent Home Office Section 95 Overview Report for 2002–2003 (so named because of the additional Section 95 clause within the Criminal Justice Act 1991 which deals with the need for the collection of data for purposes of monitoring in order to avoid unequal treatment), approximately 91 per cent of the population of England and Wales was white.[4] The black population was around two per cent of the population, the Asian population 4.5 per cent, those of mixed origin comprised 1.5 per cent, and 'Other' BME a further one per cent, making a total of nine per cent (ICPR 2004). This is somewhat higher than figures reported in earlier Labour Force Surveys and in the Policy Studies Institute's fourth survey of ethnic minorities, though it is acknowledged that earlier surveys may have underestimated the figures, notwithstanding the complexities in recording ethnicity (Modood et al. 1997). There are also indications that the BME population is a relatively youthful population: over a third of Bangladeshis and Pakistanis are under the age of 16, for instance, compared with one in five of white people (Scott et al. 2001). This is significant in that it is well known that young people are more likely than others to be involved in crime, both as victims and as offenders. We also know that over 50 per cent of BME people live in the 44 most deprived local authority areas, and that over 30 per cent of Chinese people, 40 per cent of African Caribbean and 80 per cent of Pakistani and Bangladeshi people live in households with less than half the national average income (see Modood et al. 1997; SEU 2002). At a general level, it is clear that BME groups are more likely to be unemployed than white people (Leslie *et al.* 1998) although there is some variation; unemployment is high for Black Caribbean, Bangladeshi, Pakistani and Black African groups, for example, but low for Indian and Chinese groups. However, in none of these sources are we given a detailed gender breakdown of the figures.

Few would dispute that BME women are an economically marginalised group. Ethnic minority women's place in the British economy thus cannot be equated with that of either their BME male or white female counterparts. As Mama (1984) has pointed out, black and Asian women have played a specific and unique role in the workforce and union activism. She writes that black women workers are to be found 'in the lower echelons of all the institutions where [they] are employed (this in itself reflects the patterns of a segmented labour market) where the work is often physically heavy (in the factories and the mills no less than in the caring professions), the pay is lowest, and the hours are longest and most anti-social (night-shifts for example)' (cited in Chigwada-Bailey 1997: 37). Chigwada-Bailey adds that 'the forces of "race", class and gender, work in *combination'* to the detriment of minority women. Living in a society where the dominant culture, values and institutions are 'white', and where society is devised and run by men, the privations of life at the bottom of the scale are often combined and compounded for black women (1997: 11).

There are some signs that the situation is changing, especially with regard to post-compulsory education where rates of staying in education are higher for Indian/African Asian women than for some other groups (Modood *et al.* 1997). Moreover, an exploratory analysis by Dale *et al.* (2004) into the ethnic differences in women's demographic characteristics has revealed major differences between ethnic groups in terms of employment, as well as significant changes over time. Black women have tended to remain in full-time employment throughout family formation, whereas white and Indian women have been more likely to be in part-time employment. In contrast, levels of economic activity among Pakistani and Bangladeshi women fell substantially once they had a partner and fell again when they had children. This descriptive analysis suggests it is important to take into consideration the varying demographic and family structures when analysing the economic activity of minority ethnic women; Black Caribbean, Bangladeshi and Pakistani groups of women appear to suffer a range of severe forms of discrimination, as do Black African groups, but to a lesser degree (Modood *et al.* 1997).

This said, the general position of BME women as marginalised is clear. Might we expect figures in the criminal justice system to reflect BME women's general economic disadvantage, given what we know about women's pathways into crime (Gelsthorpe 2004a)?

Black and ethnic minority women in crime and the criminal justice system

While criminal convictions are relatively common for males, they are still unusual for women. Public and media worries about increases in women's crime notwithstanding, it is still the case that women comprise only about a fifth of known offenders (Home Office 2003, 2005). In terms of self-reported offending, while it is seemingly the case that more females are committing crimes than hitherto, the basic male/female discrepancy in rates of involvement pertains (Flood-Page *et al.* 2000). The Home Office's series of Section 95 reports reveal that about 16 per cent of those arrested for notifiable offences are women, but the proportion is higher for fraud and forgery and theft and handling. More women than men are cautioned but this largely reflects the lesser seriousness of their crimes and the high rate of immediate admission of guilt. In terms of sentencing, women are more likely than men to be given a conditional or absolute discharge, or a community sentence, for indictable offences, and are less likely to be fined or sentenced to custody. In terms of community sentences, women account for about 13 per cent of those under the supervision of the Probation Service (the most common sentence for women here being the Community Rehabilitation Order) (RDS NOMS 2004). When sentenced to prison, women tend to receive shorter sentences than men.

Ethnic minority women make up about 29 per cent of the female prison population with a high proportion of these (around 20 per cent) being foreign nationals imprisoned for drug importation and then deported (RDS NOMS 2004). Moreover, the proportion of black sentenced females in prison for drug offences (75 per cent) was almost double the proportion of all sentenced female prisoners in prison for drug offences (41 per cent). Excluding foreign nationals, the proportion of black females serving sentences for drug offences (46 per cent) was still considerably higher than that of white females (26 per cent) and also that of black males (18 per cent).

The differential sentencing patterns between men and women have led some to argue that the system is lenient towards women and others to argue that the system is harsher towards women than it is towards men (Gelsthorpe 2001a). But the sentencing of women is complex and has as much to do with gender-related and offence seriousness factors and previous convictions as any straightforward sex differences.[5] Much has been claimed about the inappropriate use of gender-role stereotypes, and about decision-making that involves judgement of women as 'good' or 'bad' mothers for instance (Gelsthorpe 2001a). But none of the studies includes systematic analysis of the intervening factor of ethnicity.

A comprehensive look at the sentencing of men and women was taken in the mid-1990s, when on the basis of a statistical analysis of matched offenders (male and female) Hedderman and Gelsthorpe (1997) revealed that the magistrates' courts showed a seeming reluctance to imprison some women (depending on offence) and a difference in the use of community penalties for men and women (with sentencers being reluctant to fine women – leading to some women receiving more lenient penalties and others more severe penalties than predicted on the basis of their offences and previous convictions – depending, in part, on 'gender-appropriate behaviour' as well as offence seriousness). But while this study suggests that sentencers divide women into the 'troubled' and 'troublesome', it did not include ethnicity because the data were not available on the National Offender Index, which was used as the main database. Anecdotal evidence in the criminal justice system, however, and research studies from other areas of social policy fuel the idea that the stereotyping of black mothers as bad parents may exacerbate the negative implications of such an observation (Kennedy 1992; Bernard 1995; Chigwada-Bailey 2003).

There is certainly wide concern that receptions into women's prisons have increased enormously over the past decade (Fawcett Commission 2004). The average female population in custody increased by 173 per cent, while the average population of males in custody increased by just 50 per cent by comparison. There are various explanations for this, ranging from popular notions of more drug-related crimes being committed by BME women[6] to an apparent tendency on the part of magistrates to sentence older persistent shoplifters to custody (Gelsthorpe and Morris 2002), and from suggestions of increases in burglary committed by women (Deakin and Spencer 2003) to notions that the increase in the use of imprisonment simply reflects an increase in the number of women being convicted (Hedderman 2004). Thus we should lament the absence of detailed analysis that looks at both gender *and* race issues combined.

The Home Office's series of Section 95 reports also reveal some details in regard to criminal justice system responses to black and minority ethnic group victims and offenders. However, the most recent Section 95 report points out that many areas cannot yet provide information on cautioning rates, prosecutions and convictions broken down by ethnic group. There are particular problems in gaining data from magistrates' courts (and since 95 per cent of criminal cases are dealt with in those courts this means that any analysis based on available statistics is fundamentally flawed). Moreover, the range of national statistics that can chart the sentencing process is extremely limited. What we do know is that the number of offenders sentenced to imprisonment is over four times higher for BME groups than for white groups; however, the statistics are nowhere near sophisticated enough to be able to show *how* one might disentangle the apparent disproportionality in sentencing here.[7] Moreover, little of the analysis includes a gender breakdown, with small exception.

Generally speaking, most commentators agree that there is evidence of cumulative racial discrimination but that few studies show this on their own (Bowling and Phillips 2002). There is perhaps only one sentencing study that has attempted to disentangle the relevant factors to date (and this is rapidly becoming out of date). Hood and Cordovil's (1992) study of sentencing in five Crown Court centres in the West Midlands in the late 1980s concluded that adult male black defendants were slightly more likely to be sent to prison than white defendants and slightly more likely than would have been anticipated in light of their background features (offence seriousness, previous convictions and so on). Although Asian defendants were slightly less likely to be sent to prison than white defendants, both black and Asian offenders received longer sentences than their white counterparts. Notwithstanding criticisms of Hood's research regarding the ethnic categories and other technical queries (Halevy 1995), this is widely considered to be an important study on sentencing. Importantly, 76 black and 14 Asian female offenders were included in the analysis. Custodial sentences were used much less often for women than for men, whatever their ethnic background, but this broadly reflected differences in patterns of offending. In the one court where there was a slightly higher rate of custody for women, the differences in the sentencing of black women compared with white women could largely be explained by factors relating to offence seriousness, although the court's high use of custody compared with other courts was inexplicable. The differences in the pattern of non-custodial penalties imposed on black and white women, particularly in the use of suspended sentences of imprisonment, was found to be explained by the fact that more of the black women had characteristics that placed them in a relatively high-risk group of receiving custody. As to the issue of black women receiving different treatment from white women, however, there was little to support any idea of negative discrimination.[8]

Turning to the theme of BME group experience of probation, Morgan (Chapter 3, this volume) has also considered sentencing in regard to probation practice, ranging from research on pre-sentence reports (and their forerunners, social inquiry reports) through to possible differences in sentencing offenders to non-custodial/community disposals – which might include those that come under the auspices of the Probation Service. The general conclusion here is that there is no overall pattern to the types of non-custodial/community disposals given to BMEs since these tend to differ from one study to another (possibly reflecting general differences between courts in patterns of non-custodial disposals). There tends to be agreement that African-Caribbeans are less likely to receive probation (Moxon 1988; Brown and Hullin 1992) but commentators have come to diametrically opposite conclusions regarding explanations for this. Some have argued that African-Caribbeans are 'up-tariffed'; others argue that there is no difference in the rate of probation orders once other factors such as seriousness of offences and previous convictions are taken into account. For various reasons – small sample sizes, lack of distinction between ethnic minorities, and limited data on variables relevant to sentencing – many of the research studies have proved inconclusive. Moreover, none of these studies include ethnicity *and* gender.[9]

This is a long route to the issue of BME women on probation, but it is a necessary route given the general absence of information on the intersection of race and gender issues in sentencing studies and this is a key message in the chapter. Although there is *some* research on *both* 'race' and 'gender', the intersections of race and gender have been neglected (leaving aside social class which, in itself, may provide significant mediation of criminal justice). Analysis of sentencing, as stated, means consideration of who gets what and why. Thus we are left with pieces of a jigsaw that simply do not fit; it is rather a matter of using the pieces in impressionistic fashion. We basically do not know which BME women get probation or why, although from the preceding discussion we might conclude that there are likely to be fewer Asian women than white or black on probation. Also, broader considerations of gender and sentencing and of ethnicity and sentencing alert us to the strong possibility of negative forms of discrimination in the delivery of Probation Services to BME women.

Black and ethnic minority women on probation

Early research indicates that minority female offenders were less likely than their white counterparts to be made subject to a Community Rehabilitation Order (until 2000 known as a probation order) (Chigwada-Bailey 2003). As stated, in the most recently published statistics on community sentences it appears that in 2003 women accounted for about 13 per cent of those starting orders under supervision by the Probation Service, with the most common sentence being a Community Rehabilitation Order, while for men it was a Community Punishment Order (RDS NOMS 2004). This perhaps bears out broad conceptions of women as 'troubled' rather than 'troublesome', given the different orientations of these penalties, though it could also reflect offence seriousness and assessments of criminogenic needs. Theft and handling was the most common offence for women given a community sentence in 2003, whereas for men summary offences were most common. However, even the recent Offender Management Caseload Statistics (RDS NOMS 2004) do not include reference to ethnicity.

Thus how can we describe the *probation experience* for BME women? As long ago as 1989, Green suggested that Probation Service practice denied the racist context in which many offenders were living and the extent to which this might contribute to their offending behaviour and personal identity. Green suggested that the combination of the court's focus on individual offending rather than the social and economic context in which the offending occurred, alongside probation officers' tendency to pathologise African-Caribbean family life (contrasted with the white middle-class 'norm'), led to a narrow and unreflective institutional response that meant that recommendations to the court for sentencing were often narrow in scope.

In 1990, the National Association of Probation Officers (NAPO) identified in a practice guideline the need to challenge traditional assumptions being made about women and made particular mention of the need to guard against assumptions that women and black clients were more difficult than white men. More than this, analyses of pre-sentence reports (and their forerunners, social enquiry reports) have consistently revealed that the frames of reference within which they are produced reflect dominant white euro-centric culture (Whitehouse 1983; Gelsthorpe 1992; Denney 1992; McQuillan 1992). Thus we might easily conclude from this that BME women's experiences may reflect an alienation from the system. In one of the few studies that has involved 'consumers' of probation services, Chigwada-Bailey describes mixed perceptions of probation officers' ability to assist BME women (with some interviewees feeling that the officers were patronising them and not really understanding where they were coming from); among the 20 black female interviewees in her study there was a strong sense that black officers should 'behave black' in order to maintain legitimacy in their eyes (2003: 71–2).

More generally, there have been strong criticisms that the Probation Service, in both policy and practice, has neglected women. Successive reports have commented on this neglect. A timely focus on women in 1991, for example (given the introduction of the Section 95 clause in relation to the Criminal Justice Act 1991), revealed that few probation services had developed distinctive policy strategies in relation to women and it was largely assumed that what had been created for men would be suitable for women (HMIP 2001). A similar review of provision for women in 1996 (HMIP 1996) reported that very few probation areas had strategies or guidelines or other mechanisms to ensure that women had equal access to community sentences. Further findings included the following:

- A minority of areas provided females-only group work and community service tasks.

- The needs of women were not a priority when developing local partnership arrangements to deal with misuse of drugs and alcohol and the effect of unemployment.

- The provision of safe and secure accommodation for women (both pre-trial and post-trial) was patchy at best.

- There was sometimes a failure to consider gender-related issues in the preparation of pre-sentence reports on women. A lack of knowledge about childcare provision, for example, militated against women being sentenced to community sentences (particularly Community Service Orders as they were then known).[10]

Further work on this theme of access to services by women was developed by Imogen Brown in 1997 and it was revealed that the kinds of information available to sentencers via pre-sentence reports varied in significant respects for males and females *and*, crucially, according to ethnic group. The Thematic Probation Inspectorate Report *Towards Race Equality* (HMIP 2000) similarly made critical comment on the quality of pre-sentence reports, noting a significantly higher quality of reports overall written on white than on minority ethnic offenders. The failure to comment on the management of risk in the majority of pre-sentence reports prepared on African/African-Caribbean offenders was a major concern (HMIP 2000: 18). The report went further and noted: 'The failure by the majority of services to collect data on race and ethnic origin and monitor their performance on reports written on minority ethnic offenders contributed to inconsistent service delivery' (HMIP 2000: 18). Moreover, while the survey that led to the report identified that some services were beginning to develop culturally sensitive services to minority ethnic offenders, there was little to suggest that such initiatives included BME women offenders. Overall, this was a sobering report, all the more so in view of other reports on women offenders that demanded closer attention to issues of equality and to women's distinctive needs (Prison Reform Trust 2000; Hedderman 2004).

The characteristics of female offenders and their needs are relatively well known, but while some of these are shared with men, some are not. Women are often the victims of physical, sexual and emotional abuse at the hands of intimates or others known to them, for example. Moreover, they are often mothers and the primary care-givers in relation to children; they have less experience of education and are more often than men unemployed at the time of their offence, and many are financially dependent (Rumgay 2000). At the same time, many have addictions to drugs or alcohol as well as physical and mental health concerns (Prison Reform Trust 2000; Hedderman 2004). In short, women's pathways into crime are different from those of men, they are shorter, their institutional adjustment patterns are different and their resettlement needs are different too (Gelsthorpe 2004a; 2004b), although we know far too little about BME women's needs within this overall pattern.

As a number of researchers have suggested, criminal justice practice and probation practice in particular are increasingly dominated by notions of risk and risk-assessment (Kemshall 2003; Garland 2001). Risk is both gendered and racialised (Bhui 1999; Lupton 1999) but there is acknowledged need to go beyond the idea of simply adding a variable or two to adapt risk-assessment instruments in order to deal with race and gender issues. Such adjustments would not accurately reflect the extent of differences between men and women, nor indeed between women.

Turning back to probation provision again, a follow-up probation inspection report (HMIP 2004) followed in the wake of various national initiatives: the publication of a national service strategic statement (NPS 2001), national implementation of the Race Relations (Amendment) Act 2000 with a requirement for all probation areas to have Race Equality Schemes in place by May 2002, and the publication of *The Heart of the Dance* (NPS 2003), which involves a diversity strategy for the National Probation Service. This last report notes several areas of improvement in respect of meeting targets for BME recruitment and issuing guidance in relation to race and diversity within What Works strategies among other things, but little change in respect of the quality of reports on BME and white offenders. The NPS report *The New Choreography* (NPS 2001) enshrines three particular concepts to promote equality in provision: inclusiveness, transparency and openness. It identifies new targets in respect of the recruitment of Asian staff in general and the recruitment of BME staff to senior management, as well as women to Board chairs. More particularly, it promotes the idea that NPS services must be 'accessible, appropriate, inclusive and responsive to all offenders from minority groups in respect of service delivery and policy covering accredited programmes, hostel regimes and general case-management' (NPS 2003: 19).

In terms of basic probation provision for women in general and BME women in particular, numerous logistical difficulties are mentioned (Barker 1993; Howard League 1999). The low numbers of women given community punishment at any one time can make it difficult to bring together sufficient women for a 'working group', and as a consequence women have been attached to men's work groups or given work tasks on their own – thus denying them the benefits of working in all-women groups (see Howard League 1999; Goodwin and McIvor 2001).

Another key issue in all of this, of course, is whether or not dedicated group work or other provision for black and Asian women has been sufficiently developed. One notable survey of such programmes was conducted in 1993 when it was shown that out of 1,463 groups just three were for black or Asian offenders only – and men, at that (Caddick 1993). But a number of initiatives emerged following the review, including the Black Offenders' Initiative, set up by the North Thames Resource Unit, which shaped its activities around the needs and experiences of black and Asian offenders (Browne and Poole 1997). Other areas followed suit: Chigwada-Bailey (2003: 74) reports that the then South West Probation Training Consortium produced a training manual *Making a Difference: A Positive and Practical Guide Working with Black Offenders*. But again, these initiatives reflected the need to develop provision for men. Later surveys (Hedderman and Sugg 1997; Underdown 1998; Powis and Walmsley 2002) identify more programmes for black offenders and some for women, but none clearly discernible for BME women offenders. More recent developments still have emerged from the Home Office's Women's Offending Reduction Programme (WORP 2004), where strong intention to address women's needs and issues in relation to policy and practice is expressed. Yet it remains the case that only one programme for women has been accredited, and again, it does not give obvious attention to black and Asian women's experiences or needs (Home Office 2004). We should remind ourselves, of course, that we do not know precisely what these specific needs are, but the point here is that *any* programme should arguably address both gender issues and matters relating to ethnicity, whether these be to do with people's material circumstances and pathways into crime, or effective learning experiences.

It is generally the case that not only have BME offenders been neglected in programme development, but women offenders have too. As Shaw and Hannah-Moffat, among others, have argued, much of the discussion around the evidence based initiatives of recent years has been silent on the origins of the research on which they are based, that is, on men (Shaw and Hannah-Moffat 2004: 90). But these initiatives, reflecting rehabilitation and treatment effectiveness, and based on psychological principles, make a number of assumptions about the style and appropriateness of treatment programmes for different clients.

The problems of using so-called 'gender neutral' risk assessment instruments and programmes may well be amplified when cultural or ethnic differences are considered alongside gender differences. We know too little about the qualitative differences in the English and Welsh context of probation practice to be able to comment further here, except to say that we might usefully draw on experiences elsewhere to at least alert us to the need to consider the possibility of gender based differences being compounded by ethnic and cultural differences in circumstance, pathways into crime and criminogenic needs and risks. Writing about the Canadian experience, for example, Jackson argues that the intersection of race, gender and class presents 'a special context of difference for Aboriginal women, grounded in a colonial legacy of assimilation policies' (1999: 101). The point here is that BME women have largely been ignored in the probation context and more information is needed on their cultural and social distinctness, their personal and social histories, and their motivations for and pathways into crime.

As Shaw and Hannah-Moffat have put it, designers of programmes assume

> that those which have been developed for men will be applicable for women, that aspects of their lives other than their thinking patterns and individual deficiencies are relatively unimportant in reducing offending (and risk), and that ethnic and cultural differences are irrelevant in the grand scheme of scale reduction, predictive validity and programme delivery. (2004: 91).

Thus if offenders are the criminalised 'other' by virtue of their offending behaviour and removal from the category of 'good citizens', then BME women become the other 'other', separated off and seen through a hegemonic masculine and culturally specific white western lens. Certainly, it may be suggested that BME women have criminogenic needs that are not met by the programmes designed for 'mainstream' white, male, mentally stable offenders, although, as previously stated, we need more research on this.

Interestingly, recent research by Calverley *et al.* (2004), based on a survey of nearly 500 black and Asian male offenders, makes an important contribution to 'what works' for black and Asian offenders if only in displacing some practitioners' beliefs that such offenders *always* wish to be supervised by someone from the same ethnic group and attend programmes for groups containing only members from minority ethnic groups. Over half of the sample surveyed indicated that it would make no difference who the supervisor was, though a substantial third expressed support for the idea of supervision by someone from the same ethnic group. Of those who attended programmes, about a third indicated that the ethnic composition of the group was unimportant (most said it should be mixed).

But it would be a mistake to assume that these findings necessarily hold for BME women. Enough is known about women's experiences in general, if not BME women's experiences specifically, to suggest that gender related factors are critical to effective work with offenders (see Zaplin 1998, and McIvor 2004 for an overview). Indeed, gender related factors are a strong predictor of both offending patterns and treatment needs (McIvor 2004). But what we really need to do now is look at BME women's distinctive patterns of offending, their distinctive needs, *and* at what works for them in the probation context, logistical problems notwithstanding. If there is genuine intention to promote evidence based practice, then effectiveness should win out over economy – even if that means some creative thinking to address the issue of small numbers of female offenders, and smaller numbers of BME women still.

Durrance and Williams (2003) analyse Pathfinder programmes and argue that programme material that explicitly addresses the social and cultural context within which offending occurs might better engage black and Asian offenders. In one sense, they press the case for probation practice to acknowledge the lived realities of many offenders: poor neighbourhoods, limited opportunities and high visibility to the police through spending a good deal of time on the streets. Add to this the common internalisation of racism and we can see how this impacts on self-esteem, self-identity and self-conceptualisation (Maruna 2001). This is a welcome point. Clearly, probation practice should acknowledge gender related and ethnicity factors as key elements of the 'lived realities' to which Durrance and Williams (2003) refer. There is strong evidence to suggest that the promotion of effectiveness requires recognition of gender, social and cultural differences combined, and thus far there has been too little attention given to the issue (Gelsthorpe 2001b). In many ways, this chapter serves only to reiterate this simple point, but it cannot be overstated.

As we look to the implementation of the Criminal Justice Act 2003 it is clear that the NPS and NOMS will have to manage a range of community provision within the context of a generic community order. This means that probation officers and others involved in the probation and NOMS fields will have a great deal of discretion. It is to be hoped that new policies and practices in terms of group programmes and case management will be informed by both gender *and* race issues combined.

Equally, while Home Secretary Charles Clarke's pronouncement in March 2005 of new initiatives for women offenders in the form of two community and support centres is to be welcomed, these 'one stop shops' should not only draw on what is known about women's criminogenic needs and on the experiences of existing projects such as the Asha Centre in Worcester and Centre 218 in Glasgow (both of which already offer innovative services to women to address drug abuse, mental health problems, housing, childcare, domestic violence and other issues that can shape women's pathways into crime), but should seek out and draw on what is specifically relevant to BME women offenders too.

Women have high representation on probation caseloads. We do not know what proportion are BME women. Nevertheless, lack of acknowledgement of cultural diversity alongside gender differences may limit the legitimacy of probation interventions.

Notes

1 Kathy Daly's analysis of sentencing in New Haven, Connecticut, in the 1980s (Daly 1994) proves an exception to this – but there is no immediate transference of ideas or conclusions because of cross-cultural differences in sentencing practice.

2 Pat Carlen's (1987) discussion of the short route between 'care' and 'custody' does at least acknowledge the existence of BME girls in the system and she is careful to let them speak about their experiences. One might argue, also, that a surge of writings by black women (see Amos and Parmar 1984; Mama 1984; Bhavani and Coulson 1986 for example) contributed to the attempts to include black women's experiences in feminist writings.

3 It is arguable that where attention has been given much of it has revolved around recruitment and staffing issues. See, for example, Mavunga (1992), Home Office (2002) and NPS (2005). The Association of Black Probation Officers and the Black Workers Forum and other NPS action groups have been doing important work in this direction and in relation to training in racism awareness and cultural diversity also.

4 Section 95 was a hard fought for clause and considered to be hugely innovative at the time.

5 For an overview of critical decisions in the sentencing process see Gelsthorpe (2001a).

6 Both sweeps of the Youth Lifestyles Survey have yielded plausible estimates of involvement in offending behaviour. The 1993 sweep (Graham and Bowling 1995) found no difference between black and white respondents in terms of their involvement in the criminal process, and much lower representation of Indian, Pakistani and Bangladeshi people. See also Flood-Page et al. (2000).

7 Leaving all other matters aside, there are claims too that the ethnic identity of offenders in the criminal justice process is rarely recorded with any accuracy (Dholakia 1999). Certainly, monitoring forms, like previous national censuses, have confused geography, nationality, skin colour and culture.

8 It is only really with a recent study of ethnic minority young offenders in the youth justice system that we see a detailed focus on race and gender issues at the same time (Feilzer and Hood 2004). However, NPS involvement in YOTs is relatively low because of the agreed age cut-offs between agencies.

9 It has been agreed that monitoring throughout the criminal justice system

should be based on self-assessment using the 16-point census categories as a basis for the monitoring. This system of monitoring was implemented in April 2003 so as to ensure consistent monitoring across the agencies. It is to be hoped that the monitoring and presentation of findings will include gender differences. A problem for all currently used methods of classifying ethnic groups is that they do not give proper attention to people with mixed parentage (most of whom have one minority parent and one white one); but this issue is the focus of the following chapter.

10 Under the Criminal Justice and Courts Services Act 2000 Community Service Orders were renamed as Community Punishment Orders. Under the Criminal Justice Act 2003 such orders have been subsumed under the heading of the generic Community Order (from April 2005).

References

Amos, V. and Parmer, P. (1984) 'Challenging Imperial Feminism', *Feminist Review*, 17, 3–19.

Barker, M. (1993) *Community Service and Women Offenders*. London: Association of Chief Officers of Probation.

Bernard, C. (1995) 'Childhood Sexual Abuse: The Implications for Black Mothers', *Rights of Women Bulletin*.

Bhavani, K. and Coulson, M. (1986) 'Transforming Socialist Feminism: The Challenge of Racism', *Feminist Review*, 23, 81–91.

Bhui, H. (1999) 'Racism and Risk Assessment: Linking Theory to Practice with Black Mentally Disordered Offenders', *Probation Journal*, 46: 3, 171–81.

Bowling, B. and Phillips, C. (2002) *Racism, Crime and Justice*. Harlow: Longman.

Brown, I. (1997) 'Equity of Access for Women Offenders to Service Provision', *VISTA*, 2: 3, 177–87.

Brown, I. and Hullin, R. (1992) 'A Study of Sentencing in the Leeds Magistrates' Courts: The Treatment of Ethnic Minority and White Offenders', *British Journal of Criminology*, 32: 1, 41–53.

Browne, D. and Poole, L. (1997) *Evaluation of the New Directions Groupwork Programme*. Manchester: Greater Manchester Probation Service.

Caddick, B. (1993) 'Using Groups in Working with Offenders: A Survey of Groupwork in Probation Services of England and Wales', in A. Brown, and B. Caddick (eds) *Groupwork with Offenders*. London: Whiting and Birch.

Calverley, A., Cole, B., Kaur, G., Lewis, S., Raynor, P., Sadeghi, S., Smith, D., Vanstone, M. and Wardak, A. (2004) *Black and Asian Offenders on Probation*, Home Office Research Study 277. London: Home Office.

Carlen, P. (1987) 'Out of Care, into Custody: Dimensions and Deconstructions of the State's Regulation of Twenty-two Young Working Class Women', in

P. Carlen and A. Worrall (eds) *Gender, Crime and Justice.* Milton Keynes: Open University Press.

Chigwada-Bailey, R. (1997) *Black Women's Experiences of Criminal Justice: A Discourse on Disadvantage.* Winchester: Waterside Press.

Chigwada-Bailey, R. (2003) *Black Women's Experiences of Criminal Justice. Race, Gender and Class: A Discourse on Disadvantage* (2nd edn). Winchester: Waterside Press.

Dale, A., Dex, S. and Lindley, J. (2004) 'Ethnic Differences in Women's Demographic, Family Characteristics and Economic Activity Profiles, 1992–2002', *Labour Market Trends*, 112: 4, 13–32.

Daly, K. (1994) *Gender, Crime and Punishment.* New Haven: Yale University Press.

Deakin, J. and Spencer, J. (2003) 'Women Behind Bars: Explanation and Implications', *Howard Journal of Criminal Justice*, 42: 2, 123–36.

Denney, D. (1992) *Racism and Anti-Racism in Probation.* London: Routledge.

Dholakia, Lord H. L. (1999) *Debs*, 607, cols 991–3.

Durrance, P. and Williams, P. (2003) 'Broadening the Agenda Around What Works for Black and Asian Offenders', *Probation Journal*, 50: 3, 211–24.

Fawcett Commission (2004) *Women and the Criminal Justice System,* Commission on Women and the Criminal Justice System, chaired by Vera Baird QC MP. London: Fawcett Society.

Feilzer, M. and Hood, R. (2004) *Differences or Discrimination? Minority Ethnic Young People in the Youth Justice System.* London: Youth Justice Board.

Flood-Page, C., Campbell, S., Harrington, V. and Miller, J. (2000) *Youth Crime: Findings from the 1998/99 Youth Lifestyles Survey,* Home Office Research Study 109. London: Home Office.

Garland, D. (2001) *The Culture of Control.* Oxford: Oxford University Press.

Gelsthorpe, L. (1992) 'Social Inquiry Reports: Race and Gender Considerations', *Home Office Research Bulletin,* 32, 17–22.

Gelsthorpe, L. (2001a) 'Critical Decisions and Processes in the Criminal Courts', in McLaughlin, E. and Muncie, J. (eds) *Controlling Crime.* London: Sage/Open University.

Gelsthorpe, L. (2001b) 'Accountability, Difference and Diversity in the Delivery of Community Penalties', in A. E. Bottoms, L. Gelsthorpe, and S. Rex (eds) *Community Penalties: Change and Challenges.* Cullompton: Willan.

Gelsthorpe, L. (2004a) 'Female Offending: A Theoretical Overview', in G. McIvor (ed.) *Women Who Offend.* London: Jessica Kingsley.

Gelsthorpe, L. (2004b) ' "Making It on the Out": The Resettlement Needs of Women Offenders', *Criminal Justice Matters*, 56, Summer, 34–5, 41.

Gelsthorpe, L. and Morris, A. (1990) (eds) *Feminist Perspectives in Criminology.* Milton Keynes: Open University Press.

Gelsthorpe, L. and Morris, A. (2002) 'Women's Imprisonment in England and Wales: A Penal Paradox', *Criminal Justice*, 2: 3, 277–301.

Gilroy, P. (1987) 'The Myth of Black Criminality', in P. Scraton (ed.) *Law, Order and the Authoritarian State*. Milton Keynes: Open University Press.

Goodwin, K. and McIvor, G. (2001) *Women's Experiences of Community Service Orders*. Stirling: University of Stirling Social Work Centre.

Graham, J. and Bowling, B. (1995) *Young People and Crime*, Home Office Research Study 145. London: Home Office.

Green, R. (1989) 'Probation and the Black Offender', *New Community*, 16: 1, 81–91.

Halevy, T. (1995) 'Racial discrimination in Sentencing? A Study into Dubious Conclusions', *Criminal Law Review*, April, 267–71.

Hassan, E. and Thiara, R. (2000) *Locked Out? Black Prisoners' Experience of Rehabilitative Programmes*. London: Association of Black Probation Officers.

Hedderman, C. (2004) 'The Criminogenic Needs of Women Offenders', in G. McIvor (ed.) *Women Who Offend*. London: Jessica Kingsley.

Hedderman, C. and Gelsthorpe, L. (eds.) (1997) *Understanding the Sentencing of Women*, Home Office Research Study 170. London: Home Office.

Hedderman, C. and Sugg, D. (1997) 'The Influence of Cognitive Approaches: A Survey of Probation Programmes', in *Changing Offenders' Attitudes and Behaviour: What Works?*, Home Office Research Study 171. London: Home Office.

Heidensohn, F. (2002) 'Gender and Crime', in M. Maguire, R. Morgan and R. Reiner (eds) *The Oxford Handbook of Criminology*. Oxford: Clarendon Press.

Her Majesty's Inspectorate of Probation (1996) *A Review of Probation Service Provision for Women Offenders*. London: Home Office.

HMIP (2000) *Towards Race Equality: A Thematic Inspection*. London: HMIP.

HMIP (2001) *Report on Women Offenders and Probation Service Provision*, Report of a Thematic Inspection. London: Home Office.

HMIP (2004) *Towards Race Equality: Follow-up Inspection Report*. London: HMIP.

Home Office (2002) *Training in Racism Awareness and Cultural Diversity*, Home Office Development and Practice Report. London: Home Office, RDS.

Home Office (2004a) *Statistics on Women and the Criminal Justice System 2003*. London: Home Office, RDS. A Home Office publication under Section 95 of the Criminal Justice Act.

Home Office (2004b) *Focus on Female Offenders: The Real Women Programme – Probation Service Pilot*, Home Office Development and Practice Report. London: Home Office.

Home Office (2005) *Sentencing Statistics 2003*. London: RDS, NOMS.

Hood, R. and Cordovil, G. (1992) *Race and Sentencing*. Oxford: Clarendon Press.

Howard League (1999) *Do Women Paint Fences Too? Women's Experiences of Community Service*, Briefing Paper. London: Howard League for Penal Reform.

ICPR (2004) *Race and the Criminal Justice System: An Overview to the complete Statistics 2002–2003.* London: Institute for Criminal Policy Research, School of Law, King's College London.

Jackson, M. (1999) 'Canadian Aboriginal Women and their "Criminality": The Cycle of Violence in the Context of Difference', *Australian and New Zealand Journal of Criminology*, 32: 2, 197–208.

Kemshall, H. (2003) *Understanding Risk in Criminal Justice.* Buckingham: Open University Press.

Kennedy, H. (1992) *Eve Was Framed.* London: Chatto and Windus.

Leslie, D., Blackaby, D., Clark, K., Drinkwater, S., Murphy, P. and O'Leary, N. (1998) *An Investigation of Racial Disadvantage.* Manchester: Manchester University Press.

Lewis, D. (1981) 'Black Women Offenders and Criminal Justice: Some Theoretical Considerations', in M. Warren (ed.) *Comparing Female and Male Offenders.* London: Sage.

Lupton, D. (1999) *Risk.* London: Routledge.

Mama, A. (1984) 'Black Women, the Economic Crisis and the British State', *Feminist Review*, 17, 20–35.

Maruna, S. (2001) *Making Good: How Convicts Reform and Build their Lives.* Washington, DC: American Psychological Association.

Mavunga, P. (1992) 'Probation: A Basically Racist Service', in L. Gelsthorpe. (ed.) *Minority Ethnic Groups in the Criminal Justice System*, Cropwood Conference Series No. 21. Cambridge: Institute of Criminology.

McIvor, G. (ed.) (2004) *Women Who Offend.* London: Jessica Kingsley.

McQuillan, R. (1992) *Pre-Sentence Reports: An Anti-Discriminatory Perspective.* London: Association of Black Probation Officers.

Modood, T., Berthoud, R., Lakey, J., Smith, P., Virdee, S. and Beishon, S. (1997) *Ethnic Minorities in Britain: Diversity and Disadvantage – Fourth National Survey of Ethnic Minorities.* London: Policy Studies Institute.

Moxon, D. (1988) *Sentencing Practice in the Crown Court*, Home Office Research Study 103. London: Home Office.

NPS (National Probation Service) (2001) *A New Choreography: An Integrated Strategy for the National Probation Service for England and Wales.* London: Home Office, NPS.

NPS (2003) *The Heart of the Dance: A Diversity Strategy for the National Probation Service for England and Wales 2002–2006.* London: Home Office, NPS.

NPS (2005) *Workforce Profile Report,* Issue 2. London: Home Office.

Powis, B. and Walmsley, R. (2002) *Programmes for Black and Asian Offenders on Probation: Lessons for Developing Practice,* Home Office Research Study 250. London: Home Office.

Prison Reform Trust (2000) *Justice for Women: The Need for Reform*, The Report of the Committee on Women's Imprisonment, chaired by Dorothy Wedderburn. London: Prison Reform Trust.

RDS NOMS (2004) *Offender Management Caseload Statistics 2003.* London: Home Office.

Rice, M. (1990) 'Challenging Orthodoxies in Feminist Theory: A Black Feminist Critique', in L. Gelsthorpe and A. Morris (eds) *Feminist Perspectives in Criminology*. Milton Keynes: Open University Press.

Rumgay, J. (2000) 'Policies of Neglect: Female Offenders and the Probation Service', in H. Kemshall and R. Littlechild (eds) *Improving Participation and Involvement in Social Care Delivery*. London: Jessica Kingsley.

Scott, A., Pearce, D. and Goldblatt, N. (2001) 'The Sizes and Characteristics of the Minority Ethnic Populations of Great Britain – Latest Estimates', *Population Trends*, 105, Autumn.

SEU (Social Exclusion Unit) (2002) *Reducing Re-offending by Ex-prisoners*. London: Office of the Deputy Prime Minister.

Shaw, M. and Hannah-Moffat, K. (2004) 'How Cognitive Skills Forgot about Gender and Diversity', in G. Mair (ed.) *What Matters in Probation*. Cullompton: Willan.

Solomos, J. (1993) *Race and Racism in Contemporary Britain*. London: Macmillan.

Underdown, A. (1998) *Strategies for Effective Offender Supervision*. London: HMIP.

Whitehouse, P. (1983) 'Race, Bias and Social Enquiry Reports', *Probation Journal*, 30: 2, 43–9.

WORP (Women's Offending Reduction Programme) (2004) *Action Plan*. London: Home Office, WORP.

Worrall, A. (1990) *Offending Women: Female Lawbreakers and the Criminal Justice System*. London: Routledge.

Zaplin, R. (ed.) (1998) *Female Offenders: Critical Perspectives and Effective Interventions*. Maryland: Aspen.

Chapter 7

Not black and white: mixed heritage experiences of criminal justice

Sam Lewis and Jill Olumide

Introduction

The study of Black and Asian men on probation by Calverley *et al.* (2004) involved the completion of semi-structured interviews with 483 Black (241), Asian (172), mixed heritage (57) and Other (13) minority ethnic offenders.[1,2] The interviewers produced information about respondents' 'criminogenic needs',[3] their experiences of supervision on community rehabilitation orders and programmes, their contact with other parts of the criminal justice system, and their wider experiences of life as minority ethnic people in Britain (see Chapters 4 and 5, this volume). When the completed interview schedules were analysed a worrying trend began to emerge. The mixed heritage interviewees regularly fared worse, particularly in relation to social exclusion and deprivation, than their Black and Asian counterparts. The small numbers involved mean that many of the findings are not statistically significant. They do, however, provide initial evidence of the particular and often unfavourable experiences of mixed heritage offenders. This chapter explores mixed heritage experiences of criminal justice, with a particular focus on the findings from the study by Calverley *et al.* (2004).

The chapter appears at a time when there is growing interest in and recognition of people of mixed heritage, as evidenced by the recent inclusion of mixed heritage as a specific ethnic category in the 2001 Census and other official data. It is necessary, then, to put the discussion in context. Our efforts to 'set the scene' begin with a brief overview of the history of discussions of mixed race, before moving on to consider 'the mixed heritage identity'. This is followed by a discussion of facts and figures on the mixed heritage population of the United Kingdom, gathered from official data sources. This section concludes with a discussion of public services and people of mixed heritage.

The main body of the chapter is concerned with mixed heritage experiences of the criminal justice system, beginning with a discussion of mixed heritage experiences of victimisation, as reported in the British Crime Survey 2002/2003 (Salisbury and Upson 2004). It proceeds to discuss the findings related to mixed heritage offenders in a recently completed study of minority ethnic young people in the youth justice system (Feilzer and Hood 2004), which have relevance to work with mixed heritage offenders of all ages. Finally, attention is paid to the findings pertaining to mixed heritage offenders from the study of Black and Asian men on probation in England and Wales (Calverley *et al.* 2004).

Setting the scene

Mixed heritage: an old concept with a new relevance

Until recently, the mixed heritage population of the United Kingdom has been ignored by social policy makers and absent from government statistics. It is interesting to note, then, that the concept of mixed heritage is far from new. The scientific, political, philosophical, theological, legal, psychological and sociological literatures on race mixing are vast, and reveal that the 'problem' of race mixing has long troubled and perplexed society's movers and shakers.

Nineteenth and early twentieth century Europe witnessed claims that white races are naturally superior (see, for example, Galton 1909; Gobineau 1915). It was also contended that race should not, for physical, psychological or 'common sense' reasons be mixed, on the grounds that this would damage the superiority of 'the white type':

> The white race originally possessed the monopoly of beauty, intelligence and strength. By its union with other varieties, hybrids were created, which were beautiful without strength, strong without intelligence, or, if intelligent, both weak and ugly. (Gobineau 1915: 209)

Moving past this bleak period in European history, which also saw Nazi Germany's adoption of eugenicist breeding principles, mixed race was passed to the sociological realms for investigation. Robert Park (1928, 1931) and Everett Stonequist (1935, 1937), studied the cultural mix of people living in Chicago. Park labelled the migrant and the person of mixed heritage 'the marginal man' (1928). He stated that typically 'the marginal man is a mixed blood … because the man of mixed blood is one who lives in two worlds, in both of which he is more or less of a stranger' (1928: 893). Park was far from pessimistic about the plight of the marginal man, however, whom he deemed at the forefront of human advancement (1928: 893):

> It is in the mind of the marginal man that the moral turmoil which new cultural contacts occasion manifests itself in the most obvious forms. It is in the mind of the marginal man – where the changes and fusions of culture are going on – that we can best study the process of civilisation and of progress.

During the mid twentieth century academics paid little attention to the mixed heritage population, proceeding as if individuals were members of only one racial group (Harris 2002: 63). Towards the end of the twentieth century, however, the situation slowly began to change:

> Although the multiracial population continues to be absent from most academic studies, the research community has devoted greater attention to this group in recent years, in response to continuing increases in interracial marriage … and growing acknowledgement of 'multiracial' as a legitimate racial identity … (Harris 2002: 64)

Harris' review of studies in this area suggests that American researchers are some way ahead of their British counterparts. As the mixed heritage population of the United Kingdom continues to grow (see below), so too will the need for research to better understand the needs and experiences of mixed heritage members of society. Some dominant themes are emerging from the limited data that do exist, however. In particular, evidence of how people of mixed heritage perceive themselves, in terms of their ethnic identity, is coming to light. So too is the social exclusion, marginalisation and discrimination often experienced by members of this minority ethnic group.

The mixed heritage identity

During the 1980s and 1990s some social work professionals argued that the only suitable identity for a person of mixed heritage was that of 'Black' (see, for example, Small 1986). Considering an alternative ethnic identity was deemed a form of false consciousness and a denial of the facts of racism. This view was remarkably influential both within the social work profession and in society as a whole.

Recent British studies suggest a greater complexity (Wilson 1987; Tizard and Phoenix 1993; Alibhai-Brown 2001; Olumide 2002; Ali 2003), with mixed race people and their families embracing all manner of ethnic identities. Tizard and Phoenix (1993) controversially suggested that mixed race adolescents do not feel obliged to consider themselves to be either white or Black. Rather they are able to respond to events and to the company they are in and to act accordingly. This is akin to Root's (1996: 11) idea of 'situational ethnicity' or the ability to respond flexibly and sympathetically to the cultural milieu of the moment.

Katz and Treacher (2005: 57) considered the social and psychological development of mixed heritage children, and highlighted the difficulty with taking a psychological approach to the issue of mixed heritage identity:

> The focus on individual psychological problems gives the message that mixed race people are a problem which needs sorting out – whether by therapy or by 'celebrating' their identity. While identity is important (and to some people it is the issue that dominates their lives) we need to go beyond identity to understand the social reality of mixed race people and see it as a social phenomenon.

An understanding of the social nature of race is particularly important for people of mixed heritage, given the history of psychological and scientific 'proofs' of their abnormal state. Olumide (2005) has suggested that the phrase 'mixed racialised' might be used to convey the social nature of the mixed heritage experience: the phrase says nothing of ethnic or cultural components, or intrinsic 'identity', but rather acknowledges that an individual's ethnic identity may be the result of social processes.

The mixed heritage population of the United Kingdom: facts and figures

The 1991 Census ethnic question included nine categories: White;

Indian; Pakistani; Bangladeshi; Black Caribbean; Black African; Black Other; Chinese, and Any Other Ethnic Group (Bowling and Phillips 2002: 34). Respondents were asked to indicate which single category best described their ethnicity by ticking the appropriate box. Chris Myant, the current Director of Operations for the Commission for Racial Equality (CRE) Wales, noted that many respondents were unable to shoe-horn their ethnicity into a single category (Lloyd 1998). Some invalidated their response to this question by ticking more than one ethnic category, e.g. Black and White. Further, those who indicated that they were from an 'Other' ethnic group frequently specified that they were of mixed heritage.

The potential benefits and drawbacks of a 'mixed option' in official statistics have been well rehearsed (see, for example, Ifekwunigwe 1999; Owen 2001; Aspinall 2000, 2003; Fernandez 1996). The arguments revolve around whether it is productive to have *any* system of racial classification, and the impossibility of fitting people of mixed heritage into prescribed categories. Nevertheless, the 2001 Census ethnic question gave respondents 16 categories to choose from, including four mixed options: White and Black Caribbean, White and Black African, White and Asian; any other mixed background.[4] In addition, in 2001 the recommended output classification of ethnic group for National Statistics data sources changed to be broadly in line with the new Census categories.[5,6] These developments have been described as a 'milestone' in the history of mixed race people living in the United Kingdom (Lloyd 1998: 1; John 2002).

Thus there is now a significant body of data pertaining to people of different ethnic backgrounds, including those of mixed heritage, living in the United Kingdom. The ethnic breakdown of the population is shown in Table 7.1. Of the 59 million people recorded as living in the United Kingdom by the 2001 Census, 7.9 per cent are from a minority ethnic group. Just 1.2 per cent of the total population (14.6 per cent of the minority ethnic population) is of mixed heritage.

Minority ethnic groups have a younger age structure than the white population (see Figure 7.1), which is explained by the Office for National Statistics thus:

[This reflects] past immigration and fertility patterns. The first large-scale migration of people of minority ethnic origin came from the Caribbean shortly after the Second World War and during the 1950s. Immigrants from India and Pakistan arrived mainly during the 1960s. Many people of African-Asian descent came to the UK as refugees from Uganda during the 1970s.

Most Chinese and Bangladeshi people came to Britain during the 1980s. Many of the Black Africans came during the 1980s and 1990s. (ONS 2002: 6)

It is unsurprising that the mixed heritage group has the youngest age structure. As the number of people from minority ethnic groups arriving in and then being born in Britain has grown, so the number of inter-ethnic relationships has increased, their issue forming the

Table 7.1 Population by ethnic group, April 2001 (UK)

	Total population (numbers)	Total population (percentages)	Non-white population (percentages)
White	54,153,898	92.1	
Mixed	677,117	1.2	14.6
Indian	1,053,411	1.8	22.7
Pakistani	747,285	1.3	16.1
Bangladeshi	283,063	0.5	6.1
Other Asian	247,664	0.4	5.3
All Asian or Asian British	**2,331,423**	**4.0**	**50.3**
Black Caribbean	565,876	1.0	12.2
Black African	485,277	0.8	10.5
Black Other	97,585	0.2	2.1
All Black or Black British	**1,148,738**	**2.0**	**24.8**
Chinese	247,403	0.4	5.3
Other ethnic groups	230,615	0.4	5.0
All minority ethnic groups	**4,635,296**	**7.9**	**100.0**
All population	**58,789,194**	**100.0**	

Source: Office for National Statistics (2005)

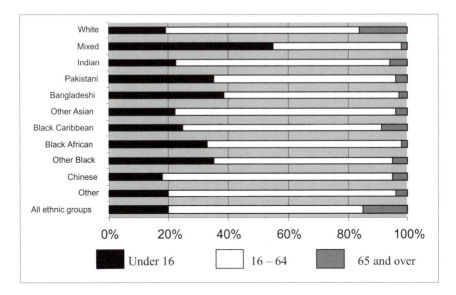

Figure 7.1 Age distribution by ethnic group, 2001/02 (UK)
Source: Office for National Statistics (2002)[7]

growing mixed heritage population. Although inter-ethnic marriages are still rare, with just two per cent of all marriages involving people from different ethnic groups (ONS 2005: 4), the rising number of inter-racial relationships means that the mixed heritage population will continue to grow.

Public services and people of mixed heritage

A paucity of statistical information has hampered consideration of governmental policies and public service practice in relation to people of mixed race (Aspinall 2000). Social services, for example, have failed until recently to collect data on mixed ethnicity in relation to children in the public care system (Barn 1999; Sinclair and Hai 2002; Aspinall 2000). Now that such information is available, it appears that mixed race children are greatly over represented in the public care system (Bebbington and Miles 1989: Rowe *et al.* 1989: Charles *et al.* 1992).

Tikly *et al.* (2004) conducted a detailed study of the educational needs of mixed heritage pupils for the Department for Education and Skills (DfES), with a particular focus on the barriers to achievement facing mixed heritage pupils with one white parent and one Black Caribbean parent. They found that many of the barriers were the same as for Black Caribbean pupils: they often came from socially disadvantaged backgrounds, were more likely to suffer discrimination from teachers in the form of low expectations, and were more likely to be excluded from school. Of particular note, however, is the finding that mixed heritage pupils also face *specific* barriers to achievement that are difficult to address:

> Low expectations of pupils by teachers often seem based on a stereotypical view of the fragmented home backgrounds and 'confused' identities of White/Black Caribbean pupils. These pupils often experience racism from teachers and their White and Black peers targeted at their mixed heritage ... The barriers to achievement experienced by White/Black Caribbean pupils operate in a context where mixed heritage identities ... are not recognised in the curriculum or in policies of schools and of LEAs. In the case of White/Black Caribbean pupils, their invisibility from policy makes it difficult for their underachievement to be challenged. (2004: 6)

The research by Tikly *et al.* (2004) is not alone in highlighting the potentially deleterious effects of the attitudes held by some professionals to people of mixed heritage. Okitikpi (1999) begins his consideration of the numbers of mixed race children in the public care by questioning the attitudes of social workers to mixed heritage children. The extent to which the attitudes of professional workers exacerbate the social exclusion and marginalisation of mixed heritage members of society remains unclear: the role of professional workers in relation to relatively powerless groups deserves further investigation (see Olumide 1997).

The criminal justice system of England and Wales has been slow to consider the salience of race and to record the ethnicity of offenders in anything but a rudimentary manner. Recent developments, in particular the annual publication of the Section 95 race and crime statistics, and the publication of the report into the death of Stephen Lawrence (Macpherson 1999) have pushed the issue of race and crime up the political agenda. Evidence now exists about the experiences of mixed heritage individuals as victims of crime (Salisbury and Upson 2004) and as offenders (Calverley *et al.* 2004; Feilzer and Hood 2004). It is to this evidence that we shall now turn.

Mixed heritage experiences of criminal justice

Discussions of mixed heritage experiences of criminal justice are hampered by various factors. First, and as other contributors to this book have noted (see Chapters 6 and 9, this volume), the recording of ethnicity within the criminal justice system is both limited and unreliable. It will be shown that particular problems exist with the statistics pertaining to mixed heritage offenders. Second, very few studies have been conducted that present information on this issue. Thus the ensuing information comes from a small number of sources: the British Crime Survey 2002/2003 (Salisbury and Upson 2004), a study of minority ethnic young people in the youth justice system (Feilzer and Hood 2004), and the study of Black and Asian men on probation in England and Wales (Calverley *et al.* 2004).

Mixed heritage experiences of victimisation

The British Crime Survey 2002/2003 found that members of all minority ethnic groups are at greater risk of victimisation than white people (Salisbury and Upson 2004). This is perhaps not surprising given the age distribution of different ethnic groups (see above), because the risk of victimisation varies with age, and people aged 16 to 34 are at greatest risk (2004: 2). After allowing for age, however, the greater risk faced by minority ethnic people *as a whole* disappeared.

Risk of victimisation varied considerably between different minority ethnic groups. Asian and, in particular, mixed heritage people were at greatest risk of victimisation. The risk of victimisation for those of mixed heritage was found to have increased significantly between 2001/02 and 2002/03. It is particularly important to note that the difference in risk persisted for mixed heritage people (but not for Asian people) when age and other socio-economic risk factors were taken into account.

The treatment of mixed heritage young offenders: differences or discrimination?[8]

The report of a recent study of minority ethnic young people in the youth justice system, entitled 'differences or discrimination?', stated that 'one cannot ignore the conclusion that those who were said to be of mixed parentage did receive differential treatment in many respects' (Feilzer and Hood 2004: 162). The concerns raised about the treatment of mixed heritage young offenders have relevance beyond the youth justice system to the work done with such offenders of all ages.

The first point to note is that the authors found 'many gaps in the data collection systems' used by the Youth Offending Teams (YOTs) involved, and 'the proportion of cases in which no information was recorded about ethnicity was far too high' (2004: 161). Of particular relevance is the following discovery (2004: 161):

> The problem was particularly acute with regard to the identification of young people as being of mixed parentage. The very large under-representation of this category in nearly all the Yot areas, compared to their representation in the local population is simply not credible.

The authors inferred that not all mixed heritage young people, and perhaps only a small proportion of them, were identified as such, the others having been classified under another ethnic group (2004: 43). They called for further research into how the ethnic classification of mixed heritage young people is conducted, and why variations occur (2004: 51, 162). It seems highly probable that these comments could have been made about the ethnic classification of mixed heritage offenders of all ages.

The report highlighted several other areas of concern. At the pre-court stage, the police have to decide whether to make a pre-court disposal (i.e. a reprimand or final warning) or recommend prosecution. Cases involving Black (81.1 per cent) and mixed heritage (90.5 per cent) males were more likely to be recommended for prosecution than those involving white males (75.6 per cent), and this finding was statistically significant. When factors that can legitimately influence the police decision to recommend prosecution were taken into account, however, the odds of a Black male being prosecuted were approximately the same as those for a white male, while the odds of a mixed heritage male being prosecuted were 'significantly higher than that of a white youth' (2004: 73).[9] This indicator of discriminatory treatment highlights a problem that may well extend beyond the youth justice system.

One result of being remanded in secure conditions is that the probability of receiving a prison sentence is 'considerably increased' (2004: 116). Higher proportions of cases involving Black (10.2 per cent) and mixed heritage (12.9 per cent) males than white (7.6 per cent) males had been remanded in secure conditions, and the differences were statistically significant. When case characteristics were held constant, the odds of a case involving a Black or a mixed heritage offender being remanded in secure conditions were still higher than that of a white male. While this finding was not statistically significant, 'the trends were unfavourable towards black and mixed-parentage males' (p.117), and while similar proportions of Black (52.1 per cent), Asian (51.2 per cent) and White (54.3 per cent) males were eventually convicted and sentenced, this figure was markedly higher for mixed heritage males (70.1 per cent). These findings raise questions about, and have implications for, criminal justice practice generally.

In relation to sentencing, raw differences in custody rates between members of different ethnic groups were largely due to differences in case characteristics. Feilzer and Hood also explored whether there were ethnic variations in the proportions sentenced to more restrictive, as opposed to nominal or less restrictive, community penalties. Higher proportions of Black (29.5 per cent) and mixed heritage (32.9) males than white (23.7 per cent) males had received a more restrictive community sentence, and both differences were statistically significant. When case characteristics were taken into account 'only the odds of a mixed-parentage male of 1.6, compared to a white male receiving such a penalty, were statistically significant' (2004: 99). While none of the findings cited here prove that the treatment received by mixed heritage offenders is discriminatory, they provide a *prima facie* indication that mixed heritage offenders receive unfavourable treatment.

Mixed heritage men on probation in England and Wales

Calverley *et al.* (2004) interviewed 483 minority ethnic men on probation, 57 (11.8 per cent) of whom were recorded as being of mixed heritage (unweighted sample). Of the 40 mixed heritage interviewees who gave details of their parents' ethnic origin, 33 (82.5 per cent) said that one parent (usually their father) was Black, while the other parent was white (unweighted sample). This discussion focuses on the findings relating to the 57 men in the mixed heritage sub-sample.

The mixed heritage identity: A fanciful concept?

A close reading of the 57 interview schedules underlined the fact that there is no single mixed heritage identity. Many interviewees, in incidental references to their ethnicity, described it as that of their minority ethnic (usually Black) parent. Others consistently referred to themselves as being of mixed heritage or mixed race. Still others used the ethnicity of their minority ethnic parent and 'mixed heritage' interchangeably to describe their own ethnicity. One interviewee made it quite clear that he saw himself as being neither Black nor Asian, but as 'English'. The following quotations help to give the flavour:

I was the only Black guy [at boarding school].

They [the police] wouldn't have called for back up if I wasn't Black.

So far they [probation supervisor] have never asked me how I feel as a mixed race person.

We [my probation supervisor and me] both know what it's like being Black ... I don't think mixed race people have any different needs really.

I don't see myself as a Black or Asian person with different needs anyway. I'm English. I've grown up around [white] English people all my life. My culture is English white culture.

The last remark appears to support Olumide's (2005) comments concerning the social processes that shape a person's ethnic identity. It is evident from these remarks that notions of a single mixed heritage identity are misleading. Criminal justice policy and practice rooted in a belief in the uniformity of mixed heritage identities, needs and experiences would in itself be a form of discrimination.

Orders, supervisors and supervision

Just under half of the 483 people interviewed for the study were on an ordinary probation order (236, 48.9 per cent, unweighted sample), while the rest (247, 51.1 per cent, unweighted sample) were on an order that included an additional requirement to attend a probation programme. There were statistically significant differences[10] in the proportions of the different ethnic groups that were on a probation order with an additional requirement to attend a programme: 39.5 per cent of Asian offenders, 51.5 per cent of Black offenders, and 65.8 per cent of mixed heritage offenders were on such orders. These differences may have been due, in part at least, to differences in OGRS[11] scores: mean OGRS scores varied considerably between the Asian (44.6), Black (49.7) and mixed heritage (62.6) groups.

Overall, the accounts given of probation supervision and programmes by the 483 interviewees were broadly positive, a finding that was reflected in the responses from mixed heritage offenders. The vast majority (85.6 per cent) of the survey participants reported having been treated fairly by their supervisor, with little variation between the proportions of Black (85.2 per cent), Asian (83.9 per cent) and mixed heritage (86.1 per cent) respondents reporting fair treatment.

Of the main supervisors, 69.2 per cent were white, 25 per cent were Black, 5.4 per cent were Asian, and less than one per cent were of mixed heritage.[12] These figures varied considerably between areas with high, medium and low proportions of inhabitants from minority ethnic groups. In high density areas, 27.5 per cent of offenders had a Black supervisor while 5.5 per cent had an Asian supervisor. In medium and low density areas combined, these figures were 8.1 per cent and 4.8 per cent respectively.

To the question of whether having a minority ethnic supervisor had (or would have) made a positive difference, 34.8 per cent of all interviewees answered that it was (or would have been) a benefit. Interestingly, a higher proportion of mixed heritage (43.1 per cent) respondents than Black (34.0 per cent) or Asian (31.4 per cent) respondents gave this response. The most frequent reasons given by the mixed heritage sub-sample were the same as for the whole sample: that a minority ethnic supervisor would be better able to understand the background, culture and experiences of a minority ethnic probationer (24.5 per cent of mixed heritage sample, 22.4 per cent of whole sample), that they would be easier to talk to (9.8 per cent, 8.3 per cent), and that they would make the interviewee feel more comfortable (7.7 per cent, 6.5 per cent):

> I think it [having a Black supervisor] would have made a bit of a difference. Especially if they were from round here, because then you would both know what it's like living in a place like this [a rural county in the South of England] and being Black.

> You can speak to them [a minority ethnic supervisor] about things you don't feel comfortable speaking to a white person about.

> My Asian probation officer is very good. I would like to speak to a person of mixed heritage … so I can identify with them. I think it's really important.

The first two quotes are typical: few of the mixed heritage interviewees specified a preference for a mixed heritage probation supervisor. Again, this emphasises the range of needs to be found within the generic category 'mixed heritage'.

Programmes

As already noted, 65.8 per cent of mixed heritage offenders were on a programme order. Those who were waiting to start their programme, and had no previous programme experience, were excluded from the analysis and are not included in the remaining findings presented under this heading.[13]

In the original study (Calverley *et al.* 2004), those who were on or had been on a programme were asked whether the ethnic composition of a group matters. Most (66 per cent) respondents said that composition is important, and most of those thought that it should be mixed. This finding was mirrored for the mixed heritage interviewees: most (70.8 per cent) of those who responded to this question (93 per cent) thought that ethnic composition is important. The vast majority (92.7 per cent) of those for whom composition mattered thought that it should be mixed (which accounts for 61.4 per cent of the mixed heritage people who were on or had been on a programme).

All programme participants were asked how they were treated by their group leaders. The responses from mixed heritage interviewees echoed the positive responses from programme participants generally. The majority (83.3 per cent) of mixed heritage programme participants (86.2 per cent of all programme participants) said that they had been treated fairly, while a small minority (4.8 per cent, 2.5 per cent of all programme participants) said that they had been treated unfairly. The rest (11.8 per cent, 11.2 per cent) said that they did not know whether their treatment had been fair, or that it had been 'mixed', or failed to respond.

Mixed heritage probationers and social exclusion

The data collected in this study indicated that the Black, Asian and mixed heritage men who took part suffered, to differing degrees, from social exclusion and disadvantage in three main areas: economic, educational and geographic. The mixed heritage interviewees regularly reported higher levels of social exclusion and discrimination than their Black and Asian counterparts.

Economic exclusion is generally related to a person's (or family's or community's) unemployment, work status, benefit dependency, lack of housing ownership, substandard quality of housing, lack of satisfactory educational qualifications, and so on. In the current study, unemployment, low income, and benefit dependency are indicators of social exclusion.

The 2001 Census found that higher proportions of Asian (9.5 per cent), Black (14.9 per cent) and mixed heritage (12.4 per cent) men than white (5.4 per cent) men were unemployed. Figure 7.2 shows

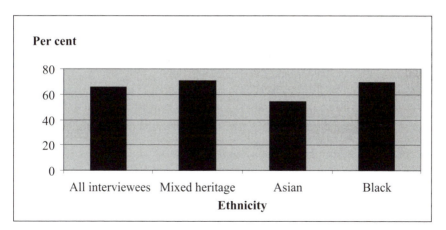

Figure 7.2   Unemployment rates for interviewees by ethnic group

the unemployment rates for the interviewees by ethnic group. The first point to note is the high rate of unemployment among all interviewees. The second point to note is the particularly high levels of unemployment among the Black (69.4 per cent) and mixed heritage (70.8 per cent) groups.[14] Interviewees were also asked to name their main source of income. The proportions of interviewees who cited state benefits as their main source of income varied according to ethnicity: a far smaller proportion of Asian (55.3 per cent) interviewees than Black (71.0 per cent) and mixed heritage (80.8 per cent) interviewees gave this response.

Educational disadvantage and exclusion relates to school experiences and educational attainment. Approximately one third (36.7 per cent) of all the interviewees who answered this question (n = 481) said that they had no educational qualifications, with little difference in the proportions of Asian (38.1 per cent), Black (35.5 per cent) and mixed heritage (39.7 per cent) interviewees who gave this response. In line with the findings of Tikly *et al.* (2004), this study found that many of the barriers to achievement faced by mixed heritage interviewees were the same as for Black respondents. Greater proportions of mixed heritage interviewees reported experiencing those obstacles, however. There was also evidence that mixed heritage interviewees faced specific barriers to achievement.

All 483 interviewees were asked how they got on at school. Most frequently the response was generally negative (40.8 per cent).[15] The proportion of respondents who gave a generally negative account varied between Asian (34.2 per cent), Black (41.7 per cent) and mixed heritage (47.2 per cent) groups. Over one third (37.2 per cent) of all interviewees who expressed feelings about their teachers (n = 223) gave a generally negative account. Again, the proportions varied between Asian (29.0 per cent), Black (36.2 per cent) and mixed heritage (47.2 per cent) groups.

One fifth (20.3 per cent) of the interviewees reported having experienced racism at school. Further details of the responses given by ethnicity are provided in Table 7.2. The following comments from mixed heritage interviewees give the flavour:

I was the only Black kid in the class. You learned to stick up for yourself. There was a lot of racist abuse.

I was treated unfairly by the teachers when me and a white kid did something wrong. I got into more trouble than a white kid, and I was also called 'Black bastard' by the other students.

I was bullied by the other kids, and I used to fight a lot, and because I was mixed race I was in the middle and it made it more difficult for me.

The remark about being 'in the middle' resonates with comments made by Gorham (2003: 35), a writer of mixed heritage, who stated that 'being mixed race can mean that you ... don't feel totally accepted by either the black or the white community'. Being 'in the middle' may be a problem for mixed heritage adults too, as one interviewee explained:

Table 7.2 Respondents who reported having experienced racism at school

	Yes, from teachers % (n)	Yes, from pupils % (n)	Yes, from both teachers and pupils % (n)	TOTAL % (n)
Asian	7.0 (6)	14.0 (12)	2.3 (2)	23.3 (20)
Black	4.5 (14)	8.7 (27)	5.2 (16)	18.4 (57)
Mixed heritage	2.8 (2)	13.9 (10)	6.9 (5)	23.6 (17)
Other	12.5 (2)	6.25 (1)	6.25 (1)	25.0 (4)
TOTAL	5.0 (24)	10.4 (50)	5.0 (24)	20.3 (98)

I was assaulted by a Black Jamaican guy and his white friend. They just came up to me and said, 'What fucking colour are you?' and they started beating me up.

Being in rented or supported accommodation may be an indicator of geographical disadvantage. All 483 people interviewed were asked about their living arrangements. While almost one fifth (18.6 per cent) of respondents from the total sample owned their own homes, this figure was far lower for mixed heritage respondents (9.7 per cent). Unsurprisingly, a smaller proportion of respondents from the total sample (64.4 per cent), than from the mixed heritage sub-sample (73.4 per cent), was in rented or supported housing.

As already noted, evidence suggests that mixed race children are greatly over-represented in the public care system (Bebbington and Miles 1989; Rowe *et al.* 1989; Charles *et al.* 1992). The findings from this study support this claim. Markedly smaller proportions of Asian (3.6 per cent) and Black (19.8 per cent) than mixed heritage (34.7 per cent) interviewees reported ever having been in care. The reasons for this general trend are unclear, and require further investigation.

Almost one third (30.0 per cent) of the whole sample reported that one or more family members had been in trouble with the law. Again, there were marked variations between the proportions of Asian (22.1 per cent), Black (29.1 per cent) and mixed heritage (48.6 per cent) interviewees who gave this response.

Mixed heritage experiences of criminal justice

All 483 people involved in the original study were asked to comment on their treatment by different criminal justice professionals. The police were particularly criticised: 62 per cent of respondents reported unfair treatment by the police. There were slight variations in the proportion of Asian (58.1 per cent), Black (62.6 per cent) and mixed heritage (69 per cent) respondents who reported such unfair treatment. The vast majority (84.2 per cent) of respondents reported having been stopped and searched by the police for no reason, with variations between the proportions of Asian (75.6 per cent), Black (85.4 per cent) and mixed heritage (90.3 per cent) respondents who made this claim.

It has already been noted that among the general population minority ethnic people are at greater risk of victimisation than white people, and mixed heritage individuals are at greatest risk (Salisbury and Upson 2004). Most of the interviewees (64.6 per cent) reported having been a victim of crime, with variations in the proportions of Asian (56.5 per cent), Black (67.2 per cent) and mixed heritage (64.4 per cent) interviewees who reported experience of victimisation. This contrasts with the situation among the general population where, as noted earlier, it is Asian and in particular mixed heritage people who are most at risk (Salisbury and Upson 2004).

Conclusion

There are a number of clear messages that emerge from the evidence presented in this chapter. First, the mixed heritage group has the youngest age structure: over 50 per cent of the mixed heritage population is less than 16 years of age (ONS 2002). Second, the mixed heritage population is growing, and this looks set to continue. Third, it is difficult to identify a single 'mixed heritage identity', just as it is difficult to argue the existence of a unitary identity for any ethnic group. Fourth, there is, however, evidence of commonality of experience among people of mixed heritage. This group does, for example, display higher levels of social exclusion and disadvantage than other ethnic groups, and is prone to being 'managed' by state agencies such as the police, social services and education. Fifth, there is emerging evidence to suggest that mixed heritage people may experience discriminatory treatment within the criminal justice system.

What are the implications of these findings? Socio-economic deprivation has been shown to be an independent predictor of delinquency (see Farrington 2002). If steps are not taken to address the high levels of disadvantage experienced by the predominantly young and growing mixed heritage population, these factors could, over time, contribute to their increased representation among the offending population. In addition, there is an urgent need to collect more reliable data on race and crime generally, and on mixed heritage offenders in particular. Further, those working with mixed heritage offenders should not assume that they all have the same needs and experiences, but should be aware of the high levels of socio-economic deprivation among this group. Thus efforts to address such needs might be as vital as, for example, work to address cognitive deficits. Finally, research is needed to assess and take steps to address the sources of disadvantageous treatment for mixed heritage people who enter the criminal justice system. Social justice and the contemporary emphasis on crime prevention demand that the 'marginal men' (and women) of history must not stay at the margins of society, or of social and criminal justice research, policy and practice.

Notes

1 For more details about the Other category, see Chapter 4, this volume.

2 These figures are unweighted. All other figures in this chapter relating to the study by Calverley *et al.* (2004) are weighted unless otherwise stated. See Chapter 4, this volume, for further details about the weighting procedures.

3 'Criminogenic needs' are characteristics of people or their circumstances which are associated with an increased risk of offending. In the study, criminogenic needs were measured in two ways: comparatively, using the CRIME-PICS II assessment instrument, and in a more qualitative way through interviews about individual experiences. In this chapter, the findings from the interviews with mixed heritage offenders are presented and discussed. The results of the CRIME-PICS II assessments can be found in Chapter 4, this volume.

4 Respondents were asked to select one section from A to E and then tick the box next to the appropriate subcategory to indicate their ethnicity: A White (British; Irish; Any other white background); B Mixed (White and Black Caribbean; White and Black African; White and Asian; Any other mixed background); C Asian or Asian British (Indian; Pakistani; Bangladeshi; Any other Asian background); D Black or Black British (Caribbean; African; Any other Black Background); E Chinese or other ethnic group (Chinese; Any other) (Bowling and Phillips 2002: 34).

5 General information about National Statistics is available from the Office for National Statistics: http://www.statistics.gov.uk/about/national_ statistics/default.asp (accessed 28 April 2005).

6 See http://www.statistics.gov.uk/about/Classifications/ns_ethnic_ classification.asp for more details about this change (accessed 26 April 2005).

7 The data from which Figure 7.1 was created is available at: http://www. statistics.gov.uk/StatBase/Expodata/Spreadsheets/D6206.xls (accessed 27 April 2005).

8 For the sake of brevity, only the findings relating to the larger sample of male offenders are discussed here. The findings relating to female offenders raise similar concerns, however.

9 A logistic regression analysis was used to control for the influence of the following variables: gravity of charges, nature of main offence, interaction between gravity and charge, number of current charges and age (Feilzer and Hood 2004: 72, n.58).

10 P<0.05.
11 OGRS, the Offender Group Reconviction Scale, is a measure of reoffending. It provides an estimate of the probability that a convicted offender will be reconvicted within two years from release from prison or from the start of a community sentence.
12 The information regarding the ethnicity of main supervisors came from the interviewees. A cautionary note must be added regarding the reliability of the proportion of supervisors said to be of mixed heritage, which is necessarily based on guesswork.
13 Thirty-seven of the 57 mixed heritage offenders in the unweighted sample were or had been on a probation order with an additional requirement to attend a programme. Three people had yet to start when they were interviewed, however, and had no other experience of a probation programme. Thus only the responses from the remaining 34 interviewees were used in the analysis. They accounted for 60.8 per cent (n = 44) of the mixed heritage offenders in the weighted sample.
14 The figures for the general population were calculated from data available from the Census 2001: National Report for England and Wales, p. 134, Table S108, using the International Labour Organisation (ILO) definition of the unemployment rate as a percentage of all those who were economically active. The unemployment figures quoted in Figure 7.2 give the number of unemployed as a percentage of all respondents. While the 'unemployment rates' cited for the general population and for the interviewees are not directly comparable, they illustrate the level of economic exclusion experienced by the interviewees (whose unemployment rate is even higher if calculated using the ILO definition).
15 Taking the sample as a whole, 35.3 per cent of responses were generally positive, 40.8 per cent were generally negative, 22.4 per cent of accounts were mixed, and 1.5 per cent of respondents said that they did not attend school at all.

References

Ali, S. (2003) *Mixed-race, Post-race: Gender, New Ethnicities and Cultural Practices*. Oxford: Berg.

Alibhai-Brown, Y. (2001) *Mixed Feelings: The Complex Lives of Mixed Race Britons*. London. Women's Press.

Aspinall, P. J. (2000) 'Children of Mixed Parentage: Data Collection Needs', *Children and Society*, 14: 3, 207–16.

Aspinall, P. J. (2003) 'The Conceptualisation and Categorisation of Mixed Race/Ethnicity in Britain and North America: Identity Options and the Role of the State', *International Journal of Intercultural Relations*, 27, 269–96.

Barn, R. (1999) 'White Mothers, Mixed-Parentage Children, and Child Welfare', *British Journal of Social Work*, 29: 2, 269–84.

Bebbington, A. and Miles, J. (1989) 'The Backgrounds of Children Who Enter Local Authority Care', *British Journal of Social Work*, 19: 5, 349–68.

Bowling, B. and Phillips, C. (2002) *Racism, Crime and Justice*. London: Longman.

Calverley, A., Cole, B., Kaur, G., Lewis, S., Raynor, P., Sadeghi, S., Smith, D., Vanstone, M. and Wardak, A. (2004) *Black and Asian Offenders on Probation*, Home Office Research Study 277. London: Home Office.

Charles, M., Rashid, S. and Thorburn, J. (1992) 'The Placement of Black Children with Permanent New Families', *Adoption and Fostering*, 16: 3, 13–19.

Farrington, D.P. (2002) 'Developmental Criminology and Risk-Focused Prevention', in M. Maguire, R. Morgan and R. Reiner (eds) *The Oxford Handbook of Criminology*. Oxford: Oxford University Press.

Feilzer, M. and Hood, R. (2004) *Differences or Discrimination? Minority Ethnic Young People in the Youth Justice System*. London: Youth Justice Board.

Fernandez, C. (1996) 'Government Classification of Multiracial/Multiethnic People', in M.P.P. Root (ed.) *The Multiracial Experience: Racial Borders as the New Frontier*. Thousand Oaks, CA: Sage.

Galton, F. (1909) *Essays in Eugenics*. London: Eugenics Society.

Gobineau, A. de (1915) *The Inequality of Human Races*. New York: G. P. Putnam.

Gorham, C. (2003) 'Mixing It', *Guardian Weekend Magazine*, 22 October 2003, 34–5.

Harris, D. R. (2002) 'Does it Matter How We Measure? Racial Classification and the Characteristics of Multiracial Youth', in J. Perlmann and M. Waters (eds) *The New Race Question: How the Census Counts Multiracial Individuals*. New York: Russell Sage Foundation.

Ifekwunigwe, J. O. (1999) *Scattered Belongings: Cultural Paradoxes of 'Race', Nation and Gender*. London: Routledge.

John, C. (2002) *Changing Face of Britain: Britain's Blurring Ethnic Mix*. Available online at: http://news.bbc.co.uk/hi/english/static/in_depth/uk/2002/race/changing_face_of_britain.stm (accessed 26 April 2005).

Katz, I. and Treacher, A. (2005) 'The Social and Psychological Development of Mixed Race Children', in T. Okitikpi (ed.) *Working with Children of Mixed Parentage*. Lyme Regis: Russell House.

Lloyd, I. (1998) *2001: A Race Odyssey*. Available at: http://www.pih.org.uk/articles/2001race.htmi (accessed 26 April 2005).

Macpherson, W. (1999) *The Stephen Lawrence Inquiry: Report of an Inquiry by Sir William Macpherson of Cluny*. Cm. 4262-1. London: Home Office.

Okitikpi, T. (1999) 'Why is There Such a High Percentage of Mixed Race Children in Care', *Child Care in Practice*, Northern Ireland Journal of Multidisciplinary Childcare Practice, 5, 4 October.

Olumide, J. (1997) *The Social Construction of Mixed Race*. PhD thesis (University of Bradford).

Olumide, J. (2002) *Raiding the Gene Pool: The Social Construction of Mixed Race*. London: Pluto Press.

Olumide, J. (2005) 'Mixed Race Children: Policy and Practice Considerations', in T. Okitikpi, (ed.) *Working with Children of Mixed Parentage*. Lyme Regis: Russell House.

ONS (Office for National Statistics) (2002) *Social Focus in Brief*. London: Office for National Statistics. Internet report only, available at: http://www.statistics.gov.uk/statbase/Product.asp?vlnk=9763 (accessed 27 April 2005).

ONS (2005) *Focus on Ethnicity and Identity*. London: Office for National Statistics. Available at: http://www.statistics.gov.uk/focuson/ethnicity/ (accessed 27 April 2005).

Owen, C. (2001) '"Mixed Race" in Official Statistics', in D. Parker and M. Song (eds) *Rethinking 'Mixed Race'*. London: Pluto Press.

Park, R. E. (1928) 'Human Migration and the Marginal Man', *American Journey of Sociology*, 33: 8, 881–92.

Park, R. E. (1931) 'Mentality of Racial Hybrids', *American Journal of Sociology*, 36: 4, 534–51.

Root, M. P. P. (1996) 'A Bill of Rights for Racially Mixed People', in M. P. P. Root (ed.) *The Multiracial Experience: Racial Borders as the New Frontier*. Thousand Oaks, CA: Sage.

Rowe, J., Hundleby, M. and Garnett, L. (1989) *Child Care Now: A Survey of Placement Patterns*. London: British Agencies for Adoption and Fostering.

Salisbury, H. and Upson, A. (2004) *Ethnicity, Victimisation and Worry about Crime: Findings from the 2001/02 and 2002/03 British Crime Surveys*, Home Office Research Findings 237. London: Home Office.

Sinclair, R. and Hai, N. (2002) *Children of Mixed Parentage in Need in Islington*. London: National Children's Bureau.

Small, J. (1986) 'Transracial Placements: Conflicts and Contradictions', in S. Ahmed, J. Cheetham and J. Small (eds) *Social Work with Black Children and their Families*. London: Batsford/BAAF.

Stonequist, E. V. (1935) 'The Problem of the Marginal Man', *American Journal of Sociology*, 41: 1, 1–12.

Stonequist, E. V. (1937) *The Marginal Man: A Study in Personality and Culture Conflict*. New York: Russell and Russell.

Tikly, L., Caballero, C., Haynes, J. and Hill, J. (2004) *Understanding the Educational Needs of Mixed Heritage Pupils*, Department for Education and Skills Research Report RR549. London: Department for Education and Skills.

Tizard, B. and Phoenix, A. (1993) *Black, White or Mixed Race?* London: Sage.

Wilson, A. (1987) *Mixed Race Children*. London: Allen and Unwin.

Part Three

Recent Developments

Chapter 8

Designing and delivering programmes for minority ethnic offenders

Patrick Williams

Introduction

In June 1999 a group of probation practitioners, voluntary sector managers, teaching consultants and research staff were commissioned to design, develop and implement a groupwork programme specifically for minority ethnic offenders being supervised by the Greater Manchester Probation Area (GMPA). Significantly, the undertaking of this journey exposed the organisation to a number of challenges to the ways GMPA intervened with its Black and Asian service users.[1] The process also challenged the organisation to revisit a number of theoretical, cultural and practice perspectives that facilitated a re-engagement with the strategic premise upon which interventions for minority offender groups were based. The development and implementation process came to fruition in the Spring of 2000 with the pilot of the Black Offender Groupwork Programme. Simultaneously, national developments were apace to provide evidence of What Works for Black and Asian offenders resulting in the development and piloting of four Pathfinder groupwork models. The practice and cultural interplay between the local probation area and the National Probation Directorate (NPD) introduced an additional set of variables, which significantly 'influenced' the delivery of services within the local area. Importantly, within GMPA there has always been a standpoint that views the pursuit of effective practice as an enterprise that is reliant upon the continuous exploration and validation of probation practice and research. Moreover, it is only through engagement with this enterprise that the organisation can claim to be responsive to the needs of the offenders and communities that it serves.

This chapter will return to the sequence of events that gave rise to the development of the Black Offender Groupwork programme. In addition, it will examine the relationship between the 'local' and the 'centre' to highlight the complexities and difficulties that arise in the provision of 'guidance' from the centre to inform practice and interventions within the local context. As will be seen, what arises are a number of disparities that have restrained the development of innovative practice at the local level and therefore render questionable the process of identifying 'what works' with Black and Asian offenders.

Probation programmes for Black Offenders

There were a number of drivers behind the development of Black offender groupwork programmes. First, there was growing evidence of a differential in the delivery of services to Black and Asian offenders. Official statistics showed a disproportionate increase in the numbers of Black offenders receiving custodial sentences (Home Office 2003). In addition, studies found a disparity in the quality of pre-sentence reports prepared on Black and Asian offenders and highlighted the concerns of practitioners about the types of interventions available (HMIP 2000, 2004). Second, the absence of 'diversionary' interventions for Black and Asian offenders, which had been implemented for the generic probation caseload, made the organisation susceptible to a charge of discriminatory practice. Third, there emerged 'dissenting voices' that questioned the legitimacy of the application of 'effective practice principles' for Black and Asian offenders which were as yet largely unproven.

Groupwork – traditional goals versus modern concerns

The use of groupwork as a mode of intervention for addressing the related needs of offenders has a long history within probation practice. Senior (1991) provides a good précis of the gradual introduction of the groupwork programme by isolating its growth into three distinct epochs, framed within the cultural and political constructs of probation work. For the purpose of this chapter I would like to focus on the seminal period of 1972 through to 1984 where it is argued that the groupwork programme was employed as a means to 'empower' the probation client.

It is during this period that groupwork was utilised as a tool for participant empowerment, reflecting the socio-political value base of the Probation Service. Within this construct, the offender was deemed a product of wider societal inequality and oppression and thus the intervention was developed to recognise and redress the social status of the client (Mitchell-Clarke 1998).

This approach was underpinned by a value-base that critiqued the 'humanistic and individualised' approach towards the engagement of clients and advanced the theory that structural disadvantage and the experience of injustice were key characteristics of the probation caseload. Moreover, the advancement of practice to be 'anti-discriminatory', 'anti-oppressive' and 'anti-sexist' provided the subtext for this political shift (Nellis and Gelsthorpe 2003). Therefore, throughout this period there was a socio-political drive to develop interventions that were responsive to and representative of the organisation's resolve to confront 'the oppression of women, Black people and other oppressed groups' (Brown 1986: 22). Increasingly, the design and development of groupwork reflected the 'strategies' employed to 'reduce, eliminate, combat and reverse negative valuations by powerful groups in society affecting certain individuals and social groups', by challenging institutional and social oppression (Payne 1991: 229).

The mid-1980s through to the 1990s saw a move away from the use of groupwork programmes to 'empower' the individual, towards its re-employment as a mechanism for the 'control' of the offender within the community. May (1994) indicates that the move to 'control in the community' reflects a paradigm shift in the political and theoretical explanations and organisational responses to offending behaviour. This saw the isolation of the individual from their social environment towards explanations of causality based solely on individual characteristics and rejecting considerations around social, political and economic justice. This shift posed a significant challenge to the culture and practice of the probation organisation. The emphasis upon 'control' was embraced by the National Probation Directorate (NPD) as a means through which the organisation could exert a claim of effectiveness in the management of offenders within the community. This re-branding implicitly required the relegation of methods that sought to engage and respond to the contextual features of offending behaviour. Within this context the exploration and impact of the societal phenomenon such as racism, sexism, class and wider forms of discrimination became peripheral to offender management.

Difference – the experience of Black people in British society

The socio-economic experiences of Black and Asian people within British society have been documented extensively (Powis and Walmsley 2002; Bowling and Phillips 2002). In 1987, Hall articulated the following:

> Black people find themselves within the bottom pile of every indicator of deprivation and disadvantage. The question of deprivation cannot be isolated from the particular and specific ways in which disadvantage affects the experience of people who are black, and is compounded by the fact of their racial identity. (Hall 1987: 46)

It still remains the case that Black and Asian people are more likely to be concentrated within deprived communities and locations, to be living within poor housing conditions, to experience unemployment or be employed within lower paid and lower status jobs. In terms of education, Black and Asian children are more likely to be represented within truancy figures, be excluded from mainstream education and attain lower examination results. Moreover, the introduction of second and third generational factors highlights the increasing complexities and strain faced by Black people. For Bowling and Phillips, the 'strain that arises from the aspirations of late-modern society, the power of consumerism expressed through the mass media and the reality of systematically blocked opportunities, destroy hope and creates despair, frustration, anger and resistance' (Bowling and Phillips 2002: 10) There is evidence that members of Black and Asian groups who find themselves at the bottom of the social pyramid sometimes display the phenomenon of 'self-hatred' and 'self-depreciation' (Tajfel, quoted in Robinson 1995: 90).

> [L]iving in a racist, white society, where blacks are viewed and treated as inferior and where they are in poverty in a powerless community leads blacks early in life to internalise negative beliefs and negative feelings about themselves and other blacks. Exposure to racism and oppression has damaged the black person's psychological make-up and most probably is reflected in their conceptions of self. (Robinson 1995: 91)

This gives a complex picture in which issues of race, ethnicity and identity are compounded by those of class and social exclusion.

The work of Calverley *et al.* (2004) provides an invaluable insight into the experiences and 'needs' of Black and Asian offenders. The stark realities of social inequality are brought to the fore through the interviews conducted as part of this study. Notably, what is reiterated within this study is that the perception and experience of social and economic inequality is as a result of wider racism and discrimination. This perception is learned and internalised within a criminogenic environment, devoid of legitimate opportunities, 'successful talk' or stories, and where the benefits afforded to the majority of society members become perceived as the preserve of 'others'. It is exposure to this environment that damages self-conception and raises implications for behaviour as the external world impacts upon the internal. In many instances the onset of offending behaviour is facilitated by a lack of pro-social strategies to manage the 'strain' that accompanies these negative life experiences. Crucially, strategies for working with Black and Asian offenders must therefore be located within the social, economic and personal constructs of the individual and be able to engage and address the multiplicity of factors addressed above.

Groupwork for Black offenders – towards empowerment

There is little the Probation Service can do to change the social environments within which offenders live, but it can assist them through the exploration of self-identity and self-conceptualisation to change their views about the choices available within those environments. Maruna argues that what distinguishes 'desisters' from 'persisters' is not 'obvious external differences in the social environment … but in the way people interpret their lives' (Maruna 2001: 32). Crucially it is these variables that are found to be more influential in facilitating desistance from offending (Maruna 2001; Rex 2001). When thinking about desistance, control theories and empowerment models offer a framework within which interventions can be constructed, interventions that can help individuals re-evaluate their lives and the opportunities open to them within their communities.

Control theories provide an explanation as to why most people stay within the confines of the law, a central tenet being that an individual's needs are infinite and that they will tend to seek fulfilment by unlawful means if they can perceive no legitimate way of achieving satisfaction. They accept that poverty and deprivation are related to offending as they weaken an individual's bond with society (Hirschi in Downes and Rock 1998: 221; Chapman and Hough 1998). However, deprivation does not inevitably lead to offending: many who live in poverty lead law-abiding lives. Control theory therefore seeks to outline the controls that keep the behaviour of most individuals within the law, seeing these as the factors that mediate between poverty and offending. As a theory it acknowledges the existence of cognitive deficits, but does not regard them as central. In 1967 Reckless itemised external controls such as the existence of reasonable limits, the availability of meaningful roles and relationships and 'several complementary variables such as reinforcement by groups and significant supportive relationships, acceptance, the creation of a sense of belonging and identity' (quoted in Lilly *et al.* 1989: 95). Internal controls, however, are thought to be particularly important as their impact endures independently of the environment. Reckless saw these as a strong self concept as a law- abiding person; a goal orientation focused on legitimate, achievable goals; high frustration tolerance on the realisation that different opportunities are available to different groups; and an absence of norm erosion that may occur when previously accepted social rules come to appear less legitimate (Lilly *et al.* 1989: 96–8).

There could be a problem here, since if the society of which one is a member has criminogenic values, then increasing social bonds could lead to an increase in offending. But this argument assumes that those who live within sections of society that tend to produce the highest levels of criminal activity necessarily hold values that favour offending, and this view has been challenged (Maruna 2000; Sykes and Matza 1996). As Sykes and Matza argue, the need to develop 'techniques of neutralisation' to facilitate offending or minimise its seriousness presupposes a need to distance oneself from one's anti-social acts (1996: 206).

Bowling and Phillips (2002) also argue that illegal acts sometimes result from situations where individuals feel they have no legitimate alternative rather than from a commitment to criminal values, a view endorsed by attendees at a Black self-development group in London (Durrance *et al.* 2001). One strategy for assisting desistance then is through helping offenders identify positive roles within their communities through which they can achieve status without offending. Maruna's work wholeheartedly endorses this as a recognised route out of offending (Maruna 2000).

Empowerment programmes, then, seek to reduce the propensity of individuals to offend through fostering the development of social controls. While many Black and Asian people achieve a positive racial identity as family and community supports lead to the development of effective survival skills, it is likely that some people on probation may feel alienated from, or marginal to, wider society. Black empowerment therefore involves the development and application of skills based on 'information sharing' while centralising the importance of 'we' rather than 'I'. Critically, the empowerment process requires that the individual looks at their own situation from their own perspective to assist in the development of strategies to empower and improve their situation (Frances-Spence 1994 in Mitchell-Clarke 1998). Thus an empowerment model

> must assist the individual in his/her understanding of the historical, social, economic and individual factors which have and will impact on the process of change, aid in the setting of realistic and achievable goals and assist in removing negative traits of behaviour. The individual must also be provided with an opportunity to identify strategies for coping with events that influence his/her lifestyle but for which he/she does not have ultimate control for change. (Duff 2002: 10)

This involves focusing upon the extent to which group participants may have internalised negative stereotypes and racist attitudes and the possible ways this may impact upon their own behaviour, as a first step towards promoting a more positive view of the self.

Though variations existed, empowerment programmes for Black and Asian offenders tended to be multi-faceted, with explorations of racism, social exclusion and discrimination providing the springboard from which discussions around personal responsibility to the self and others within the community could be explored. In this respect, far from allowing offenders to abnegate responsibility, the process encouraged them to take responsibility for their actions, to be less of a victim and more of an agent. Typically, programmes included sessions on Black and Asian history, providing a positive image of Black achievements unlikely to have been experienced elsewhere in the school curriculum or the media. Some included education, training and employment (ETE) components and links with community organisations, thereby providing routes through which newly developing confidence could be channelled, and sources of support that Black and Asian people could access without having to offend (Durrance *et al.* 2001).

Specifically, a model of empowerment developed within GMPA consisted of five programme sessions with the aim to 'explore the levels and types of internal, external and institutional racism', and how these attitudes may 'impact upon the offenders' social and criminogenic attitude'. In addition, session content ranged from discussions around the historical context of Black people within Greater Manchester, focusing on 'how we came to be here', to sessions in relation to 'self definition' and 'how we see ourselves'. Other sessions facilitated discussion around 'survival strategies from slavery to the present' and sought to highlight the process and features of decision-making taken by significant figures throughout history. Importantly, empowerment sought to present the historical context of racism and discrimination within a modern framework relevant to programme participants, leading to an examination of the nature and role of citizenship in the present. Structured programme sessions were delivered by Black tutors, with programme learning consolidated through the use of community based mentors to assist the participant in the execution of newly acquired skills and confidence within the community (Williams 2001).

It is, though, important to recognise that exploring aspects of identity within a separate group is not for all Black and Asian offenders. In Jeffers' study, some offenders saw splitting off Black and Asian offenders from white as inherently racist (Jeffers 1995: 27). When asked about their experience of being in all-Black groups, offenders gave mixed reactions, from the very positive to the negative (1995: 28). This spread of reaction is only to be expected, as it reflects the heterogeneity of this client group and the different meanings that individuals ascribe to elements of their social environment.

By way of addressing difference, local probation areas have introduced processes to ensure that full information is provided to all offenders who are eligible for such programmes. For example, within the Greater Manchester area offenders were assessed and given the 'informed' choice of attendance at either a specific Black offender groupwork programme or at the 'generic' offending behaviour programmes delivered within local probation offices. During the period January to December 2003, 177 Black and Asian offenders who met the eligibility criteria were referred to offending behaviour programmes and of these 35 (19.7 per cent) opted to attend the generic programme within local probation offices instead of the empowerment programme (Williams 2003). Conversely, Calverley *et al.* (2004) found that only five per cent of the interview sample favoured groups for ethnic minority participants only.

The evaluations of local programmes highlight that the completion rates for Black empowerment groups compare favourably with those currently achieved for general offending behaviour programmes. Within the London probation area, programme completion consistently attained levels of approximately 68 per cent at a time when attendance was voluntary (Durrance et al. 2001: 28). Moreover, this figure was sustained when attendance on the group became enforceable. Elsewhere, completion rates of between 50 per cent and 70 per cent were realised for groups run in the West Midlands and Greater Manchester probation areas (Dunn 2000; Williams 2003). These comparable completion rates appear to reflect the positive comments made by the participants of Black empowerment groups. In many cases, this is the first opportunity offenders have ever had to discuss issues around race, being Black, and their needs in relation to offending and race within a safe, supportive environment (ILPS 1993; Williams 2001; Durrance et al. 2001). Equally, programme participants are able to relate the issues covered in the programme to their offending. Participant feedback also provides evidence of the way empowerment programmes get offenders to look at their self-perceptions and values:

> The course made me realise that I had some self-development issues to deal with. Before I started this course I thought I knew what I had to do and where I was going in life. (Durrance et al. 2001: 46)

Empowerment programmes can also impact upon their offending:

> Prison doesn't stop you offending. It makes you angry and frustrated at the way they treat you. Coming to this group has helped me to look at my offending. (Durrance et al. 2001: 39)

Offenders also comment on wanting to continue the work they have started:

> More self development groups, to continue to the end of our orders in general for everyone to attend. It's really important to learn about Black history and to feel good about yourself. (Durrance et al. 2001: 52)

Some participants in a Black self-development module that preceded a general offending behaviour programme suggested they would like 'an after-course that was less strict on attendance' (Williams 2002). In the case of programmes where the Black self-development module was short or comprised one component of a larger programme, offenders reported feeling frustrated by there being insufficient time for working through these issues (Powis and Walmsley 2002; Williams 2001; ILPS 1993).

The evidence supporting empowerment groups reflects that contained in the broader criminological literature relating to desistance from offending. Various researchers have considered the development of a non-offending identity as central to the cessation of offending:

> [E]x-offenders need to develop a coherent, prosocial identity for themselves. As such, they need to account for and understand their criminal pasts ... and they also need to understand why they are now 'not like that anymore'. Ex-offenders need a coherent and credible self-story to explain (to themselves and others) how their checkered pasts could have led to their new, reformed identities. (Maruna 2001: 7–8)

This can only be achieved through locating their experience within their social context as 'these narratives cannot be understood outside of their social, historical, and structural context ... self narratives are developed through social interaction' (Maruna 2001: 8). This belief is echoed by Rex (2001: 67), who states that 'for rehabilitative programmes to be effective ... there is at least an equally pressing need to pay attention to offenders' social environments, and the normative processes that support non-offending choices'. As illustrated above, for many Black and Asian offenders this process will include their experience of racism and discrimination. Similarly, Gove (in 1985) includes increasing comfort in social relations, increasing concern for others in the community rather than self-absorption, and increasing concern with issues regarding the meaning of life as being linked to desistance from crime (cited in Maruna 2001: 34). It has been noted that the cessation of offending can often be related to acquiring something that one values and is subsequently unwilling to relinquish, whether this be a job, a relationship or a new self-image (Farrall 2002: 11; Rex 2001: 73).

Local and national drivers – different song sheets

The development and use of groupwork programmes was accepted within probation practice as a means of reversing the ever-increasing numbers of offenders being given custodial sentences.

The development of the 1a2 condition as part of a Probation Order (*sic*), as enacted through the 1991 Criminal Justice Act, facilitated the introduction of a number of groupwork programmes with the aim of providing the courts with a rigorous alternative to custody. By 1998, probation areas had acquired an impressive portfolio of groupwork programmes. For example, within GMPA the following programmes were being delivered to offenders: Offence Focussed Problem Solving Groupwork Programme; Anger Management Programme; Drivers Impaired by Alcohol (DIAL); Alcohol Related Offending; Disqualified Drivers; Drug Users Programme; Women's Programme; Domestic Violence Programme; Sex Offender Groupwork Programme. These programmes were delivered from a single location, which fuelled the assumption that effectiveness is an isolated and specialist area of practice. In the circumstances, the absence of a groupwork programme for Black and Asian offenders appeared somewhat confusing.

The overwhelming evidence of an over-representation of Black and Asian people throughout the criminal justice system and specifically within the prison population suggests that the 'additional requirement' would be of benefit to this group. By way of emphasis, a national survey of groupwork programmes found that of 1,463 groupwork programmes being delivered, only three were being delivered specifically for Black offenders (Caddick 1993). This finding prompted the following conclusions.

> It is impossible to accept that groupwork which gives such scant attention to race as a cultural factor is seriously addressing the real experiences and consequent needs of Black offenders and, in light of the considerable over-representation of Black offenders in the criminal justice system, this finding is painfully ironic ... the existence or non-existence of such groups conveys something important about the [probation] service's attention to anti-discriminatory practice and about its approach to offenders generally. (Caddick 1993: 28)

Moreover, the replication of these findings some ten years later clearly highlights the continued lack of suitable provision for Black and Asian offenders (Powis and Walmsley 2002). Given the diversionary basis for the development of programmes for offenders, the above clearly suggests that the history of Probation Service provision to Black and Asian people was at best 'patchy' and at worst discriminatory. Preceding the Caddick study, Hood produced an influential study into the impact of race on sentencing. This study provided the clearest indication that ethnicity can have an influence on sentencing by increasing the likelihood of a custodial sentence for Black and Asian offenders. Hood (1992) stated that 'many people's lives are being severely damaged and their future prospects impaired for no reason other than they are black'. The challenge this presented for the Probation Service was clearly elucidated by Poole and Browne (1997: 29):

> Black people are having bad experiences with the Criminal Justice System. What is the Service doing to show its commitment to addressing this imbalance?

In the absence of a national strategy and with the voicing of practitioner concerns as illustrated above, local probation areas began a process of developing groupwork interventions for Black offenders. Importantly, the pursuit of 'equity' in the delivery of groupwork programmes was facilitated by the genuine concern with the inequality of specific provision of practitioners who felt that the Probation Service was not fulfilling its obligations to addressing the needs of Black and Asian offenders within their communities (Briggs 1995; Poole and Brown 1997). Clearly, then, the features and needs that gave rise to the development of specific groupwork programmes for Black and Asian offenders from local probation areas represented a genuine drive and concern that sought to redress the experiential inequalities of the offender as a means through which to empower the individual and to develop strategies to reduce future involvement in offending behaviour.

Importantly, the implementation of these programmes was only the start of the developmental process. Underlying the implementation of these initiatives was the realisation that the pursuit of 'what works' for Black and Asian offenders was not a static enterprise and therefore revision and adaptation of policy and practice would be central in this regard. Essentially, local practice anticipated the findings of the national diversity enterprise to assist in the implementation of strategies that were proven to be effective in our work with Black and Asian offenders.

The Macpherson Report into the death of Stephen Lawrence (Macpherson 1999) clearly identified institutional racism within the criminal justice system and highlighted the need for a greater focus on 'diversity' within the agencies that make up that system. It contained important lessons for how the Probation Service might best address the needs of all minority ethnic people. Under the auspices of the government's Crime Reduction Programme the Home Office commissioned a study to explore the possibility of developing an intervention programme specifically for Black and Asian offenders (Powis and Walmsley 2002). In addition, a research study was to be undertaken by researchers from Glamorgan, Lancaster, Lincoln and Swansea Universities, to explore the criminogenic needs of Black and Asian offenders (Calverley *et al.* 2004).

The study by Powis and Walmsley (2002) found little information in relation to interventions specifically for Black and Asian offenders, with the result that the authors were unable to say what type of intervention was likely to be effective in reducing offending behaviour. In response to this problem, the Home Office decided to take the agenda forward by developing and testing out a number of Pathfinder models (Stephens *et al.* 2004). As discussed elsewhere within this book, a core component of the Pathfinder programmes was the inclusion of Black self-development models in the wider context of standard general offending behaviour programmes currently running within the Probation Service. Within the general offending behaviour programmes, criminal behaviour is deemed symptomatic of 'cognitive deficits' that have resulted from a deficient socialisation process and learned behaviour. These cognitive deficits lead to a lack of well-developed problem-solving techniques and social skills. Teaching these skills is seen as one way of addressing offending because they can help offenders to modify and control their own behaviour (McGuire 1996).

Concurrently, there had been a significant change in the theory base underpinning the delivery of probation practice to offenders. The emergence of the What Works theory base isolated a number of key principles upon which all probation interventions were to be built. The acceptance of these principles by the National Probation Service (NPS) resigned many 'locally developed' initiatives, or 'legacy' programmes as they became known, to the margins of probation practice, to be replaced by accredited programmes that, it was claimed, had been rigorously evaluated and were proven to be effective in reducing the offending behaviour of participants. Where the 'kudos' of implementing accredited programmes was not sufficiently motivating for local areas to ensure their wide implementation into probation practice, the subsequent introduction of 'cash-linked' targets based on the number of offenders who commenced and completed programmes certainly was.

There emerged a number of theoretical and cultural conflicts between the ambitions and pursuits of local probation areas when juxtaposed with the national approach. First, the Pathfinder models promote an individualistic explanation for offending behaviour and therefore place a greater emphasis on the pathology of the individual, paying scant regard to the social context within which the behaviour exists (Durrance and Williams 2003). This has resulted in the disengagement of the individual from their social, personal and cultural context, which undermines the significance of racism, discrimination and inequality for offending behaviour. Where effective practice principles thrust the crime causal nexus onto the individual, structural theories postulate that supposedly 'pathological' forms of behaviour are 'functional adaptations' to the reality of the offenders' socio-economic and personal environment (Bowling and Phillips 2002). Therefore, locally, the drive to utilise the groupwork programme as a mechanism to address inequality and discrimination was curtailed with the implementation of the Pathfinder process.

Implicitly the Black and Asian Pathfinder models illustrate the shifts in probation values and culture through the use of terminology and, more significantly, movements in the utility of empowerment as a mechanism for facilitating compliance (Stephens *et al.* 2004). The Pathfinder models make redundant the language of 'empowerment' for the less menacing 'preparatory' to describe the sessions undertaken prior to the offending behaviour module of the Pathfinder programmes. The aims of the 'preparatory' sessions are to aid the compliance of the participant through the programme, by acting as a motivator to engage programme participants (Stephens *et al.* 2004). Given the comparable completion rates for empowerment programmes, the Pathfinder employment of preparatory sessions to facilitate offender motivation and completion is somewhat misguided. Moreover, the partial inclusion of the experiential effects of racism, discrimination and wider societal inequality, within preparatory sessions, as a mechanism to facilitate programme compliance is inappropriate.

Second, Stephens *et al.* (2004: 9) noted a 'perceived lack of input in training and in the programme material specific to, or acknowledging, Asian culture'. In addition, there was a question raised regarding where 'the responsibility lay for input on aspects of diversity – nationally, locally or with the individual' (2004: 9). Where programmes are developed in an attempt to respond specifically to the heterogeneity of Black and Asian offenders then the focus of intervention may become lost. Within the local probation area, definitions have encompassed an inclusive and common definition for programme participants, focusing on the shared experiences of racism and discrimination. Programme materials were developed to be responsive to all programme participants and included references to both Black and Asian participants. Clearly, the increasing heterogeneity of Black people, as evidenced through the continuing diversification of British society, significantly reduces the capacity to include materials to meet the cultural, religious and ethnic needs of all eligible groupwork participants for whom empowerment would be beneficial. As a local practitioner stated recently, the responsibility for managing the increasing diversity of the groupwork environment is centred on the 'skills, knowledge and responsivity of the programme tutor and the extent to which she can draw the required knowledge from the programme participant'. It is therefore important that the increasing diversification of the programme participants is not utilised as a justification for not pursuing an empowerment approach by rendering impractical the pursuit of offender empowerment.

Conclusion

From a national perspective, the research enterprise to identify what works for Black and Asian offenders has provided a number of valuable contributions to the debate. However, given the less than conclusive findings to emerge from the Home Office study into the impact of interventions on offending behaviour (Home Office 2004) the development and application of learning from this evidence has proven disappointing. The enthusiasm generated at the beginning of this journey has been dissipated by a lack of courage and innovation in the application of the findings. Logically, the lack of evidence to inform the development of programmes for Black and Asian offenders has led to the development of the Pathfinder pilots. Yet, as suggested by Durrance and Williams (2003), the missed opportunity for consideration of an alternative approach has resulted in the stagnation of the research enterprise. In light of the high levels of racism and discrimination reported by those interviewed by Calverley *et al.* (2004), which resonated with earlier research (Lawrence 1995), it is clear that programmes must focus on the negative feelings that arise as a result of these experiences before the process of empowerment can begin. The exploration of self-identity, the challenging of negative views of the self and the wider community, the re-framing of the offender perception from that of victim to agent, and facilitating the development and exploration of pro-social (and pro-community) choices are prerequisites to reduce the feelings developed as a result of the experiences of racism, discrimination and socio-economic inequality. Moreover, it is exposure to the empowerment process that can facilitate the desistance process.

Further, there is an imminent threat to the continuation of the Pathfinder enterprise in relation to Black and Asian offenders. The arrival of the National Offender Management Service (NOMS) has led to a restructuring of the Research, Development and Statistics Directorate (RDS), which had previously been committed to the evaluation of the projects. Regrettably, this has resulted in the devolution of research responsibility for the Pathfinder projects to local probation areas. The capacity of local research departments to fully engage with the issues discussed within this chapter is questionable, given the constraints on local resources and in light of the revised methodologies employed that confine the evaluation to monitoring the throughput of participants in the Pathfinder models. Clearly the celebration and pursuit of 'equitable, fair and accessible practices both within the [probation] workforce and for those receiving its services' is being undone through an overemphasis and reliance upon micro-managerialist methodologies to push through the objectives of the NPD Diversity Strategy (Nellis and Gelsthorpe 2003).

Simultaneously, while we pursue these objectives, the stubborn differential and negative experiences of Black and Asian people throughout the agencies of the criminal justice system remain. Furthermore, given the disproportionate numbers of Black and Asian people within prison institutions, the individual and community effects are of great concern. In light of the challenges to the Probation Service and specifically the Pathfinder enterprise discussed above, the responsibility to address these effects will again fall upon the local probation areas that are responsible for the offenders, victims, communities and stakeholders they serve. The NPD must now facilitate local areas to reconnect with their communities and develop effective interventions that match the community's needs. It is clear that this must be undertaken at a local level, as the composition of race and ethnicity varies by locality. This will require us to embrace and acknowledge the centrality of the social, personal and identity constructs of *all* offenders to illustrate our commitment to addressing offending behaviour in all its forms. A wider question that requires exploration is the extent to which issues discussed in this chapter relate also to the generic probation caseload – whether there is an urgent need to revisit and engage with the interplay of class and the dynamics of social exclusion as a context for all probation clients in relation to offending behaviour.

Acknowledgements

This chapter draws on previous arguments and discussions developed collaboratively with Pauline Durrance of the London Probation Area.

The author wishes to thank Rebecca Clarke and Sam Lewis for their helpful comments and suggestions. Any remaining errors are the sole responsibility of the author.

Note

1   For the purpose of clarity the term 'Black and Asian' will be employed, throughout this chapter, to describe all people of African, African-Caribbean, and Asian descent who have a common experience of racism and discrimination. Use of the singular 'Black' is employed in relation to probation policy and practice to again denote the common experiences of Black and Asian people and not ethnicities.

References

Bowling, B. and Phillips, C. (2002) *Racism, Crime and Justice*. London: Longman.

Brown, A. (1986*) Groupwork*. Aldershot: Gower.

Briggs, C. (1995) 'Policing Moss Side: A Probation Service Response, *Probation Journal*, 42: 2, 62–6.

Caddick, B. (1993) 'Using Groups in Working with Offenders: A Survey of Groupwork in the Probation Services of England and Wales', in A. Brown, and B. Caddick (eds) *Groupwork with Offenders*. London: Whiting and Birch.

Calverley, A., Cole, B., Kaur, G., Lewis, S., Raynor, P., Sadeghi, S., Smith, D., Vanstone, M. and Wardak, A. (2004) *Black and Asian Offenders on Probation*, Home Office Research Study 277. London: Home Office.

Chapman, T. and Hough, M. (1998) *Evidence Based Practice: A Guide to Effective Practice*. London: HMIP.

Downes, D. and Rock, P. (1998) *Understanding Deviance: A Guide to the Sociology of Crime and Rule Breaking*. Oxford: Clarendon Press.

Duff, D. (2002) *A Programme for Change and Rehabilitation: Black Self-Development Groupwork Manual*. London: LPA.

Dunn, M. (2000) *Recidivism: Report of the Black Offender Group Pilots*. Birmingham: West Midlands Probation.

Durrance, P., Hignett, C., Merone, L. and Asamoah, A. (2001) *The Greenwich and Lewisham Self-Development and Educational Attainment Group: Evaluation Report*. London: London Probation Area.

Durrance, P. and Williams, P. (2003) 'Broadening the Agenda Around What Works for Black and Asian Offenders', *Probation Journal*, 50:3, 211–24.

Farrall, S. (2002) *Rethinking What Works with Offenders: Probation, Social Context and Desistance from Crime*. Cullompton: Willan.

Hall, S. (1987) 'New Ethnicities', in J. Donald and F. Rattansi (eds) *Race, Culture and Difference*. London: Sage.

Home Office (2003) *Statistics on Race and the Criminal Justice System 2002*. London: Home Office.

Home Office (2004) *The Impact of Corrections on Re-offending: A Review of 'What Works'*, Home Office Research Study 291. London: Home Office.

Hood, R. (1992) *Race and Sentencing*. Oxford: Clarendon Press.

HMIP (Her Majesty's Inspectorate of Probation) (2000) *Towards Race Equality: A Thematic Inspection*. London: Home Office.

HMIP (2004) *Towards Race Equality: Follow-up Inspection Report*. London: Home Office.

ILPS (Inner London Probation Service) (1993) *The Black Groups Initiative 1992–93: Evaluation*. London: ILPS.

Jeffers, S. (1995) *Black and Ethnic Minority Offenders' Experience of the Probation Service*. London: ILPS.

Lawrence, D. (1995) 'Race, Culture and the Probation Service', in G. McIvor, (ed.) *Working with Offenders*. London: Jessica Kingsley.

Lilly, J R., Cullen, F. T. and Ball, R. A. (1989) *Criminological Theory: Context and Consequences*. London: Sage.

Macpherson, W. (1999) *The Stephen Lawrence Inquiry: Report of an Inquiry by Sir William Macpherson of Cluny*. Cm. 4262-1. London: Home Office.

Maruna, S. (2001) *Making Good: How Ex-convicts Reform and Rebuild Their Lives*. Washington: American Psychological Association.

May, T. (1994) 'Probation and Community Sanctions', in M. Maguire, R. Morgan and R. Reiner (eds) *The Oxford Handbook of Criminology*. Oxford: Clarendon Press.

McGuire, J. (1996) *Cognitive-behavioural Approaches: An Introductory Course on Theory and Research*. Course Manual. Liverpool: University of Liverpool.

Mitchell-Clarke, V. (1998) *Groupwork with Black Offenders*, unpublished Masters dissertation. Leicester: Scarman Centre.

Nellis, M. and Gelsthorpe, L. (2003) 'Human Rights and the Probation Values Debate', in W. H. Chui and M. Nellis (eds) *Moving Probation Forward*. Harlow: Pearson.

Payne, M. (1991) *Modern Social Work Theory*. Basingstoke: Macmillan.

Poole, L. and Brown, D. (1997) *Evaluation of the 'New Directions' Groupwork Programme*. Manchester: Greater Manchester Probation Service.

Powis, B. and Walmsley, R. K. (2002) *Programmes for Black and Asian Offenders on Probation: Lessons for Developing Practice*, Home Office Research Study 250.

Rex, S. (2001) 'Beyond Cognitive-Behaviouralism? Reflections on the Effectiveness Literature', in A. Bottoms, L. Gelsthorpe and S. Rex (eds) *Community Penalties: Change and Challenges*. Cullompton: Willan.

Robinson, L. (1995) *Psychology for Social Workers: Black Perspective.* London: Routledge.

Senior, P. (1991) 'Groupwork in the Probation Service: Care and Control in the 1990s', *Groupwork*, 4 (3): 284–95.

Stephens, K., Coombes, J. and Debidin, M. (2004) *Black and Asian Offenders Pathfinder: Implementation Report.* Home Office Development and Practice Report 24. London: Home Office.

Sykes, G. M. and Matza, D. (1996) 'Techniques of Neutralization', in J. Muncie, E. McLaughlin and M. Langan (eds) *Criminological Perspectives: A Reader.* London Sage.

Williams, P. (2001) *Evaluation of the Black Offender Groupwork Programme.* Manchester: Greater Manchester Probation Service.

Williams P. (2002) *Second Evaluation of the Black Offender Groupwork Programme.* (unpublished) Manchester: Greater Manchester Probation Service.

Williams, P. (2003) *Evaluation of the Think First Black and Asian Offenders Programme.* Manchester: Greater Manchester Probation Service.

Chapter 9

What Works with Black and minority ethnic offenders: solutions in search of a problem?

Rachel K. Walmsley and Kate Stephens

Following the destruction of the Earth in order to make way for a hyperspace bypass, Arthur Dent in Douglas Adams' *Hitch-hiker's Guide to the Galaxy* sets off on a surreal quest to find the answer to life, the universe and everything. At the end of the quest, the incredibly powerful computer, Deep Thought, provides the answer – 42. Deep Thought points out that the real problem was to find out the question. The Earth – now destroyed – had been created for this purpose. It turns out that the real challenge, in determining answers to big issues, is to clarify the question to which an answer is sought.

Arthur Dent's science fiction quest provides a humorous parallel for thinking about research and developing practice with Black and minority ethnic (BME) offenders. If programmes for BME offenders provide a solution for community interventions, what is important is determining the problems they are intended to solve. This chapter reviews how the question 'What Works with BME offenders?' has been interpreted in recent Home Office and other research, and discusses what questions remain to be addressed.

Do Black and minority ethnic offenders benefit from special interventions?

Before the creation of a National Probation Service (NPS) and the introduction of nationally accredited interventions to reduce reoffending, some area Probation Services ran home-grown programmes for BME groups. In 1999 the Probation Unit (now the National Probation Directorate – NPD) commissioned the Home Office research directorate, Research, Development and Statistics (RDS), to investigate what was known about the criminogenic needs of BME offenders, the Probation Service provision available at the time, and the effectiveness of any approaches in reducing reoffending.

This study (Powis and Walmsley 2002) comprised: a literature review of published research; a survey of all Probation Services in England and Wales to identify the extent and nature of previous, current and planned provision for BME offenders; and case studies of ten interventions that were identified in the survey. The study found a dearth of strong evidence on the need for different interventions for BME offenders and on the effectiveness of these interventions in reducing reoffending or achieving other positive outcomes.

Literature was identified suggesting that BME offenders might have different motivations for offending compared to white offenders; for example, probation programmes for BME offenders often seemed to be built around the premise that offending was the product of racism and required specialist rehabilitation focusing on empowerment and related issues (Lawrence 1995). However, there was no hard evidence that the criminal behaviour of BME offenders was related to their experiences of racism. Previous qualitative research based on interviews with offenders and criminal justice practitioners reported findings that racism might be related to the offending of BME groups (Denney 1992; Fisher and Watkins 1993). However, other similar studies found that, in interviews, offenders were less likely to give racism as a reason for their offending (Lawrence 1995; ILPS 1996).

Powis and Walmsley identified a number of programmes for BME offenders that had been run previously or were still being delivered within the Probation Service. Many of these were described as Black empowerment groups that were stand-alone programmes specifically designed to address issues of racism and how racism related to offending behaviour. Staff interviewed felt that these programmes were effective in reducing reoffending among Black and Asian offenders. However, evidence of effectiveness was limited to a small number of probation in-house studies. In these studies, outcomes were only provided for small samples, typically without comparison groups, and focused on samples of groupwork completers. This made it impossible to draw any general conclusions as to whether interventions of this type were effective in reducing reoffending.

Do Black and minority ethnic offenders benefit from separately delivered treatment?

Powis and Walmsley also considered the question of whether BME offenders benefited from the separate delivery of mainstream interventions to BME only groups, as opposed to mixed groups. Arguments were found both for and against the delivery of interventions to separate BME groups. Denney (1992) reported the results of a study of a mixed group probation programme that found that Black men and women often found it difficult to relate to others in the groups and sometimes reported feelings of isolation and disconnection. Other research suggested that there should be more than one Black member in a mixed group to reduce the possible sense of isolation that one Black person on his/her own might experience. Findings indicated that if BME members were a minority within a group, they felt less able to discuss issues from their perspective (Akhtar 2001; Fisher and Watkins 1993). However, research was limited by small sample sizes, with Fisher and Watkins relying partly on speculation by the authors rather than empirical evidence.

Powis and Walmsley also reviewed research suggesting that groups with a significant number of BME members, or that were all minority ethnic, could be more supportive. This research reported that offenders in BME groups gave support to each other and developed a sense of belonging. The positive experiences of some minority ethnic members was said to give encouragement to others who doubted their chances of succeeding within a hostile system (Raynor *et al.* 1994; Fisher and Watkins 1993).

However, other research suggested that some BME offenders did not like the idea of all BME groups and stated preferences to be in mixed groups that included both Black and white members (Akhtar 2001; Tuklo Orenda Associates 1999). Tuklo Orenda Associates (1999) found that some Black offenders felt that all-Black groups were a form of segregation or made them feel that they were being picked out. Some Black offenders also said that they had the same experiences as white offenders and therefore felt that there was no need for separate groups.

Interviewees from Powis and Walmsley's study who were running programmes for BME offenders suggested that separate provision provided a safe, supportive environment for offenders to discuss sensitive issues around racism and how this had impacted on their lives and offending behaviour. Staff interviewed felt that groups including white offenders were often characterised by undercurrents of racism that made it difficult for BME offenders to address the issues of racism and the impact this may have had on their offending behaviour. However, staff also pointed to difficulties experienced in all BME groups if they were made up of offenders from a diversity of minority ethnic backgrounds. These groups were recognised as being more challenging to the facilitator who had to ensure the needs of all attendees were being met and that their culture was being represented in the course. On the basis of their experience of running programmes, some staff said that having both Black and Asian offenders in the same group could sometimes be problematic. They saw the main problem as the racism that may exist between the two cultures and felt that Asian offenders, who were often in the minority, might feel marginalised. On the other hand, other programme deliverers felt that culturally diverse groups were more effective. They suggested that the group participants all had common experiences of racism that they could share and that the group would challenge their own prejudicial views.

Although the search of the literature found arguments both for and against running separate groups for BME offenders, it found little empirical evidence to substantiate the view that separate provision was generally the most effective approach. Interviews with staff delivering interventions for BME offenders found no overall consensus as to whether it was better to provide separate groups for each ethnic group or to provide a single group for all offenders identified as being from a minority ethnic background.

Do Black and minority ethnic offenders benefit from being tutored by BME staff?

Powis and Walmsley's study was unable to find any strong evidence that better outcomes were achieved if offenders were tutored by staff from similar ethnic groups. Nevertheless, staff interviewed generally agreed that programme deliverers should be of a similar minority ethnic background to group participants. However, interviewees discussed the difficulty of achieving this kind of 'match' between the facilitators and participants where the group was composed of offenders from many different ethnic backgrounds. Virtually all staff interviewed felt that programme staff should be from a minority ethnic background so that facilitators would provide positive role models to offenders. It was also felt that BME staff had common experiences of racism that they could share with group participants, and they were considered to have a greater empathy and understanding. Interviewees also thought that because BME tutors had a greater knowledge of minority ethnic cultures, they would be more likely to identify situations when an offender was likely to reoffend.

However, many of those staff interviewed stressed that being of the same ethnic background as programme participants was not a sufficient qualification to be a tutor on groups for Black and Asian offenders. They felt it was more important for facilitators to have a good understanding of racism and its impact on an offender's behaviour. Staff interviewed also thought that programme tutors needed to have considered the impact of racism on their own behaviour and to have resolved any issues they might have around such experiences. It was also felt they needed a good understanding of their own culture and other minority ethnic cultures.

Do Black and minority ethnic offenders have different criminogenic needs?

If evidence was available that BME offenders had different criminogenic needs from white offenders, this would support the argument for separately provided or different provision. In 2001, given the lack of strong empirical evidence in the Powis and Walmsley review, the newly created National Probation Directorate (NPD) commissioned research into the criminogenic needs of BME offenders. This research (Calverley et al. 2004) was conducted by a consortium that included researchers from the Universities of Glamorgan, Lincoln, Swansea and Lancaster. Interviews were conducted with a sample of 483 offenders under probation supervision. The interviews collected information about offenders' criminogenic needs; their experiences of supervision on community rehabilitation orders and programmes; their contact with other parts of the criminal justice system; and their wider experiences of life as Black and Asian people in Britain.

The methodology and findings of this study are discussed in detail in other chapters in this volume (see particularly Chapters 4, 5, 7 and 10). However, among the findings was the clear conclusion that Black, Asian and mixed heritage offenders showed statistically significantly *fewer* crime-prone attitudes and beliefs and lower levels of self-reported problems than relevant comparison groups of white offenders. This evidence does not support the idea that BME offenders have distinctly different or greater criminogenic needs than white offenders. The study by Calverley et al. (2004) was not designed to investigate whether the experience of racism was itself a criminogenic need, as this would have required the use of comparison groups of non-offenders drawn from Black and Asian communities, and would have been a much larger study. However, the interviews did explore offenders' perceived reasons for disadvantage and adverse experiences. BME offenders tended to attribute these negative circumstances to racial prejudice, hostility or discrimination. The researchers concluded that when such experiences occurred within the criminal justice system, this could affect the perceived legitimacy of criminal justice agencies and possibly compliance with their requirements (see Chapter 5, this volume).

The interviewees in this study were also asked what their opinions were on separate groups for BME offenders. Their results showed that 54 per cent of offenders thought groups should be mixed. This was 87 per cent of those who thought that composition mattered at all. There was very limited support for groups containing only members from minority ethnic groups. The authors suggested that their findings supported a policy of running mixed groups rather than groups consisting of only minority ethnic offenders. However, they were concerned about the isolating effects of singleton placements, and they also noted that the Service needs to be aware of the needs of mixed heritage offenders who may suffer discrimination without a sense of acceptance by a minority ethnic community. The sample only included 24 offenders who had personal experience of Black or Asian groups, so the preferences expressed for particular group compositions were often not based on experience; however, those who had attended all-BME programmes were not significantly more likely to say that they preferred them (Calverley *et al.* 2004: 36).

Is compliance with accredited programmes enhanced by special or separately provided interventions?

At the same time as the research by Calverley *et al.* (2004) was being undertaken, the NPD also began a number of Pathfinder projects for Black and Asian offenders. At that time the NPD was in the process of implementing a suite of nationally accredited interventions supported by international effectiveness research, and an ongoing programme of independent outcome research.

In the absence of any strong contrary outcome evidence, the policy position taken by the NPD (Probation Circular 76/2001) was that all offenders, including those from BME groups, should have access to the same programmes nationally, provided they met the relevant eligibility and suitability criteria. The premise was that accredited programmes could be delivered in ways that responded appropriately to the diversity of offenders, with adaptations monitored through a national change control process. The Black and Asian offender Pathfinders were conceived as a group of 'add-ons' or responsive modes of delivery for accredited programmes, in particular Think First and the Drink Impaired Drivers Programme, and were intended to maximise the impact of the programmes.

Through national project group meetings the Pathfinder drew upon the experiences of several of the practitioners and managers who had been involved in earlier initiatives, in particular staff from Greater Manchester, West Midlands and Leicestershire areas. In all, nine areas were involved: one planning to deliver the Drink Impaired Drivers Programme to groups of Asian offenders and all the others working in various ways with Black and Asian offenders eligible and suitable for accredited Thinking Skills programmes. Of these, five areas aimed to implement a mentoring scheme that was intended as an approach to support Black and Asian offenders through accredited programmes in areas with low BME density, where separate groupwork was not a practical option. In the three other areas a four-session groupwork module, the Preparation Module (sometimes known locally as an Empowerment Module, or the Preparation Sessions) was implemented.

The groupwork module comprised exercises and scenarios relating to ethnic identity and experiences of (and ways of dealing with) racism. The module aimed to assist participants to increase their awareness of the way in which life experiences such as racism and cultural difference impact upon beliefs and feelings, within a cognitive -behavioural framework. The content was developed from work in use prior to the introduction of nationally accredited programmes in the context of some of the programmes surveyed by Powis and Walmsley, but included new material enabling links to be made with the forthcoming cognitive-behavioural treatment programme. In the RDS research design, the success of the sessions would be indicated by a range of measures, including reconviction and impact on attendance and completion of the Think First programme. There were two models of delivery for the Preparation Module: in Greater Manchester it was agreed to deliver the Preparation Module and Think First to BME-only groups of offenders, while in the other two areas, the Preparation Module was followed by attendance on a mixed Think First programme.

The NPD had invited areas to participate which believed they could achieve a sufficient number of completions for evaluation purposes. In a period of considerable upheaval for the NPS, some of these beliefs proved to be over-optimistic about what could be delivered. The Drink Impaired Drivers Programme suffered from too few referrals and problems in finding suitable staff to deliver the programme, leading to long wait times for groups to start. The mentoring strand suffered from the small size of the potentially eligible and suitable caseload in participating areas, attrition of trained mentors, and difficulties in matching offenders appropriately to their mentors. By the end of the first year, across all five participating areas, and despite recruitment and training of mentors having taken place, only three offenders had started mentoring. Managers reported reluctance of offenders to take part, in some instances due to a lack of perceived need on the part of offenders.

The most successfully implemented aspect of the Pathfinder was the Preparation Module. During the first year, several groups finished with a high percentage of starters completing. Numbers of referrals seemed potentially adequate to meet the planned target throughput within the Pathfinder period. Despite some optimism about implementation, there were still some obstacles. The supply of adequately trained and motivated Black and Asian staff was one important constraint for areas which chose to use Black and Asian staff to deliver the Pathfinder. In research conducted by Powis and Walmsley (2002), interviewees reported that it was particularly difficult to recruit staff to deliver programmes for Asian offenders because Asian staff were under-represented within the Probation Service. Despite advances made in staff representation (see Chapter 3 in this volume), the Pathfinder project also found that finding ethnically appropriate, suitably trained and enthusiastic staff (particularly sufficient numbers of Asian staff) was a constant problem. This problem was partly due to tutor attrition and the time-lag involved in training up staff in response to local demand. Stephens *et al.* (2004) also reported that while some staff gained professionally from their involvement in the Pathfinder, this sometimes meant they advanced to other roles, and replacements with the same energy and commitment took time to find. Other staff felt typecast in being required to be involved in the Pathfinder simply because of their ethnic identity, sometimes indicating that they felt that involvement restricted their professional development. Stephens *et al.* commented that while matching offender and staff ethnicity may be desirable, it can be seen as asking minority ethnic staff to carry the responsibility of responding to diversity, when this should really be a whole Service responsibility.

The implementation report also indicated a perceived lack of input in training and in the programme material specific to, or acknowledging, Asian cultures. Anxiety among tutors about their own limited diversity experience and knowledge was common. Some Black tutors felt they lacked knowledge about Asian communities. Some input on diversity issues was provided in national training, but this was not expected to meet the full range of local needs. While some funding was provided for local provision, areas were aware of further training needs that they sometimes did not appear confident about addressing. For example, some tutors commented on gaps in understanding of the changing local context for British Asian youth, and quickly changing patterns of cultural identity. The implementation report discussed the probability of the level of detailed local information need being fulfilled by the centre, recommending greater local input drawing on up-to-date local knowledge and experience of BME communities.

In assessing levels of programme attrition, consistent ways of monitoring this locally were still needed. Participating areas have been funded by the NPD to provide follow-up reports on cohorts of sentenced offenders referred to the programme. This is important information supplementary to group completion rates. Once this information is available for participating areas, assessment will be needed of how much of the drop-out before programme start is due to structural or organisational issues (such as staffing issues, or difficulty in assembling sufficient numbers to start groups) and how much is due to offender motivation issues, in order to assess whether continuation is a feasible option.

Was an outcome study of the Pathfinder interventions feasible?

The first phase of the Pathfinder project illuminated some of the practical feasibility issues involved in implementation of special interventions for BME offenders, and provided some information on tutor, service manager and offender views. However, it was severely limited in its ability to deliver generalisable outcome findings. Some of these limitations were due to obstacles to implementation that have been discussed above. Others were due to inherent research design problems that would have existed even if implementation had gone to plan.

To generate strong outcome findings, an intervention needs an appropriate comparison. In the Pathfinder, comparison was intended between the different implementation models. However, these comparisons would only be meaningful if there was confidence that there were no important differences in implementation other than those planned in the design. That is, the Black and Asian only and mixed Think First models would need to be delivered to comparable groups and in the same way in all important respects, other than the delivery condition being tested.

In practice, the evaluators could not be confident that this was the case. The two main participating areas had different arrangements for referral (described as 'automatic' for one area and following a process of pre-sentence assessment in the other). Moreover, the two areas had quite different sentencing options available to the courts. In one area, following pre-Pathfinder practice, the courts sentenced directly to 'Think First Black and Asian' where this was recommended following assessment by specialist assessors (including an element of choice by the offender). In the other area the courts gave a community sentence with a generic programme condition: once sentenced, Black and Asian offenders were described as 'automatically' referred to the Preparation Sessions.

In addition to this, consistent delivery of the same material across the two areas was compromised. First, the programme materials were still in development during the process of the trial. While there obviously needed to be a period of development in the light of experience, any changes to the material were not consistent with a fair outcome test. Second, treatment management was an issue. The Pathfinder practitioner group had a strongly held belief that tutors would benefit from treatment management by Black and Asian staff. In practice, suitably trained staff (who met all three conditions of being trained in Think First treatment management, being Black or Asian, and having been trained in the Pathfinder module) were not easy to find. Delivery on one site was effectively without a treatment manager for most of the first year following promotion of the original treatment manager.

The Black and Asian offenders' Pathfinder research approach comprised a complex and ambitious design, from which service managers hoped to gain knowledge about comparative outcomes. The relatively small numbers on which this was hoped to be achieved, even on optimistic projections, meant that opportunity for matching of offenders for outcome comparison would be limited.

One possible solution to the problem of comparing completion outcomes for the intervention sites might have been comparing outcomes for each site to comparison groups taken from the same site: for example, comparing the Black and Asian referred group in one area to the white group in that area. However, it would not be possible to know whether any observed difference was due to the intervention or to some other factor. One reason for this was because baseline data for any differences between race/ethnic groups were not available. While Pathfinder area discussions sometimes assumed different levels of need with regard to participating in and completing programmes, there was no quantitative evidence to support this.

There are several reasons for this. While national and local data collection systems require the supply of ethnicity data, this was often found to be missing. Also, management information reporting systems on the programmes database were, at the time of conducting this work, not able to deliver programme completion reports broken down by ethnicity. The provision of this level of management information report remains a priority for the NPD. By the end of April 2005 it was mandatory for all probation areas to report on programmes' performance via the Interim Accredited Programmes Software (IAPS) and this was expected to include information on ethnicity (along with gender and age). If the quality of data can be assured, this would throw some light on what (if any) differences exist between ethnic groups in successful accredited programme completion. The availability of baseline data would inform understanding of the 'problem' that initiatives for specific groups are designed to address. If, for example, BME offenders were shown to have overall higher completion rates than white offenders, then the reasoning behind providing the preparation module would need some review.

The Black and Asian offenders' Pathfinder has not been alone in suffering evaluation design limitations. There is a general need for good designs for intervention outcome studies (Friendship *et al.* 2004). Notwithstanding externally commissioned research, at present there is not a strong evidence base for the effectiveness of general offending behaviour programmes in this country. This is partly because evaluations to date have relied on the use of matched comparison groups to establish treatment effect. This design is limited because of the possibility of selection bias or other differences between the treatment and comparison groups. It has been the only available design for commissioned independent studies on accredited programmes to date, partly due to perceived difficulties of implementing better designs.

Many problems in outcome studies could be overcome by the use of a randomised controlled trial (RCT). In RCTs participants are randomly assigned to either a control group (who do not receive the treatment) or a treatment group, and the groups are then compared over time. This method controls for selection bias and other differences between the groups that might affect the outcomes. The use of RCT in testing for effectiveness of interventions is now a priority for the Home Office. In 2005 the Home Office commissioned a feasibility study into using an RCT to evaluate the effectiveness of one of the offending behaviour programmes currently used in prison or the community. But before reaching the conclusion that an RCT for this Pathfinder could have delivered results, other questions need to be considered.

Is it appropriate to treat **BME** offenders as a homogenous group?

In working group discussions for the Black and Asian offender Pathfinder, the issue of eligibility was discussed. Historically, BME empowerment interventions had drawn on the idea of experience of racism as an eligibility criterion. This meant that any BME person (including groups other than the Black or Asian categories as used in NPS monitoring) could potentially participate, and this was the working solution reached by the Pathfinder. Combined with the desire to reach projected targets and the practice of 'automatic' referral in at least one area, this meant that the target group was potentially very broadly defined.

While there are some generalisable socio-economic differences between BME and white groups, there are also important differences within the BME group with respect to a range of factors that may be indirectly related to offending and order compliance. These factors may include culture and religion, educational background and achievement, language use and competence, employment status, and so on. These factors could render some BME people at greater risk of offending, and some at lesser risk of offending than the white group.

For example, it is widely reported that minority groups are socio-economically disadvantaged compared to white people, with groups of Pakistani, Bangladeshi, Black African and Black Caribbean underachieving in education, with direct, indirect and institutionalised discrimination contributing to unequal outcomes (Bowling and Phillips 2002; Phillips *et al.* 2003). Evidence gathered by the Department for Education and Employment in 2000 showed a pattern of continuous underachievement for certain ethnic groups that starts in early education, continues through further and higher education, and persists in the labour market (Pathak 2000). However, these differences are considerably varied across different ethnic groups. School exclusions are disproportionately high among Black Caribbean pupils. Proportionately more Black, Pakistani and Bangladeshi pupils are recorded as having special educational needs compared to white, Chinese and Indian pupils. Indian and Chinese pupils are more likely to achieve the expected level compared with other ethnic groups at all Key Stages (Bhattacharyya *et al.* 2003). There are also differences of gender and age within all groups.

While BME groups may share experiences of racism, and be disproportionately socio-economically disadvantaged, diversity within this broad group is important to consider. The variation within the broad BME grouping on some characteristics may be as wide as the variation between BME and non-BME groups. The problem of within-group compared to between-group variation is a classic issue for experimental design. If there is wide variation within the treatment group on factors related to outcomes, then treatment effects for the group as a whole will be difficult to observe. Combined with the relatively small sample sizes, as well as the likely small scale of effect for what is a relatively minor adjustment of intervention, the problems of achieving outcome results in the absence of the best possible design are magnified.

Where is the decision best made about separately provided or specialist provision for different race/ethnic groups?

Projects such as Pathfinder have attempted to find ways of supporting the effectiveness of accredited programmes for BME offenders that could then be considered nationally for all BME offenders, depending on local patterns of feasibility. With the creation of the National Offender Management Service (NOMS), and the likely separation of offender manager/commissioner roles from intervention provider, and a regional focus for commissioning services, there appears to be an opportunity to consider again the question of where decisions about best value are placed.

At the time of writing, much about NOMS is still unknown, so some of what follows is speculation. It seems likely that there will remain a national accreditation role, although the scope of this is not known. Now may be an appropriate time to consider whether decisions about implementation of intervention of the type of the Black and Asian offender Pathfinder (that is, enhancements to accredited interventions focused on known criminogenic factors, as opposed to distinctly different types of intervention) are best left to local area management. It is at the local level that practitioner knowledge about local communities is most likely to be held. However, local decisions would be better made in the light of good-quality management information on the needs, offending patterns and compliance rates for groups of offenders, and quality of intervention delivery, based on data collected and reported on to nationally agreed and quality assured data standards.

What analysis and research is now needed?

There is a pressing need for good-quality, consistent and complete management information to throw light on where additional work with different groups of offenders may be needed. The NPS has struggled with the lack of common IT systems and good nationally agreed reporting tools, processes and standards. While the vision for NOMIS (National Offender Management Information System), the NOMS case information IT system under development, is to fill this gap, interim solutions are still needed. This is a priority not only for day-to-day management and communication within a contested service environment, but also to provide an essential foundation for complex analyses and further data collection to inform national policy decisions.

Some analysis might benefit from being conducted locally, to standards that are agreed nationally. It would be useful to have local patterns of criminogenic need broken down by ethnicity to complement the Calverley *et al.* (2004) study. It would also be helpful to drill down into local cultural patterns that may affect the impact of interventions, such as language use, educational background, employment patterns and religious belief. Local areas may differ in their patterns of racial tension, which could lead to individual differences in terms of identity and empowerment, indicating a need for different, more flexible approaches to intervention enhancement. These patterns could point to new areas for innovative motivational work to enhance compliance with orders and programmes. Good local qualitative or quantitative/descriptive work could support the regional commissioning of interventions for local communities.

More work also needs to be done in terms of establishing programme attrition rates and whether or not these differ for BME groups compared to white offenders. This needs to be monitored centrally but would also benefit from local studies that might indicate trade-off between more complex referral processes and overall completion rates for an eligible cohort. Some established groups in this Pathfinder showed promising rates of completion for starters. Analysis is needed to see what is going on here and whether more general lessons could be learned about how group dynamics can motivate offenders to comply. While nationally commissioned work to support national policy decisions should be conducted to the highest technical standards, more local work to inform what are essentially implementation issues may be needed. Locally conducted work would need to be fit-for-purpose, ensuring focus on implementation issues as they arise, and capability to produce results within practical management decision-making cycles.

With the creation of NOMS there is an opportunity to reassess role boundaries and standards for research and information work conducted at different levels. During 2004, RDS, now restructured and embedded within NOMS, underwent a review of projects against service objectives. What Works research projects commissioned in recent years had suffered from being conceived in 'silos', and had often failed to deliver outcome results due to implementation and design issues. Following this, RDS NOMS refocused its attention on four longitudinal large-scale offender tracking projects, which are all subject to initial feasibility studies. In addition to this, the issue of RCTs is being taken seriously, as a way of testing the effectiveness of general offending behaviour programmes in the British context. The strength of RDS lies in large-scale, complex and technically advanced analyses, which often require longer timescales to produce results, and which may have a significant impact on the longer term development of national policy. This still leaves a space for analysis to support locally focused performance improvement project work, which may be relatively small-scale and conducted in shorter timescales.

It is also worth considering that many of the first BME programmes were historically conceived as initiatives to divert BME offenders from custody. This was due to evidence that people from BME groups were more likely to have contact with the criminal justice system. For example, Black people are just over six times more likely to be stopped and searched, three times more likely to be arrested, and seven times more likely to be in prison than white people (Home Office 2005). The research is still inconclusive as to the causes of this apparent disproportionality. However, evidence suggests that this imbalance is not simply the result of people from BME groups committing a disproportionate number of crimes (Bowling and Phillips 2002).

Other factors that may be linked to the over-representation are the high levels of deprivation among BME communities (for example, in terms of education, employment and housing) and the impact of institutional racism in the criminal justice system. If this latter argument is true, there is likely to be a lower threshold of criminality among BME offenders in prison and on probation. Calverley *et al.* (2004), in their discussion on the lower levels of criminogenic need they found among BME groups, speculate about the possible role of differential sentencing.

Anecdotal evidence from practitioners suggests that much of the activity around earlier special interventions for BME offenders had been aimed at raising sentencer awareness and influencing sentencer behaviour. If one objective were to convince sentencers that credible community interventions exist, then the concordance of sentencing with community intervention proposals could be one meaningful outcome measure. This was not specifically one of the aims of the Pathfinder, but appeared to remain a factor in some practitioner thinking. In the NOMS environment, monitoring of delivery in terms of sentencing levels is likely to become more important. It could become an important area for research alongside impact on compliance, criminogenic need and reoffending.

'What Works for BME offenders?' is a good slogan to rally support around the ideal of using empirical evidence to inform policy and practice. It is not, however, a good research question without further elaboration. This chapter has reviewed some of the research that has been conducted in recent years relating to BME offenders. In doing so it has probably raised more questions than it has provided answers. While this may appear a frustrating position to be in, it is better than mistakenly believing an answer has been found, before the underlying questions themselves have been properly understood.

References

Adams, D. (1985) *The Hitch-hiker's Guide to the Galaxy.* London: Pan.

Akhtar, S. (2001). *An Evaluation of the Prison Service Sex Offender Treatment Programme, Enhanced Thinking Skills Programme, Reasoning and Rehabilitation Programme: To See if the Treatment Needs of Black Offenders are Being Met.* Unpublished report.

Bhattacharyya, G., Ison, L. and Blair, M. (2003) *Minority Ethnic Attainment and Participation in Education and Training: The Evidence,* Department for Education and Skills Research Topic Paper RTP 01-03. London: DfES.

Bowling, B. and Phillips, C. (2002) *Racism, Crime and Criminal Justice.* Harlow: Longman.

Calverley, A., Cole, B., Kaur, G., Lewis, S., Raynor, P., Sadeghi, S., Smith, D., Vanstone, M. and Wardak, A. (2004) *Black and Asian Offenders on Probation,* Home Office Research Study 277. London: Home Office.

Denney, D. (1992). *Racism and Anti-Racism in Probation.* London: Routledge.

Fisher, K. and Watkins, L. (1993) 'Inside Groupwork', in A. Brown and B. Caddick (eds) *Groupwork with Offenders.* London: Whiting and Birch.

Friendship, C., Street, R., Cann, J. and Harper, G. (2004) 'Introduction: The Policy Context and Assessing the Evidence', in G. Harper and C. Chitty (eds) *The Impact of Corrections on Re-offending: A Review of 'What Works',* Home Office Research Study 291. London: Home Office.

Home Office (2005) *Race and the Criminal Justice System: An Overview to the Complete Statistics 2003–2004.* Available online at: www.homeoffice.gsi.gov. uk.rds

ILPS (Inner London Probation Service) (1996) *Black and Ethnic Minority Offenders' Experience of the Probation Service: June 1995.* London: ILPS.

Lawrence, D. (1995) 'Race, Culture and the Probation Service', in G. McIvor (ed.) *Working with Offenders.* London: Jessica Kingsley.

Pathak, S. (2000) *Race Research for the Future: Ethnicity in Education, Training and the Labour Market,* Research Topic Paper. London: DfEE.

Phillips, C., Bowling, B. and Annand, K. (2003) *The Experiences of Crime and Criminal Justice among Minority Ethnic Groups: A Review of the Literature.* Unpublished RDS report.

Powis, B. and Walmsley, R. K. (2002) *Programmes for Black and Asian Offenders: Lessons for Developing Practice,* Home Office Research Study 250. London: Home Office.

Raynor, P., Smith, D. and Vanstone, M. (1994) *Effective Probation Practice.* London: Macmillan.

Stephens, K., Coombs, J. and Debidin, M. (2004) *Black and Asian Offenders Pathfinder: Implementation Report,* Home Office Development and Practice Report 24. London: Home Office.

Tuklo Orenda Associates (1999) *Making a Difference: A Positive and Practical Guide to Working with Black Offenders.* Written for South West Probation Training Consortium, 1999, with support from the Home Office Probation Unit.

Chapter 10

Minority ethnic experiences of probation supervision and programmes

Sam Lewis

Introduction

In June 2000 a study of the then 54 Probation Services in England and Wales was conducted to determine the extent and nature of provisions for minority ethnic offenders (Powis and Walmsley 2002). The study found notable gaps in knowledge, particularly in relation to criminogenic needs, the effectiveness of probation interventions, and the need for specialist or separate provisions. The research by Calverley *et al.* (2004) was intended to fill some of these gaps, and to provide evidence about the best form of service provision for minority ethnic offenders.

Calverley *et al.* (2004) conducted semi-structured interviews with 483 minority ethnic men on probation in England and Wales. A detailed account of the research methodology, and of the characteristics of those in the sample, can be found elsewhere in this volume (see particularly Chapters 4, 5 and 7). This chapter is concerned with the findings that relate to minority ethnic experiences of probation supervision and programmes. (All figures in this chapter are weighted to reflect the actual distribution of minority ethnic probationers in England and Wales, as explained in Chapter 4.) The findings answer some of the questions raised by Powis and Walmsley (2002), and highlight further issues to be addressed. Evidence from the Black and Asian Pathfinder research study is expected to add to the growing knowledge base (see Stephens *et al.* 2004; and Walmsley and Stephens, Chapter 9, this volume).

Particular attention is paid to whether the supervising officer, and the content of supervision and programmes, recognised and addressed respondents' needs and experiences as Black and Asian offenders in accordance with the 'responsivity principle' of effective practice. 'Responsivity', put simply, refers to the 'fit' between programme provision (and by extension probation interventions generally) and the needs and learning styles of offenders (McGuire and Priestley 1995). Chapman and Hough (1998: para. 4.15) state:

> While well-designed and executed programmes are an essential prerequisite to effective supervision, ultimately effectiveness depends upon the individual's active participation in a process of change. In the final analysis offenders must be prepared to involve themselves sufficiently to benefit from the programme. It is the failure to gain this participation which often accounts for disappointing outcomes and rates of attendance and completion.

Thus, probation work with Black, Asian and mixed heritage offenders must be built on an understanding of the needs, experiences and learning styles of such offenders, in order to produce the active involvement and engagement needed to produce successful outcomes.

This chapter begins with an account of the findings concerning the completion of supervision plans. It proceeds to consider interviewees' experiences of probation orders, supervisors and supervision. This is followed by a discussion of the views expressed by the sub-sample of interviewees who were (or had been) on a probation programme about their experiences as programme participants. The impact of probation supervision and programmes is then considered. The chapter concludes with a discussion of the implications of the findings for policy and practice.

Supervision plans

The National Standards for the Supervision of Offenders in the Community (revised in 2002) state that a written supervision plan must be completed within 15 days of the start of a community rehabilitation order, and that offenders should be involved in its formulation (Home Office 2002a). Of the 97 per cent of interviewees who answered the relevant question, 77 per cent reported having seen a plan, while the rest said that they had not. This compares favourably with the findings of Mair and May (1997); in their study of 1,213 mainly white[1] offenders on probation, 66 per cent said that a supervision plan had been drawn up, 19 per cent said that it had not, and 15 per cent could not remember.

Offenders were asked whether their views had been considered during the formulation of the plan. Of the 72 per cent of offenders who had seen a plan and who answered the relevant question, 57 per cent (41 per cent of the whole sample) said that their views had been taken into account, 24 per cent said that they had not been, and 19 per cent did not know. Mair and May (1997) report that three-quarters of offenders said that their probation officer had asked what they thought should go into the plan, the remainder of respondents saying that they had not been asked or could not remember.

Interviewees were asked whether they had talked with their main supervisor about their feelings and needs as a Black or Asian offender. Ninety-nine per cent of interviewees responded, and 30 per cent of these said that such a conversation had taken place. A greater proportion of those with a white supervisor rather than a minority ethnic supervisor reported having had such a discussion (34 per cent and 28 per cent respectively), although the difference was not statistically significant. In over half of the conversations, the issues discussed were not actually related to being Black or Asian (52 per cent, or 15 per cent of whole sample). Where relevant matters were discussed, the topics most commonly mentioned were racism (18 per cent, five per cent of whole sample) and cultural needs and issues (six per cent, two per cent of whole sample).

The lack of attention paid to the particular needs and experiences of minority ethnic offenders is a cause for concern. First, the responsivity principle suggests that probation supervisors should make every effort to understand offenders' needs and experiences, including those pertaining to ethnicity, in order to facilitate engagement, involvement and a positive outcome. Second, many interviewees reported experiencing racial discrimination, and it has been suggested that the effects of racism may be a type of criminogenic need (Durrance and Williams 2003).[2] The study by Calverley *et al.* (2004) found *lower* levels of crime-prone attitudes and self-reported problems among the interviewees than among comparable groups of white offenders, at statistically significant levels. Stephens *et al.* (2004: 14) concluded that whilst the study 'raised expectations of findings related to racism as a criminogenic', '[t]his was not supported in the research findings'. However, the analysis by Calverley *et al.* (2004) did not directly address the suggestion that experiencing racial prejudice may be criminogenic, and *the findings do not in themselves disprove this.* Clearly, further research is required to clarify the issue.

Orders, supervisors and supervision

The vast majority of interviewees – 86 per cent – reported having been treated fairly by their supervisor,[3] with little variation in the positive response rates between members of different minority ethnic groups.[4] The most frequent reasons for saying that they had been treated fairly were that they had been treated with respect, as a 'normal' person, equally, etc. (18 per cent of the whole sample), they could talk to their supervisor or their supervisor listened to them (14 per cent), and they received help with needs and problems (13 per cent).

In the unweighted sample,[5] 72 per cent of main supervisors were white, 22 per cent were Black, six per cent were Asian, and less than one per cent were of mixed heritage. These figures varied considerably between different density areas. In high density areas, 27 per cent of offenders had a Black supervisor while six per cent had an Asian supervisor. In medium and low density areas these figures were eight per cent and four per cent respectively. Since 89 per cent of all probation officers on 31 March 2002 were white, while just seven per cent were Black and two per cent were Asian (Home Office 2002b: Table 7.10), high density probation areas in particular seem to have operated a policy of allocating minority ethnic offenders to minority ethnic supervisors.

Interviewees were asked whether having a minority ethnic supervisor had (or would have) made a positive difference. Thirty-five per cent of participants[6] said that it was (or would have been) a benefit. Interestingly, less than half (41 per cent) of those being supervised by a Black or Asian probation officer gave this response. Fifty-six per cent said that supervisors' ethnicity made no difference, ten per cent said that they did not know, and two per cent were opposed to the idea.[7] Offenders interviewed by Black and Asian researchers were significantly[8] more likely than those interviewed by white researchers to report favouring a minority ethnic supervisor. This was one of the very few situations in which the ethnicity of interviewers may have affected responses, but its impact on overall findings was limited by the fact that most interviews were not carried out by white researchers.

The most frequent reasons given for wanting a supervisor from a minority ethnic group were that he or she would be more able to understand the background, culture and experiences of a Black or Asian person (22 per cent of the whole sample), that they would be easier to talk to (eight per cent), and that they would make the interviewee feel more comfortable (six per cent):

> [Having an Asian supervisor makes a difference] because he understands me fully, we're from the same place ... For example he knows that in our communities you can't speak openly about our problems. I'd feel ashamed if I did but in front of him you can say what you need to and he knows the pressures I've been under. You wouldn't get that understanding of my situation from a white supervisor.

> When I'm trying to explain things in my own slang he knows what I'm saying. I'd prefer to have a Black supervisor but I don't really mind. I think it's easier and more comfortable. Sometimes you talk about deep stuff and perhaps a white person wouldn't understand my upbringing. I don't know how they can help you if they don't know your way of life.

The following randomly selected comments came from people who said that having an ethnic minority supervisor had (or would have) made no difference:

> I've been brought up by white people, taught by white people, grown up with them. It makes no difference.

> I think Black, white – it's just a colour thing. They are both doing the same job so it shouldn't make a difference.

> I've had a white probation officer and an Asian probation officer and it's all the same really.

> If they don't care what is happening to you – don't want to bother with you – that is what makes the difference. They can do that if they are Black or white, can't they?

The following remarks came from interviewees who expressed concern about having a minority ethnic supervisor:

> [Having a Black supervisor] could go either way. They could understand you better than a white officer ... But it might also mean that they'll be unfair and hard on you because they are trying to show their white colleagues they are not soft.

> I prefer to have a white case manager because if my case manager was an Asian she could not keep my privacy. They will hear you and then go to others and talk about it. I would not be comfortable to talk about my offence with an Asian person because he or she will reveal your private things among Asian people.

When asked whether minority ethnic offenders should have supervisors from the same ethnic background, 36 per cent of respondents agreed, 43 per cent disagreed, and 21 per cent were indifferent (n = 475). It should be noted that offenders interviewed by minority ethnic interviewers were significantly[9] more likely than those seen by white researchers to agree with this assertion, which again suggests that responses were affected by interviewers' ethnicity.

Interviewees were asked what made a good supervisor of a Black or Asian person. The most frequent responses were that a good supervisor should be easy to talk to or should listen to the offender (27 per cent of the whole sample); be understanding and sympathetic (27 per cent); and understand the offender's needs, feelings and experiences as a Black or Asian person (20 per cent). Just three per cent of interviewees defined a good supervisor as one who was Black or Asian, and there was no evidence that the ethnicity of the supervisor was significantly related to the perceived helpfulness of supervision, or to whether the order was breached.

When asked what they liked about their supervision, the most common responses were having someone to talk to or someone who listens (17 per cent of the whole sample), and receiving help with needs and problems (21 per cent). Thirty-five per cent of participants said that there was nothing that they had liked.[10] When asked what they had not liked about their supervision, 12 per cent reported disliking having to attend at all, seven per cent said that it had not been helpful, had made no difference, or had been a waste of time, and seven per cent said that it was restrictive and inconvenient. Thirty-eight per cent of interviewees said that they had not disliked anything about their supervision.[11]

The findings concerning the ethnicity of supervisors merit further discussion. As already noted, it seems that some areas were operating a policy of 'matching' minority ethnic offenders and supervisors. However, while there was some support for the idea that it would be helpful to have a minority ethnic supervisor, there was no consensus on this. Over half of the interviewees appeared indifferent, and a small minority expressed concern at the prospect. It was also unclear from the findings whether those who expressed a preference for a minority ethnic supervisor would have been content with someone from any minority ethnic background, or would have preferred someone of their own ethnicity. While a Black supervisor might have a greater understanding of and empathy for Asian offenders' experiences of racial victimisation, s/he may be no better equipped than a white supervisor to understand their cultural needs and experiences.

Further, it should not be assumed that minority ethnic staff will be content with a policy of 'matching' minority ethnic offenders and supervisors. Stephens *et al.* (2004: 7) found that some staff involved in the Black and Asian Pathfinders felt 'typecast to do work with minority ethnic groups at the expense of their professional development'. Similarly, minority ethnic staff working in an area that operates a policy of ethnic matching might object to being 'ghettoised' as specialists in work with minority ethnic offenders. Perhaps the lesson in relation to both offenders and staff is that it is wrong to make assumptions about individuals' needs and preferences, and that the answer is to ask them.

Programmes

Almost half of the unweighted sample was or had been on an order with an additional requirement to attend a probation-led programme (49 per cent). This group accounted for 52 per cent of the weighted sample. The majority (63 per cent) were, or had been on, or were due to do Think First or Think First for Black and Asian Offenders (57 per cent and six per cent respectively). Other programmes attended included Anger Management Programmes (ten per cent), Enhanced Thinking Skills (five per cent), Reasoning and Rehabilitation (five per cent), and the Black Self-development Programme (four per cent). Just ten per cent of the programme sample had been on programmes that were exclusively for minority ethnic offenders. Those who were waiting to start their programme, and had no previous programme experience, were excluded from the analysis and are not included in the remaining findings reported in this chapter.[12]

When asked why they had been put on the programme, respondents said that it was to stop them committing crime (40 per cent of the programme sample), to help them to think first and be less impulsive (31 per cent), and to help with anger management (ten per cent). Just four per cent mentioned punishment as being among the reasons why they had been required to attend a programme.

When asked whether the programme leaders had explained the purposes of the programme, the vast majority (90 per cent) of programme participants who responded (96 per cent of the programme sample) said that they had. These were most often given as to teach participants to be less impulsive and to think of the consequences of their actions (33 per cent of the programme sample), to help offenders to avoid trouble and crime, and to consider their offending behaviour, etc. (28 per cent), and problem-solving (11 per cent). When asked what they and the group leaders did, the most common responses were role-plays, 'dilemmas', problem-solving, etc. (59 per cent of the programme sample); consideration of offending behaviour (22 per cent); learning to be less impulsive and to think of the consequences of actions (15 per cent); and raising empathy and victim awareness (eight per cent).

Ninety-six per cent of programme participants described the ethnicity of their programme leaders. The ethnicity of the probation teams delivering these programmes was as follows for the unweighted (and weighted) sample: 51 per cent all white staff (42 per cent); 34 per cent (39 per cent) both white and minority ethnic staff; 16 per (19 per cent) cent minority ethnic staff only. When asked whether the group leaders were aware of their needs as a Black or Asian person on probation, 40 per cent of those who responded (93 per cent) said yes, 49 per cent said no (in some cases because they did not see themselves as having special needs), and the remainder did not know. A significantly[13] higher proportion of those on programmes designed exclusively for ethnic minority offenders said that the group leaders were aware of their needs (77 per cent). Ninety-five per cent of programme participants described the ethnic composition of their programme group, the majority (72 per cent) of which were 'mixed', containing white and minority ethnic offenders. Some groups were made up entirely of participants from minority ethnic groups (17 per cent).

Eleven per cent of respondents, usually in medium or low density areas, reported being the only minority ethnic participant. Such singleton placements proved to be an uncomfortable experience for some, as illustrated by one interviewee who said, 'I felt isolated'. Nevertheless, in areas where minority ethnic people make up a small proportion of the population, singleton placements would sometimes be the only alternative to effectively excluding offenders from programmes, which would itself be undesirable. This appears to be an issue for individual assessment and discussion with the probationer rather than for 'one size fits all' policies.

When asked whether the ethnic composition of a group matters, most (66 per cent) of those programme participants who responded (94 per cent) said that composition is important.[14] The vast majority of those for whom composition mattered (87 per cent, 54 per cent of the whole programme sample) thought that it should be mixed:

> [The composition of the group] has got to represent life out there, hasn't it? If you were ... in a group with no Black people you'd feel out of place. [There would be] no one to relate [to] on your level or understand about being Black in this country. [At the] same time if you went in a group and they were all Black you'd think 'why do only Black people get on these courses?' [Groups] need to be mixed.

Some of those who wanted mixed groups were more specific, preferring mixed groups with more than one person from each minority ethnic group (13 per cent of the programme sample), or with an equal split between members of different minority ethnic groups (four per cent):[15]

> When there is an even number of each race, people would be more comfortable to talk about themselves, and they can't make fun of each other.

> If I was the only Black [person] in the group I [would] just feel like they are talking behind my back. I [would] think that I am [being] left out and I would be very shy to talk about myself.

The most common reasons for wanting a mixed group were that participants would feel more relaxed (22 per cent of the whole programme sample), that a mixed group would provide a good learning experience (ten per cent), and that participants would be more likely to talk about themselves (nine per cent).

Just eight per cent of those who said that group composition is important favoured groups for ethnic minority offenders only (five per cent of the whole programme sample). As already noted, just ten per cent of programme participants had actually been on programmes that were exclusively for minority ethnic offenders. Interestingly, these individuals were not significantly more likely to say that they favoured groups specifically for minority ethnic offenders than the remainder of the programme sample.[16]

Eighty-six per cent of the programme participants said that their group leaders had treated them fairly, while just three per cent said that they had been treated unfairly. The remaining 11 per cent said that they did not know whether their treatment had been fair, or that it had been 'mixed', or failed to respond. The most common reasons for giving a positive account were that all participants were treated equally (23 per cent of the whole programme sample), with respect, as a 'normal person', etc. (18 per cent), and that the facilitators were friendly, patient, down to earth, etc. (13 per cent). Just three per cent of participants reported being treated unfairly by other members of the group.

Participants were asked what they liked about their programme. The most frequent responses were that it was educational and informative (16 per cent of the whole programme sample), that they had made new friends, met old friends, and got on well with other group members (13 per cent), that they had liked the group discussions (11 per cent), and that they had addressed their offending behaviour (nine per cent). A substantial minority of participants said that they had not liked anything about their programme (22 per cent).[17]

When participants were asked what they had disliked, the most common complaints were that the programmes were not relevant, a waste of time, or had not helped (17 per cent of the whole programme sample), they were boring or repetitive (16 per cent), that participants were treated like children or it was like being at school (11 per cent), and that the programmes were restrictive and prevented participants from doing other things (nine per cent).[18] Eighteen per cent of all participants said that they had not disliked anything.[19] Twelve per cent of participants failed to complete their programme. Two-thirds of these non-completions were due to the offender's misbehaviour.[20] The remainder were due to circumstances beyond his control.[21]

When asked what kind of programme could best address the needs of Black and Asian offenders, many participants said that programmes should provide practical help and advice (24 per cent of the whole programme sample), and should deal with Black or Asian issues (20 per cent) such as racism and Black history. Eight per cent of the sample suggested that programmes should be tailored to the individual, saying that generic 'one style fits all' programmes did not suit everyone. Seven per cent of participants said that a programme run exclusively by and for Black and/or Asian people would best meet the needs of Black and Asian offenders. It is interesting to note that almost all of those making this comment had not actually attended a programme specifically designed for minority ethnic offenders, and most had been in mixed groups.

It is important to note the sometimes paradoxical nature of the findings pertaining to programmes, and to consider their implications for practice. There was very little support for programmes comprising minority ethnic offenders only, but rather more support for the idea that programmes might include issues of relevance to minority ethnic offenders, such as consideration of the effects of racism, or a discussion of Black history. What are the implications for specialist provisions (such as the Black empowerment approach discussed by Williams, Chapter 8, this volume) and for separate provisions (such as Think First for Black and Asian Offenders)? The delivery of such programmes is costly, over-reliant on minority ethnic staff who may begrudge being responsible for minority ethnic service provision, and remains a contentious subject in many probation areas. Are these findings a sound premise on which to make the decision not to deliver specialist and separate provisions?

Patrick Williams,[22] another contributor to this volume, is of the firm opinion that this is not the case. Williams' work on one of the Black and Asian Pathfinder projects has led him to believe that some Black and Asian offenders, perhaps conscious of wider societal issues (such as the mainstreaming of racist politics evidenced by the increased support for the British National Party, the antagonism expressed in the right-wing press towards asylum seekers, etc.), may not wish to 'rock the boat' or give an impression of having 'a chip on their shoulder', be keen to 'fit in', and feel that it is simpler and easier to state that one does not want or need to attend such programmes. That those interviewed by Calverley *et al.* (2004) were significantly more likely to say that group composition matters when interviewed by a minority ethnic researcher adds credence to Williams' argument.

Lewis and Olumide (Chapter 7, this volume) emphasise the social nature of race, arguing that a person's ethnic identity is shaped by social processes. Similarly, Williams has suggested that minority ethnic offenders who have white family members, or who have been raised in predominantly white areas, may not feel the need to engage with issues of race and ethnicity.[23] However, such individuals are not immune from experiencing racial hostility. Williams cited a mixed heritage offender who regularly suffered verbal racial abuse from a white family member but who, being unable to discuss the matter with someone of his own ethnic background, 'just got used to it'. Williams believes that Black empowerment programmes may facilitate a better understanding of such experiences.

The evidence, then, does not provide unanimous support for simply discarding specialist and separate provisions. Rather, it suggests that these programmes may be of real benefit *to some people*, and underlines the importance of targeting such programmes accurately rather than making them the automatic choice for all minority ethnic populations. Walmsley and Stephens (Chapter 9, this volume) state that in one of the Black and Asian Pathfinder areas specialist assessors discussed the options available with eligible offenders and made recommendations to the court about whether to sentence an individual to Think First for Black and Asian Offenders. Whether, as a result of being able to make an informed choice, a greater proportion of these offenders opted for Think First for Black and Asian Offenders than stated a preference for separate provisions in the study by Calverley *et al.* (2004), remains to be seen.

The impact of probation and programmes

Interviewees were asked whether being on probation had changed the way that they thought about or approached problems. Of those who responded (98 per cent), the majority (67 per cent) said that it had. There was no significant difference in the positive response rates of Black and Asian respondents, or of those at the early and late stages of an ordinary order. Among the programme sample, those who had completed a programme were significantly[24] more likely to give a positive response than those who had yet to start. Twenty-two per cent of the whole sample said that they were less impulsive or more likely to consider the consequences of their actions.[25] Sixteen per cent said that they were trying to refrain from anti-social or criminal behaviour and seven per cent said that they had addressed or were now trying to address their substance misuse problems. Thirty-three per cent of respondents said that the order had not affected their thinking, claiming that it had been a waste of time, irrelevant, had not helped, etc. (seven per cent of the whole sample), and that they still had practical problems to be addressed (four per cent).

Interviewees were asked how helpful they had found their contact with the Probation Service as a Black or Asian person. Sixty-three per cent of those who responded (96 per cent) said that it was helpful, 16 per cent said that it was unhelpful, and the remainder described their experience as 'mixed'. There was no significant difference in the positive response rates of Black and Asian respondents. In a study of mainly white probationers by Mair and May (1997), 87 per cent of respondents described their probation order as useful. In the current study, the most frequently cited reasons for giving a positive response were that probation had provided practical help and advice, or help with needs and problems (30 per cent of the whole sample), that it had helped them to stay out of trouble or prison (ten per cent), and that it was good to have someone to talk to or someone who listens (six per cent). These resemble the findings of Mair and May (1997).[26] Interviewees giving a negative response often said that they had not gained anything from the order, it had been irrelevant to them or had been useless (eight per cent of the whole sample), and that they had not received sufficient help with practical problems (four per cent).

On the whole, then, the accounts given of supervision and programmes were mostly positive. This result is in line with the findings of other recent (post-1991) studies of white or mainly white groups of probationers. Mair and May (1997) found that 87 per cent of their 1,213 mainly white and male respondents thought probation helpful, as compared to 63 per cent in this study. Farrall (2002) found that 52 per cent of his 199 mainly white and male probationers thought that their 'obstacles' or problems were successfully resolved during their probation orders. In Mantle's (1999) similar sample of 492 probationers, 71 per cent found their probation officer helpful; Bailey and Ward (1992) found 15 out of 22 expressing a similar view, while Rex (1997) found that 52 of her 60 mainly white and male subjects saw themselves as receiving guidance from their probation officers, and 37 said they received active help. Similarly, 89 per cent of the white male programme completers of the STOP programme (Raynor and Vanstone 1997) found it helpful. The positive attitude to probation shown by the majority of respondents was therefore comparable with results from a number of studies of mainly white probationers, but towards the lower end of the range.

Conclusion

The findings pertaining to minority ethnic experiences of probation supervision were broadly favourable, in line with other consumer studies covering mainly white probationers. According to the interviewees, a good supervisor is easy to talk to and listens, is understanding and sympathetic, and understands the needs and experiences of minority ethnic offenders. There is long-standing evidence that supervisors who display such qualities may facilitate better outcomes: Truax and Carkhuff (1967) found that empathy, concern, genuineness and concreteness are the cornerstones of effective helping relationships.

The evidence concerning the benefits of 'matching' minority ethnic offenders and supervisors was less clear. About a third of the interviewees thought that it would be best for Black or Asian offenders to be supervised by someone from the same ethnic group; the remainder disagreed or thought it unimportant. In any case, a nationwide policy of ethnic matching is probably unworkable, given the over-representation of certain minority groups among the probation population, and the lower proportions of minority ethnic probation staff. However, as Patrick Williams has noted,[27] supervisors of all ethnicities must be competent at assessing, and facilitating work to address, socio-economic and criminogenic needs. This will necessitate an understanding of cultural and religious needs and experiences, and their impact upon offending behaviour. Williams stated that in the Greater Manchester Probation Area (GMPA) there exist various partnership agencies that probation supervisors can access and utilise when working with minority ethnic offenders. He cited the Pakistani Resource Centre (PRC) in Manchester, which can, for example, provide advice to case managers writing pre-sentence reports, and undertake one-to-one work with offenders where appropriate, as one such agency. Such partnership working may better enable probation supervisors to identify and incorporate ethnicity-specific factors into their work with offenders.

Probation programmes attracted favourable comments, although a substantial minority of interviewees made criticisms. Most programme staff were said to have treated probationers fairly. The evidence pertaining to the ethnic composition of programme groups was less clear. There was widespread support for mixed groups: over half of the programme sample expressed a preference for this form of provision. There was very little support for programme groups comprised entirely of minority ethnic offenders, but there was rather more support for the idea that programmes might include consideration of issues relevant to minority ethnic offenders, such as Black history or the effects of racism. Calverley *et al.* (2004: 57) concluded that these findings 'tend to support a policy of running mixed programme groups rather than groups consisting only of minority ethnic offenders'. It has been argued in this chapter, however, that the findings do not provide grounds for completely discarding specific or specialist provisions for minority ethnic offenders. Such programmes may be of benefit to some offenders. The important thing is to ensure that they are targeted accurately.

The programme participants interviewed by Calverley *et al.* (2004) were attending (or had attended) a variety of programmes, including accredited and non-accredited designs. Only a small proportion of the programme sub-sample had attended specialist or specific programmes for minority ethnic offenders. As the research did not involve outcome measures, the findings cannot provide much guidance about effectiveness or 'what works' with minority ethnic offenders. Much of the What Works research funded under the Crime Reduction Initiative involved large-scale studies designed to determine the effectiveness of different ways of working with offenders (see, for example, Hollin *et al.* 2002; Lewis *et al.* 2003; McMahon *et al.* 2004; Rex and Gelsthorpe 2002; Rex *et al.* 2004). As Walmsley and Stephens have noted (Chapter 9, this volume), however, several of these studies failed to deliver outcome results because of design and implementation problems. It is hoped that any such problems encountered by the Black and Asian Pathfinders will not prevent the evaluation of these schemes from throwing light on 'what works' with minority ethnic offenders.

One final point to note is that the findings by Calverley *et al.* (2004) have implications for work with offenders of all ethnicities. Given the number of sizeable studies of effectiveness that have been conducted under the What Works banner in recent years, and the decision by RDS to focus on four large-scale longitudinal offender tracking projects in an effort to gather further evidence of 'what works', it is important to note the limitations of the findings from such studies. They tell us *what tends to work* with particular groups, citing reductions in overall levels of criminogenic needs, reconviction rates, or other factors as evidence of success. They do not tell us whether what tends to work will work with any given individual. As Calverley *et al.* (2004) have shown, however, the needs and experiences of minority ethnic offenders (and by extension all offenders) are wide and varied. Thus a careful assessment of the specific needs of individual offenders is vital to determine whether what tends to work will do so in a given case. While the results of large-scale studies may legitimately shape the general direction of policy and practice, work with individual offenders must be rooted in a clear understanding of their particular needs and experiences.

Acknowledgements

The author wishes to thank Peter Raynor, David Smith and Patrick Williams for their helpful comments and suggestions. Any remaining errors and omissions are the sole responsibility of the author.

Notes

1 Ninety-three per cent of offenders were white.
2 Opinions differ on whether experience of racism is criminogenic. Contrast the views of Durrance and Williams (2003) with Stephens *et al.* (2004).
3 Ninety-seven per cent of the 429 probationers surveyed by Ros Harper in a study published by Middlesex Probation Service (Harper 2000), of whom 84 per cent were male and 58 per cent were white, reported having been 'treated fairly' by probation staff.
4 Eighty-five per cent of Black respondents, 84 per cent of Asian interviewees, and 86 per cent of mixed heritage respondents reported having been treated fairly or very fairly.
5 The weighted figures are as follows: 69 per cent of main supervisors were white, 25 per cent were Black, five per cent were Asian, and less than one per cent were of mixed heritage. In high density areas, 28 per cent of offenders had a Black supervisor while six per cent had an Asian supervisor. In medium and low density areas these figures were eight per cent and five per cent respectively.
6 This group did not differ from the rest of the sample in relation to offence profile. Just 8.9 per cent of this group had participated in programmes exclusively for minority ethnic offenders, while the rest had not. They did score significantly higher on the CRIME-PICS II G ($p<0.05$), A ($p<0.01$) and E ($p<0.05$) scales, however. This is probably because the majority (80.9 per cent) of those favouring a minority ethnic supervisor were Black or mixed heritage, and these groups had the highest average CRIME-PICS II scores.
7 Percentages do not add up to 100 because a small number of respondents said that having a minority ethnic supervisor might be a good thing *and* a bad thing.
8 $p<0.01$.
9 $p<0.01$.
10 Of the 160 participants who said that there was nothing that they had liked about their supervision 37 also said that there was nothing that they had disliked, suggesting indifference towards rather than a particular like or dislike of their supervision.
11 Of the 184 interviewees who said that they had not disliked anything about their supervision 37 also said that there was nothing that they had liked, again suggesting indifference.

12 Within the unweighted sample 236 were or had been on a probation order with an additional requirement to attend a programme. At the time of interview, however, 37 people had not started and had no other experience of a probation programme. Thus only the responses from the remaining 199 interviewees were used in the analysis, accounting for 45 per cent of the weighted sample.

13 $p<0.01$.

14 Respondents were significantly ($p<0.05$) more likely to say that group composition matters when interviewed by a minority ethnic researcher, indicating the presence of bias.

15 It is possible that some of those who said that groups should be 'mixed' would have preferred there to be more than one person from each ethnic group, or an equal split between members of different ethnic groups, but their responses were too vague to code as such.

16 This was calculated using Fisher's exact test.

17 Four of the people who said that there was nothing that they had liked also said that there was nothing that they had disliked, suggesting indifference rather than a particular like or dislike of their programme.

18 Similar comments were made by some of those attending a probation programme who were interviewed for the STOP research (Raynor and Vanstone 1997: 54–5).

19 See n.17.

20 For example, his being removed from the programme for non-compliance, or because he was sent to prison.

21 For example, as a result of the offender's illness, or inability to speak English.

22 Williams expressed these views in June 2005, in personal correspondence.

23 See n.22.

24 $p<0.05$.

25 This again echoes the findings of Raynor and Vanstone (1997): in their study of 64 white men on the Straight Thinking on Probation programme, 'thinking before acting, speaking or offending' and 'thinking of consequences' were the first and third most frequently self-reported changes in thinking.

26 In the study by Mair and May (1997), the most frequently cited 'good points about being on probation' were having someone independent to talk to (54 per cent), getting practical help and advice (33 per cent), and being helped to keep out of trouble (19 per cent).

27 See n.22.

References

Bailey, R. and Ward, D. (1992) *Probation Supervision: Attitudes to Formalised Helping*. Nottingham and Belfast: Centre for Social Action and Northern Ireland Probation Service.

Calverley, A., Cole, B., Kaur, G., Lewis, S., Raynor, P., Sadeghi, S., Smith, D., Vanstone, M. and Wardak, A. (2004) *Black and Asian Offenders on Probation.* Home Office Research Study 277. London: Home Office.

Chapman, T. and Hough, M. (1998) *Evidence Based Practice: A Guide to Effective Practice.* London: Home Office. Available online at: http://www.homeoffice.gov.uk/docs/ebp.html

Durrance, P. and Williams, P. (2003) 'Broadening the Agenda Around What Works for Black and Asian offenders', *Probation Journal*, 50: 3, 211–24.

Farrall, S. (2002) *Rethinking What Works with Offenders.* Cullompton: Willan.

Harper, R. (2000) *Quality of Service Survey.* London: Middlesex Probation Service.

Hollin, C., McGuire, J., Palmer, E., Bilby, C., Hatcher, R. and Holmes, A. (2002) *Introducing Pathfinder Programmes into the National Probation Service: An Interim Report,* Home Office Research Study 247. London: Home Office.

Home Office (2002a) *National Standards for the Supervision of Offenders in the Community.* Revised 2002. London: Home Office. Available online at: http://www.probation.homeoffice.gov.uk/files/pdf/national_standards.pdf

Home Office (2002b) *Probation Statistics England and Wales 2001.* London: Home Office.

Lewis, S., Vennard, J., Maguire, M., Raynor, P., Vanstone, M., Raybould, S. and Rix, A. (2003) *The Resettlement of Short-term Prisoners: An Evaluation of Seven Pathfinders,* RDS Occasional Paper No. 83. London: Home Office.

Mair, G. and May, C. (1997). *Offenders on Probation,* Home Office Research Study 167. London: Home Office.

Mantle, G. (1999) *Control, Help and Punishment,* Occasional Paper 1. Witham: Essex Probation Service.

McGuire, G. and Priestley, P. (1995) 'Reviewing "What Works": Past, Present and Future', in J. McGuire (ed.) *What Works: Reducing Reoffending.* Chichester: Wiley.

McMahon, G., Hall, A., Hayward, G., Hudson, C., Roberts, C., Fernández, R. and Burnett, R. (2004) *Basic Skills Programmes in the Probation Service: An Evaluation of the Basic Skills Pathfinder,* Home Office Research Findings 203, London: Home Office.

Powis, B. and Walmsley, R. K. (2002) *Programmes for Black and Asian Offenders on Probation: Lessons for Developing Practice,* Home Office Research Study 250. London: Home Office.

Raynor, P. and Vanstone, M. (1997). *Straight Thinking on Probation (STOP): The Mid Glamorgan Experiment,* Probation Studies Unit Report 4. Oxford: Centre for Criminological Research.

Rex, S. (1997) 'Perceptions of Probation in a Context of Just Deserts', unpublished PhD thesis, University of Cambridge.

Rex, S. and Gelsthorpe, L. (2002) 'The role of Community Service in Reducing Offending: Evaluating Pathfinder Projects in the UK', *Howard Journal*, 41: 4, 311–25.

Rex, S., Gelsthorpe, L., Roberts, C. and Jordan, P. (2004) *What's Promising in Community Service: Implementation of Seven Pathfinder Projects*, Home Office Research Findings 231, London: Home Office.

Stephens, K., Coombs, J. and Debidin, M. (2004) *Black and Asian Offenders Pathfinder: Implementation Report*, Home Office Development and Practice Report 24. London: Home Office.

Truax, C. B. and Carkhuff, R. R. (1967) *Towards Effective Counselling and Psychotherapy: Training and Practice*. London: Aldine Books.

Chapter 11

What might work with racially motivated offenders?

David Smith

Introduction

Chapter 2 discussed attempts in the Probation Service to develop work with racially motivated offenders, and suggested that there had been progress towards more informed and sensitive practice, but that this had been slow and remained uneven, with many probation officers remaining uncertain about their ability to work effectively with this group of offenders and, as a result, inclined to avoid doing so. Practitioners were not helped by inconsistent messages from the centre, which, following the publication of the Macpherson Report (1999), initially appeared committed to the development of specialist programmes that could be delivered both to groups and one-to-one (Dixon 2002). For various reasons, however, including uncertainty about the number of racially motivated offenders likely to be available to be worked with, and the lack of evidence that the criminogenic needs of such offenders were substantially different from those of generalist offenders, it was concluded that there was no case for accrediting a specialist programme. Instead, on advice from the Correctional Services Accreditation Panel, the National Probation Directorate decided in 2002 that work should progress down three 'pathways'. First, the impact of general offending behaviour programmes on the attitudes and beliefs of racially motivated offenders was to be tested over a two-year period. Second, new elements that might be relevant to racist motivation were to be gradually incorporated into existing programmes. Third, if experience with the first two approaches suggested it was necessary, a new one-to-one programme specifically for offenders convicted of racially aggravated offences could be added to the established One-to-One programme (Pillay 2003). By the end of 2004, it appeared that the official line was that One-to-One was the programme recommended for racially aggravated offenders, and it was being adapted, with a 'practical guide', to improve its relevance for work with this group (NPS 2004).

Part of the work reported by Dixon (2002) was a literature review that aimed to establish what was known about the criminogenic factors associated with racist offending, and about what 'worked' with those who perpetrated it. The review drew a blank on both counts. It concluded, however, that the three-tier model of primary, secondary and tertiary measures, familiar from thinking about crime prevention (Brantingham and Faust 1976), could be applied to racist offending. Primary measures would aim to reduce the prevalence of racist ideas in the population as a whole, secondary measures would aim to reduce the risk of racially motivated offending among populations of known offenders, and tertiary measures would aim to reduce the reoffending risk among the population convicted of racially aggravated offences, or offences with a clear racist element. While the focus of this chapter is mainly on tertiary interventions, possibilities for primary and secondary level work are considered in the conclusion.

Racism as a risk factor

Dixon, describing the work of the group of which she was a member, that was set up to produce a programme for racially motivated offenders, says (2002: 209) that the group concluded that 'racial identity was a potential dynamic risk factor'. While it might be clearer and more direct to describe the risk as coming from racist attitudes and beliefs, there can be little doubt that this conclusion was justified. One of the ways in which racism might increase the risk of offending was well described from a practitioner perspective by Gill and Marshall (1993: 56):

> ... a black person, as a potential target of an offence, is made more vulnerable by the racist views of the potential offender. Any thought about the possible effects on the victim will be moderated by the belief that the victim does not have as much worth as a white person. This might never be a conscious thought process, but we believe it is very real and powerful.

> Compare the number of people who make off without payment from black owned and run restaurants and take-aways, or taxis driven by black drivers, and consider whether the numbers are comparable with white owned businesses.

In other words, denial of the victim, one of the techniques of neutralisation famously described by Sykes and Matza (1957), becomes easier when the victim is accorded a diminished status by virtue of his or her perceived membership of the ethnic group that is the target of racist hatred, resentment and hostility.

Another important insight from Gill and Marshall's work is that the racist offenders who come into contact with the Probation Service will very rarely be 'specialists' in this type of offending, and racism will rarely manifest itself in a pure and readily recognisable form, as the sole motive for an offence (one reason why racial aggravation is difficult to prove, and why the attrition rate between charge and conviction for such offences is high (Burney and Rose 2002)). Racist offenders are far more likely to be 'generalists', who commit other offences as well as those with a discernible racist motivation, and whose overall profile (including their criminogenic needs) is very similar to that of other offenders on the probation caseload. This is one of the main lessons to be drawn from the development of practitioners' knowledge described in Chapter 2, and, as suggested there, it means that the classic image of 'hate crime' – the term now universally but misleadingly used by the police in England and Wales to cover racially motivated offending – will usually not apply to the offences probation officers have to deal with. Among the other lessons drawn at the end of Chapter 2 was that offenders will usually deny racist motivation, even when the evidence of its presence is strong: '"I didn't mean it and he knew that" was a typical response to interview questions about racially abusive remarks in the context of violent offences' (Ray *et al.* 2003: 123). Offenders are unlikely to need to be told that racism is morally wrong; many, at a conscious, cognitive level, believe this themselves, but there is a disjunction between what they think and what they feel. Racist offending usually has its roots in powerful but unacknowledged emotions that are at odds with offenders' conscious, rational beliefs, and this has implications for practice that are explored later in this chapter.

The local specificity of racism

Another issue noted in Chapter 2 deserves further discussion here, because it suggests that it may not be productive to think in terms of a single programme that could be universally applied. This is that the expression of racism is often locally specific and shaped by specific histories of relationships, by patterns of residence, and by local definitions of the nature of the problem. Dixon and Court (2003) note the symbolic importance for the expression of racist sentiments of the memorial stone to Stephen Lawrence in Eltham in south-east London, and Ray and Smith (2004) explore the particular way racist violence was defined in Oldham, that produced a local understanding of the problem quite distinct from that of other parts of Greater Manchester. Although Oldham shared many characteristics with the other 'Pennine towns' discussed by Rees and Phillips (1996), notably a high degree of residential segregation on ethnic lines, from the mid-1990s the annual police figures on racist incidents showed Oldham well out of line with the other ten police divisions. Oldham was consistently exceptional in the sheer number of incidents recorded, and in the fact that in a high proportion of them – in some years, a majority – the victims were recorded as white and the suspects as Asian. This made Oldham unique in Greater Manchester and, according to Ken Livingstone (2001), in the country, when after the riots of the spring of 2001 the peculiarities of Oldham began to attract attention in the national media.

In Oldham, the main problem of racist violence was defined as hate crime perpetrated by young Asian men. This definition was persistently offered by the local paper, the *Oldham Evening Chronicle*, which, when reporting on the issue, typically quoted the then police divisional commander as its authority. For example, the *Chronicle* of 17 March 1998, under the headline 'Fears growing over plague of racist attacks by Asian gangs', ran a story that quoted Chief Superintendent Eric Hewitt as saying: 'Anyone seems to be a target if they are white and they are vulnerable.' With this powerful ratification, the belief that Oldham had a special problem of Asian-on-white violence permeated the official response, appearing, for example, as a taken for granted if inexplicable fact in the borough's 1999 Crime and Disorder Audit (Oldham Metropolitan Borough 1999). To whatever extent the repeatedly cited figures reflected what was really happening – and it would be unreasonable to deny that some young Asian men perpetrated acts of violence against whites that fitted the classic model of hate crime (Ray and Smith 2004) – it is useful also to consider the impact this representation of the problem could have on local patterns of racial tension and violence, and on the response of official agencies. First, it encouraged a high level of activity in Oldham by the British National Party, which did better in the two Oldham seats than anywhere else in the 2001 general election (and, along with other far right groups in Britain and abroad, made Chief Superintendent Hewitt into something of a folk hero). Second, it is probable that this definition of the problem encouraged whites to report victimisation which they saw as racially motivated, while discouraging Asians from doing so (because they were liable to be perceived by the police as the source of the problem). Third, recorded racial incidents in Oldham were more likely than elsewhere to involve conflict between groups rather than individuals, and white racist offenders interviewed in Oldham were more likely than those from other parts of Greater Manchester to show knowledge of far right political organisations (Ray and Smith 2004), suggesting a degree of collectivity in the expression of racist attitudes and the enactment of racist violence that was not evident elsewhere.

Oldham may be an extreme case in the extent to which the local definition of the problem of racist violence differed from that used anywhere else, but it is important to remember that local factors will always shape the volume and type of racially motivated offending. One such factor, highlighted in the wake of the riots in Bradford, Burnley and Oldham in early 2001, is the degree of residential segregation on ethnic lines (Home Office 2002a, 2002b). According to the 1991 census (Rees and Phillips 1996) these towns were among the most highly segregated areas in Britain. If racism is in part a product of alienation and estrangement (Heitmeyer 1993; Ray *et al.* 2004), then one would expect that the highest levels of inter-ethnic suspicion, fear, resentment and hostility would be found in such areas, since there is no – or minimal – everyday contact between ethnic groups, and negative stereotypes therefore remain unchallenged.

The ethnic group that typically becomes the target of racist violence will also differ across localities, as a result of demographic, economic and cultural variations. In Greater Manchester, for example, the victims of racist violence perpetrated by whites were almost always south Asians (Ray *et al.* 2003; 2004); offenders saw Black people as more like themselves in terms of culture and their position in the economic structure, but saw south Asians as culturally alien and threatening, and as economically successful beyond anything they deserved by virtue of hard work. The interviews that produced these results were conducted before the attacks of 11 September 2001, and it is likely that hostility towards south Asians, liable to be indiscriminately considered as 'Pakis' and therefore as Muslims, increased after that. By way of contrast, the Metropolitan Police (2001) reported that 'equal proportions of victims ... were either African Caribbean or Indian/Pakistani in ethnic appearance', and in Greenwich, for example, racist hostility appears mainly to be directed against Black African and Black Caribbean people (Dixon and Court 2003).

There may also be area-specific histories of inter-ethnic conflict, such as the conflicts in Keighley in West Yorkshire over the use of social space between young Asian and young white people described by Webster (1996); both groups employed vigilantist methods to defend what they saw as their territory, and Webster complained of the unstated assumption in much of the literature that in inter-ethnic violence the victims are invariably Black or Asian – an issue that has barely been noticed in discussions of such violence in the probation context. Again, the pattern found in Keighley may be unusual, but with the other examples (see also Back 1996), it illustrates the point that racist violence takes different forms in different places, and the justifications, meanings and motives of its perpetrators will also differ. An effective Probation Service response will need to be informed by an understanding of locally specific patterns of offending and the collective understandings and traditions from which they emerge. The importance of place for probation practice has recently been stressed by commentators from the United States (Clear 2005; Smith 2001), and its implications for work on racism are discussed towards the end of this chapter.

Direct work with racist offenders

The most plausible conclusion, from practice experience and research on racist offenders, is that their criminogenic needs will not usually differ substantially from those of the total population serving community penalties, but that their racist attitudes, and their capacity to express these in violence, constitute an additional risk factor that ought to be the subject of specific attention. Past experience also suggests, however, that rarely if ever will be there be enough offenders in a local area who are known to be racially motivated for it to be feasible to run a groupwork programme for them alone. Even if it were feasible, it would arguably be risky: Rosenbaum (1987: 121), discussing the group dynamics of Neighbourhood Watch, cites evidence that 'groups made up of racist individuals have become even more racist after having the opportunity for discussion'. There must be a risk that without firm, authoritative direction a group of racially motivated offenders would behave in the same way – and firm, authoritative direction might well have the inhibiting effect discussed by Sibbitt (1997), and deter them from acknowledging their racism at all. What follows, then, assumes that a structured one-to-one programme, as recommended by the leadership of the National Probation Service, is the most promising as well as the most feasible approach.

Given that the racist offenders with whom the Probation Service will come into contact are generalists, there seems no reason to suppose that what stands the best chance of working with other offenders will not also stand the best chance with them. This is not the place to rehearse at any length the well-known characteristics of work that qualifies as evidence based practice, but these can be briefly summarised as follows (Chapman and Hough 1998: 6). The intensity and duration of intervention should be proportional to the risk of reoffending (the risk principle); the focus of work should be on needs that are related to offending (the need principle); and work should be adapted to offenders' learning styles and provide opportunities for their active participation (the responsivity principle). The most effective practice is likely to employ a variety of methods, be focused on the development of cognitive and other skills, including those related to employability, provide models of pro-social behaviour, be well planned and structured, be based in the community, and be subject to monitoring and evaluation. In addition, practitioners need to be well trained and supported, and clear and confident about their purposes and methods – which has certainly not always been the case in interventions with racist offenders.

The appeal of racism

A good starting point in thinking about what might be needed, on top of these generic features of good practice, to engage effectively with the additional risk factor of racist motivation is to consider the nature of the appeal of racist ideas and attitudes. A recurring finding from research is that racism is at its most intense, and the risk of racist violence highest, in poor, environmentally run-down areas of housing whose residents – overwhelmingly white – feel overlooked, disregarded and under-valued. The research of Ray *et al.* (2003) in Greater Manchester, for example, found that racist offenders were disproportionately concentrated in a few outlying estates in which violence was apparently regarded as an acceptable means of routine problem-solving. They describe visits to two such estates as follows:

> On a visit ... to one of these estates (built in the 1950s to house the families of workers at nearby petro-chemical plants, many of which had closed) we found that all three pubs were closed and boarded up, licences having been withdrawn as result of persistent violence; a visit to another estate coincided with a local news story that the (South Asian-owned) fish and chip shop had caught fire on the evening before, and that arson was suspected. (Ray *et al.* 2003: 118)

All but one of the shops on the second estate were in fact owned by south Asians, though their owners certainly did not live above the premises.

In discussion groups with residents – mainly women – of this and another estate, racist sentiments were expressed by many, though not all, of the participants. In particular, they expressed resentment at the supposedly preferential treatment of south Asians, and compared this with their own sense of disadvantage and neglect. When, in interviews, offenders complained of their sense of injustice and grievance, they were drawing upon a locally available cultural resource in which poor white people, and not the south Asian targets of their hostility, were cast as the real victims. Offenders could thus appeal to a general local sense of unfairness to justify their actions, as Sibbitt (1997) also found. For example, a group of women on one estate discussed the inequitable way in which the term 'racist' was used:

> They [south Asians] scream about the police and that's the first word out of their mouths, 'racist'.
> It's just 'racist' on their lips all the time, doesn't matter what the problem is.
> That gets me, honestly, that gets my back up, honestly, when they shout 'racist' for everything. It isn't always racist. I mean we don't go about saying, 'I'm white' ... If you called me white I wouldn't shout 'racist', would I?

They also echoed the sentiments of many offenders when they compared their own situation with what they imagined about that of south Asians:

> They [south Asians] go on the dole and they draw on ... It was in the paper, he's got two houses and two families and he's getting over £3,000 a week to keep his two families.
> We don't get anything like that, do we?
> Nothing like it. (Ray *et al.* 2004: 361)

Racist offenders, then, are not usually peculiarly pathological individuals with an idiosyncratic sense of hostility towards minority ethnic people; their views are widely shared within their local communities, whose residents, while not condoning racist violence, are inclined to regard it as intelligible. As noted above, this is consistent with previous findings that racism flourishes in poor white neighbourhoods whose residents feel threatened by demographic and economic changes. For example, Taylor (1982) found the highest levels of electoral support for the fascist National Front in predominantly white areas adjacent to areas with larger minority ethnic populations (a finding that is consistent with the pattern of support for the British National Party in Burnley more than 20 years later); Hewitt (1996) similarly found that racist attitudes were most prevalent where white residents felt under territorial threat. In Germany, too, Heitmeyer (1993) identified anxiety, uncertainty, isolation and a sense of powerlessness as important in understanding the appeal of racist ideas. A sense of identity under threat, against a background of economic and cultural deprivation, has consistently been found to be a central element in racist motivation. Where the local cultural milieu accepts violence as a resource, at least for young men, immediate situations of conflict – for example, over payment for goods or for a taxi fare – are readily transformed into physical confrontation, in which underlying hostility and resentment are expressed as an assault.

Perpetrators as victims

An important conclusion to be drawn from this analysis is that the traditional definition of racism as 'prejudice plus power' is at best an oversimplification. The definition was essentially a political one, used first in the USA and then in Britain as part of a necessary argument that racism was a problem of whites' attitudes and behaviour towards

Blacks. But, though it is certainly true that minority ethnic people continue to experience disadvantages that even poor, ill-educated, unskilled whites do not, racist offenders certainly do not experience themselves as powerful. They see themselves as victims rather than victimisers (Ray *et al.* 2004; Webster 1997), of unfairness, injustice, persecution (by the police) and neglect (by other public authorities). In contrast, the offenders in Greater Manchester perceived their south Asian victims as powerful, supported by cultural and familial solidarity, economically successful (though without having done the hard work that would make success deserved), arrogant and contemptuous. Ray *et al.* (2004) note disturbing parallels between the language they used about south Asians and the language, consistent over centuries, of anti-semitism; although they had never read anti-semitic literature, the interviewees' emotions – of resentment, grievance, distress and a sense of being devalued, ignored and neglected – were those that have historically animated anti-semitic rhetoric. Like anti-semitism, the racism of these interviewees was often expressed not in terms of race hatred – which they tended to disavow – but in terms of class hatred, since the south Asians owned the local shops, takeaways and taxis, and were seen – unlike Blacks – as by definition not 'hard grafters'; racist motivation was thus reworked as the justified resentment of the poor and weak for the illegitimately rich and powerful (Ray *et al.* 2003: 120–1).

This interpretation of their offending allowed interviewees to employ the technique of neutralisation (Sykes and Matza 1957) of 'denial of the victim'; the victims' moral status and claims were denied; instead, properly understood, the offenders were the real victims. The other four of Sykes and Matza's techniques of neutralisation appeared in offenders' accounts, as perhaps they would also in the accounts of other offenders: denial of injury (no one got hurt), denial of responsibility (as a result of drunkenness or some other temporarily incapacitating condition), appeals to higher loyalties (standing up for your mates), and condemnation of the condemners (the claim that they were no more racist than anyone else, and certainly no more than the police). Denial and disparagement of the victim, however, were central to these accounts, as one would expect if racism is conceived as a risk factor, and this suggests a possible avenue for intervention: the promotion of victim empathy, perhaps through the provision of information about the realities of economic and working life for the owners of small businesses and their families, and, in appropriate cases, by victim–offender mediation.

Emotions and violence

It is important, though, that any intervention should be based on an understanding of the powerful and complex emotions that underlie much racist offending. Most perpetrators of racist offences will agree (at least when asked by probation officers) that racism is morally wrong and has undesirable social effects. They are unlikely to feel any affinity with, for example, the political programme of the British National Party, or with its members. At a rational, cognitive level, they sincerely deny that they are racists. But the analysis above suggests that the emotions behind their offending are close to those that have motivated racist and fascist political movements. The social sciences have tended to favour explanations of human conduct that are cognitive rather than emotional (Barbalet 2001), and the cognitive-behavioural emphasis of much writing on 'what works' with offenders has – perhaps belatedly – introduced the same bias into probation theory and practice. The image of the 'reasoning criminal' (Cornish and Clarke 1986) has also been a powerful influence on thinking about crime prevention. In the process, the emotions – including those that may be unconscious or only brought to conscious acknowledgement with difficulty – risk being ignored in probation practice; at the very least, it has become more difficult to write about them with the kind of confidence that characterised the era of psychoanalytically influenced 'treatment' of offenders (Bottoms and McWilliams 1979). There are, however, recent signs of an effort within sociology to redress the balance, and to recognise that much human interaction cannot be fully explained in conventionally cognitive, rational terms.

Ray *et al.* (2004) argue that the work of Thomas Scheff (e.g. Scheff 1994; 1997) and Suzanne Retzinger (1991) is helpful in providing a framework for understanding the accounts of the offenders interviewed in Greater Manchester. In the work of Scheff and Retzinger, violence is interpreted as the result of the transformation of shame into rage and humiliated fury. This is liable to happen when shame, a universal human emotion, remains unacknowledged, as a result of denial or repression. In a state of shame (conceived as the opposite emotion to pride), we feel ourselves as the objects of scorn and ridicule, reduced and belittled, passive, childish and helpless. We experience the other, seen as the source of our shame, as laughing, powerful, in control, adult and active. In the interview tapes from Greater Manchester, both verbal and non-verbal 'cues' for this experience of shame appeared frequently, and in some cases the transformation of that shame into rage towards those who were perceived as the source of it – south Asian people – could be heard during the course of the interview itself (Ray *et al.* 2004). An act of racist violence can be conceived as an attempt to transform shame – a sense of weakness and dispossession – into pride – a (fleeting) experience of mastery and control.

According to Scheff (1994), this escalation of unacknowledged shame into rage is at the root of all human conflict, from the interpersonal level through group conflict to the world wars of the twentieth century. It is not necessary to make such a large claim for the theory, however, in arguing that it can be helpful in understanding racist violence and in informing a response to it. It should be made clear, however, that Scheff's use of the terms 'shame' and 'pride' is not exactly that of everyday usage. For Scheff, shame arises from the weakening or breaking of our bond with others, producing alienation and estrangement (cf. Heitmeyer 1993); 'true' pride arises from a secure bond to others, from relationships of mutual respect, acceptance and understanding, and could be defined as appropriate self-esteem. This clarification is important as Dixon (2002: 213), while prepared to acknowledge that the brief account of this theory by Ray *et al.* (2002) could be helpful in practice, worried that 'offenders encouraged to develop a sense of pride in their white cultural heritage and identity might … slip into demonstrations of aggressive and racist "white pride" ' – very far from appropriate self-esteem.

Ray *et al.* (2004) argue that the unacknowledged shame of perpetrators of racist violence arises from low self-esteem, and that this in turn is associated with a sense of anxiety and loss. Cohen (1972), in his powerful analysis of the origins of the skinhead subculture in east London in the late 1960s, wrote of the tension and threat to identity experienced by young men whose internalised conception of masculinity found no opportunities for expression in the real world; the traditional means of becoming a man had disappeared along with jobs in the traditional workplace, the docks. Cohen argued that the aggressive masculinity of the skinhead style, and the xenophobia and racism that went with it, could be understood as a 'magical' solution to this loss of traditional identity, in which the skinheads sought to re-establish a relationship with an imagined past. The interviewees in Greater Manchester also expressed fears and anxieties about change, and while their conception of themselves involved hard manual work, their biographies showed that most had little real experience of work of any kind. Those who were visibly different – and apparently more successful – readily became scapegoats for the interviewees' sense of insecurity, anxiety and failure; hence the attacks on south Asians, against a background of widespread local resentment and envy of their (supposedly undeserved) achievements.

Implications for practice

What this understanding might indicate for practice, then, is that offenders could be helped to acknowledge the ways in which they feel powerless, dispossessed and unhappy – that is, to acknowledge their shame. This will not be easy, since in modern societies we are, so to speak, ashamed of shame, and tend to avoid discussing it or even using the word (Braithwaite 1989; Scheff 1997). But a recognition that, at its simplest, racist offenders do not feel good about themselves, or about their racism, may be a necessary first step in helping them to understand, and potentially to change, the roots of their racist hostilities and resentments. A further stage, more familiarly cognitive-behavioural in style, would be to explore with them the situations in which these emotions find expression in violence. While these may vary locally, there was a strong tendency in Greater Manchester for offences to occur in situations of conflict that brought to the fore the offenders' conception of themselves as victims. Typical sites of violence were corner shops, restaurants, takeaways and taxis, and typical contexts were disputes over payment and a sense of being ignored, disapproved of, or treated with contempt. Violence was particularly likely to erupt when the victim failed to show the passive acquiescence that was attributed to south Asians; and on many, though not all, occasions the offenders had been drinking. A better understanding of these situational factors could help offenders avoid high-risk settings, or, if they cannot do so, be aware that these settings require them to exercise more than normal self-control. More generally, practitioners might explore the local cultural acceptability of violence as a means of routine conflict resolution, and propose less damaging alternatives.

All offences happen in particular places, and the situational understanding proposed here depends on workers' knowledge of the local area – for example, of where the relevant shops, restaurants and taxi ranks are, and what public transport is available. More generally, violence and racism are also characteristics of localities and not simply of individuals. There is convincing evidence that residential segregation on ethnic lines is associated with increased interracial suspicion and hostility and with a heightened risk of violence (Home Office 2002a, 2002b); this is what one would expect, too, from Scheff's (1994; 1997) account of the origins of conflict, since segregation reduces opportunities for the formation and maintenance of secure social bonds. It also tends to produce, among all ethnic groups, a sense of urban space as racialised, and hence a defensive and sometimes aggressive sense of territoriality (Webster 1996), and other segregations, for example in schools, follow from residential separation. Within Greater Manchester, it is Manchester itself that has the highest proportion of minority ethnic people in its population (at 19 per cent), but levels of segregation are low, and there was no concentration of racist offenders there (Manchester City Council 2003). The official Home Office view, based on the local reports on Bradford, Burnley and Oldham, tends to be that this segregation is the result of various kinds of choice: 'white flight' from deprived areas, for example, is complemented by a defensive self-segregation on the part of south Asians. But the degree to which one can speak meaningfully of choices is problematic. Webster (2003), for example, cites research that shows that the housing preferences of Asian and white people are very similar: ethnic composition is less important than quality of life, defined in terms of good housing and local amenities, low levels of crime and disorder, and having 'decent' people as one's neighbours. Many south Asians would 'flee' from poor, run-down, segregated town centre housing if they could afford to; but they would not regard social housing on an all-white outlying estate as being among their choices.

Racism is closely associated with deprivation, poverty and disadvantage, problems that are beyond the scope of the Probation Service to influence directly. Probation staff do, however, have opportunities to work with others to reduce the mutual suspicion and isolation of ethnic groups that result from segregation. In Oldham, for example, the Probation Service could have been among the organisations that argued that the police and local media's version of the problem of racist violence was, at best, partial and divisive. Knowledge of local circumstances should allow the Service to take advantage of comparable opportunities elsewhere. Even if schools remain segregated, further education need not (and in practice does not), and probation staff could encourage those they work with to attend local colleges, and perhaps themselves contribute to the curriculum. And, although the processes that led to residential segregation will not be quickly undone, the Probation Service could encourage local providers of social housing to pursue strategies for increasing its accessibility and attractiveness to Black and minority ethnic people, guided by a principled commitment to the reduction of segregation (see, for example, Mullins *et al.* 2004).

What is proposed here for the Probation Service may sound daunting. This chapter has argued that an effective response to racist violence is likely to require substantial local knowledge – of the distribution of racist incidents in time and space, of who the perpetrators and victims are, of the relationship between them, and of local understandings of the problem. It has also suggested that direct work with the perpetrators of racist violence is likely to entail a painful acknowledgement of their shame and humiliation, before moving on to work more directly linked with their offending behaviour. And it has argued that if this work is to be more than first aid, and the Service is to attempt to reduce the local prevalence of racist violence in the longer term, it will need to contribute, on the basis of its particular knowledge and skills, to strategies designed to reduce and eventually remove the destructive effects of racial segregation. The emphasis has been on aspects of probation practice that are at some remove from recent mainstream thinking, with its stress on the importance of enforcement of orders and the delivery of proper punishment. A stress instead on the importance of community involvement and of understanding and engaging with the emotions that underlie offending may seem to some readers to belong to the past of the Probation Service rather than its future. But, as noted above, the importance of place in understanding and responding to offending has been the theme of some recent work (Clear 2005; Smith 2001), and emotions are central to the work of Maruna *et al.* (2004) in their exploration of the implications for practice of work on desistance. The traditional aspirations and interests of the Service have not quite disappeared into the dustbin of history.

References

Back, L. (1996) *New Ethnicities and Urban Culture: Racisms and Multiculture in Young Lives.* London: UCL Press.

Barbalet, J. (2001) *Emotion, Social Theory and Social Structure: A Macrosociological Approach.* Cambridge: Cambridge University Press.

Bottoms, A. E. and McWilliams, W. (1979) 'A Non-treatment Paradigm for Probation Practice', *British Journal of Social Work*, 9:2, 159–202.

Braithwaite, J. (1989) *Crime, Shame and Reintegration.* Cambridge: Cambridge University Press.

Brantingham, P. J. and Faust, F. L. (1976) 'A Conceptual Model of Crime Prevention', *Crime and Delinquency*, 22, 130–46.

Burney, E. and Rose, G. (2002) *Racist Offences – How is the Law Working? The Implementation of the Legislation on Racially Aggravated Offences in the Crime and Disorder Act 1998*, Home Office Research Study 244. London: Home Office.

Chapman, T. and Hough, M. (1998) *Evidence Based Practice: A Guide to Effective Practice.* London: Home Office.

Clear, T. R. (2005) 'Places not Cases? Re-thinking the Probation Focus', *Howard Journal of Criminal Justice*, 44:2, 172–84.

Cohen, P. (1972) 'Subcultural Conflict and Working Class Community', *Working Papers in Cultural Studies*, 2 (Spring), 5–51.

Cornish, D. B. and Clarke, R. V. G. (eds) (1986) *The Reasoning Criminal: Rational Choice Perspectives on Offending.* New York: Springer Verlag.

Dixon, L. (2002) 'Tackling Racist Offending: A Generalised or Targeted Approach?', *Probation Journal*, 49:3, 205–16.

Dixon, L. and Court, D. (2003) 'Developing Good Practice with Racially Motivated Offenders', *Probation Journal*, 50:2, 149–53.

Gill, A. and Marshall, T. (1993) 'Working with Racist Offenders: An Anti-racist Response', *Probation Journal*, 40:2, 54–9.

Heitmeyer, W. (1993) 'Hostility and Violence Towards Foreigners in Germany', in T. Björgo and R. Witte (eds) *Racist Violence in Europe* (Basingstoke: Macmillan), 17–28.

Hewitt, R. (1996) *Routes of Racism.* Stoke-on-Trent: Trentham Books.

Home Office (2002a) *Building Cohesive Communities: A Report of the Ministerial Group on Public Order and Community Cohesion.* London: Home Office.

Home Office (2002b) *A Report of the Independent Review Team Chaired by Ted Cantle.* London: Home Office.

Livingstone, K. (2001) 'Comment', *Independent*, 30 May, p. 5.

Macpherson, W. (1999) *The Stephen Lawrence Inquiry: Report of an Inquiry by Sir William Macpherson of Cluny.* Cm. 4262. London: The Stationery Office.

Manchester City Council (2003) *Planning Studies: Key Facts and Figures about Manchester*. Available online at: http://www.manchester.gov.uk/planning/studies/keyfacts.htm#Ethnic%20groups, accessed 17 May 2005.

Maruna, S., Porter, L. and Carvalho, I. (2004) 'The *Liverpool Desistance Study* and Probation Practice: Opening the Dialogue', *Probation Journal*, 51:3, 221–32.

Metropolitan Police (2001) *Understanding and Responding to Hate Crime: Factsheet on Racial Violence* Available online at http://www.met.police.uk/urhc/racial_fact.pdf, accessed 5 May 2005.

Mullins, D., Beider, H. and Rowlands, R. (2004) *Empowering Communities, Improving Housing: Involving Black and Minority Ethnic Tenants and Communities.* London: Office of the Deputy Prime Minister.

NPS (National Probation Service) (2004) '1–1 focus day – 1 October 2004', *What Works News*, 19, 4–5.

Oldham Metropolitan Borough (1999) *Crime and Disorder Audit.* Oldham: Chief Executive's Policy Unit.

Pillay, C. (2003) 'Racially Motivated Offenders', *NAPO News,* April, p. 5.

Ray, L. and Smith, D. (2004) 'Racist Offending, Policing and Community Conflict', *Sociology*, 38:4, 681–99.

Ray, L., Smith, D. and Wastell, L. (2002) 'Racist Violence and Probation Practice', *Probation Journal*, 49:1, 3–9.

Ray, L., Smith, D. and Wastell, L. (2003) 'Understanding Racist Violence', in E. A. Stanko (ed.) *The Meanings of Violence*. London and New York: Routledge, 112–29.

Ray, L., Smith, D. and Wastell, L. (2004) 'Shame, Rage and Racist Violence', *British Journal of Criminology*, 44:3, 350–68.

Rees, P. and Phillips, D. (1996) 'Geographical Patterns in a Cluster of Pennine Towns', in P. Ratcliffe (ed.) *Ethnicity in the 1991 Census Volume 3: Social Geography and Ethnicity in Britain: Geographical Spread, Spatial Concentration and Internal Migration*. London: Office of National Statistics, 27–93.

Retzinger, S. M. (1991) *Violent Emotions: Shame and Rage in Marital Quarrels*. London: Sage.

Rosenbaum, D. P. (1987) 'The Theory and Research Behind Neighborhood Watch: Is it a Sound Fear and Crime Reduction Strategy?', *Crime and Delinquency*, 33:1, 103–34.

Scheff, T. J. (1994) *Bloody Revenge: Emotions, Nationalism and War*. Boulder, CO: Westview Press.

Scheff, T. J. (1997) *Emotions, the Social Bond and Human Reality: Part/Whole Analysis*. Cambridge: Cambridge University Press.

Sibbitt, R. (1997) *The Perpetrators of Racial Harassment and Racial Violence*, Home Office Research Study 176. London: Home Office.

Smith, M. (2001) 'What Future for "Public Safety" and "Restorative Justice" in a System of Community Penalties?', in A. Bottoms, L. Gelsthorpe and S. Rex (eds) *Community Penalties: Change and Challenges*. Cullompton: Willan.

Sykes, G. and Matza, D. (1957) 'Techniques of Neutralization: A Theory of Delinquency', *American Sociological Review*, 22, 664–70.

Taylor, S. (1982) *The National Front in English Politics*. London: Macmillan.

Webster, C. (1996) 'Local Heroes: Violent Racism, Spacism and Localism Among White and Asian Young People', *Youth and Policy*, 53, 15–27.

Webster, C. (1999) 'Inverting Racism', paper to the British Criminology Conference, Liverpool.

Webster, C. (2003) 'Race, Space and Fear: Imagined Geographies of Racism, Crime, Violence and Disorder in Northern England', *Race and Class*, 80, 95–123.

Part Four

Conclusions

Chapter 12

Race and community penalties: conclusions and next steps

Sam Lewis, Peter Raynor, David Smith and Ali Wardak

This collection of papers represents an overview of recent research on issues of racial equality as they affect the delivery of community penalties by the Probation Service. It brings together the most recent research on the needs of the Black and Asian offenders it supervises; the history of attempts to provide them with a better service; the difficulty of developing an evidence based approach to this work, and the parallel problems of developing an appropriate response to the white racially motivated offender. This final chapter is an attempt to summarise the central messages of these studies for the future. While they all have their particular distinctive findings, there are also some common themes that are likely to prove important for the next steps forward in addressing these issues.

Black and Asian probationers

Three chapters (4, 5 and 10) are based on the Home Office funded study that originally brought this editorial team together, and three (the Introduction, 7 and 9) draw substantially on it. This study was the first large-scale survey of Black and Asian probationers and provided the beginning of an evidence base for work with them – or, as the editor of the *Probation Journal* put it, 'an early staging post in the development of knowledge about black and Asian perspectives in the criminal justice system' (Bhui 2004: 265). Its detailed findings are described in earlier chapters, but some that have wider relevance are worth revisiting here. For example, the criminogenic needs study indicated that the Black and Asian offenders supervised by the Probation Service are, on average, a *less* problematic and anti-social group than their white contemporaries. If this is correct, why are they receiving the same sentences, and why are their probation orders, on average, longer? The probable explanation is that some of them are receiving rather more severe sentences than similar white offenders. This points to differential treatment that is outside the Probation Service's control (though not perhaps completely beyond influence, given the continuing importance of pre-sentence reports in sentencing).

In addition, although our respondents were broadly positive about how probation officers had treated them, most could point to experiences of disadvantage and social exclusion and of perceived unfair treatment by criminal justice personnel, much of which they attributed to racial prejudice. This is particularly worrying when viewed in the light of the growing international literature concerning perceived legitimacy and compliance with the law (for example, Tyler 1990): people are more likely to comply with the law if they are treated fairly. Although the Black and Asian probationers in our study were not more disadvantaged than other studies have shown white probationers to be, the fact that their disadvantages were often accompanied or generated by racism places an extra obligation on the Probation Service to show that it takes their experiences seriously and is visibly committed to fairness and equality.

How to show this in practice is the theme of several contributions to this volume. Vanstone and Morgan show how the Probation Service has tried to engage with these issues, and to make sure that rhetorical commitments are matched by actual services. Williams, Walmsley and Stephens describe a number of practical steps taken to develop work in this area. The history of wrong turnings, blind alleys and promising initiatives that are not sustained is not unique to this area of practice, and is probably an inescapable part of trying to address difficult problems with limited knowledge and resources. Here the evidence based approach provides an important route to *generally applicable* knowledge.

In fields where innovators and developers are motivated by strong personal convictions derived from personal experience, there can be a tendency to assume that these provide a template for other people's experiences of the same problem, and that the same solutions will make sense. One advantage of undertaking a large survey is that it can show the range of experience and opinion existing among minority ethnic probationers, and our study was able to show that some long-standing assumptions (for example, that Black and Asian probationers would generally prefer to undertake programmes in groups that contained only probationers from the same ethnic group) were not generally shared by the offenders themselves. They generally preferred mixed and multiracial service models (although they clearly also wanted to see more Black and Asian staff). In general, overconcentration on average needs can obscure the wide variations that exist between individuals: the fact that all Black people in Britain are likely to have had some similar experiences does not mean they all have the same needs. However, they clearly have the same rights to skilled individual assessment, responsive supervision and fair treatment.

The wider reach of disadvantage

Comparing Black, Asian and white probationers showed the latter to be a comparably disadvantaged group. The research on racially motivated offenders reported in Chapters 2 and 11 shows some of the consequences of the exclusion, devaluation and hopelessness experienced by some white offenders. These offenders are found to be not radically different from others under probation supervision, and on the whole it is wrong to regard them as an especially violent or dangerous group. Again the Probation Service has been slow to develop a generally accepted approach to work with this group, and promising developments have tended to remain local rather than being generalised as elements of good practice. Some long-standing aspects of good practice seem to be relevant: for example, there seems little point in confrontational and condemnatory approaches, and staff need to be able to recognise and cope with the strong negative emotions that motivate much racially aggravated offending. The most promising current approaches seem to involve additional specialised sessions in one-to-one programmes, informed by and adapted to reflect the specific local contexts of racist offending; but it is (again) not clear whether any adequate evaluation will accompany these efforts so that lessons can be learned from their successes or failures.

Other groups are also likely to require some particular awareness of their likely needs and difficulties. Offenders of mixed heritage, who sometimes saw themselves as belonging neither to white nor to Black communities, emerged from the survey as having more problems than other minority ethnic offenders, and Chapter 7 explores the particular difficulties of their situation. Black female offenders, who make up a hugely disproportionate segment of the population in women's prisons, have suffered from the system's tardiness in recognising the particular needs of both minority ethnic people in general and women in general. As Gelsthorpe makes clear, a failure to acknowledge and address *both* cultural *and* gender based needs may impact upon the legitimacy of probation work with minority ethnic women. Again, promising initiatives may provide some hope for the future, but are far away from generalisation as a standard response.

Evidence based or managerial approaches?

All the chapters describing what the Service has tried to do about this broad range of problems share a particular characteristic: they document, to varying degrees, how the development of policy and practice has fallen short of the evidence based ideal. The conscious commitment of the Service to an evidence based approach goes back at least to 1995 and the launch of the Effective Practice Initiative, later known as What Works (Home Office 1995); ten years later we are beginning to see how difficult it is to implement such a strategy in a consistent and comprehensive way. Many of the practical projects described in this book show precisely the characteristics that the evidence based approach was intended to confront: insufficiently researched aims, poor resource planning, uneven implementation, poor recording and documentation, and either no adequate evaluation at local level or a national evaluation frustrated by the poor quality of local information.

This is the opposite of a learning organisation (Vanstone 2004): in spite of the dedication and ingenuity of individual practitioners, experience does not accumulate, hypotheses are not tested, mistakes are more likely to be repeated than avoided, and promising initiatives are vulnerable to local shifts in circumstances or resources. Walmsley and Stephens conclude that significant responsibility for monitoring and evaluation must be handed back to local areas, informed by local knowledge, closeness to the data and control over its quality – precisely the role for local areas in the evidence based approach that was intended when the Home Office funded the development of a handbook for area based evaluative research (Merrington and Hine 2001). A prerequisite for local evaluation is a more consistent, reliable and detailed system for recording ethnicity. According to the Home

Office (2005:13), 'No information has been available on the ethnicity of offenders supervised by the national probation service in recent years.' For the last quarter of 2003–2004, following the introduction of the 2001 Census categories, which itself led to problems for local information systems, information was available for 37 probation areas. The quality and completeness of the information remain to be tested, however, and the experience of Calverley *et al.* (2004) is not encouraging in this respect. Given its official commitment to recognising diversity, it is a basic requirement that probation areas should develop systems that allow them to plan and implement appropriate services.

In practice, area based research has not been the main line of development for evidence based approaches. Instead they have been developed at the centre and implemented in a top-down managerialist manner (Nellis 2004): partly this has reflected the nationalisation of the Service in 2001 and the rapid growth of the National Directorate, and partly it has reflected the pressure created by over-demanding government targets imposed as part of the Crime Reduction Programme (Raynor 2004). It makes no sense to allocate blame, and it is often not clear what else national managers could have done, given their proximity to the Home Office and consequent vulnerability to political gestures. However, in many local areas staff clearly believe that the substantial amount of information they collect is for central use rather than their own, and that research has become a central function. This predominance of the central over the local has in many areas reversed the development of local research and disabled one of the Service's major learning strategies. It is time for this trend to be reversed: local and national research should complement each other. Many of the research questions that emerge from this book could benefit from skilled local investigation, and it is hoped that the capacity and resources can be found to do this.

Criminal justice and social justice

We have seen how the disadvantages and exclusion of some Black and Asian offenders, and the resentment and racism of some white offenders, are fuelled by wider patterns of social inequality and deprivation. Criminal justice cannot correct wider social injustice, and British society has become more unequal under recent governments, including those of 'New Labour', in spite of the creation of a Social Exclusion Unit with close links to Downing Street. This may change:

a new publication from a think-tank close to government points to the need to address the social justice agenda with more vigour, including (belatedly) a proposal for a more progressive tax regime (Pearce and Paxton 2005). Constructive social and economic policies can affect the opportunities and life chances of offenders, and of minority ethnic offenders in particular. Given an advantageous policy context and a continued commitment to evidence based improvement in services, much could be achieved. Sadly, the recent proposals to establish the National Offender Management Service (NOMS) have had little to say about this issue: the over-representation of minority ethnic offenders in the criminal justice system is not mentioned in either the Carter Report (Carter 2003) or the government's response to it (Home Office 2004) as a problem requiring attention. We hope this book will help to draw attention to this omission.

References

Bhui, H. S. (2004) 'Black and Asian Perspectives on Probation', *Probation Journal*, 51: 3, 264–5.

Calverley, A., Cole, B., Kaur, G., Lewis, S., Raynor, P., Sadeghi, S., Smith, D., Vanstone, M. and Wardak, A. (2004) *Black and Asian Offenders on Probation*, Home Office Research Study 277. London: Home Office.

Carter, P. (2003) *Managing Offenders, Reducing Crime: A New Approach.* London: Home Office and Strategy Unit.

Home Office (1995) *Managing What Works: Conference Report and Guidance on Critical Success Factors for Probation Supervision Programmes*, Probation Circular 77/1995. London: Home Office.

Home Office (2004) *Reducing Crime, Changing Lives.* London: Home Office.

Home Office (2005) *Race and the Criminal Justice System: An Overview to the Complete Statistics 2003–2004.* London: Home Office.

Merrington, S. and Hine, J. (2001) *A Handbook for Evaluating Probation Work with Offenders.* London: Home Office.

Nellis, M. (2004) 'Into the Field of Corrections: The End of English Probation in the Early 21st Century?', *Cambrian Law Review*, 35, 115–133.

Pearce, N. and Paxton, W. (eds) (2005) *Social Justice: Building a Fairer Britain.* London: Politico's and Institute for Public Policy Research.

Raynor, P. (2004) 'The Probation Service "Pathfinders": Finding the Path and Losing the Way?', *Criminal Justice*, 4: 3, 309–25.

Tyler, T. R. (1990) *Why People Obey the Law.* New Haven: Yale University Press.

Vanstone, M. (2004) 'What Works and the Learning Organisation', *VISTA*, 8: 3, 177–81.

Index

Aboriginal women 113
ABPO (Association of Black
    Probation Officers) 12, 18, 53
accredited programmes 157
    compliance with 169–72
African-Asian communities 42–3
Afro-Caribbeans 42
    economic activity amongst
        women 103
    family life 108
    income 102
    likelihood of receiving probation
        107
    and pre-sentence reports (PSRs)
        47–9
    school experiences 87, 88, 176
    unemployment among offenders
        84
    United Kingdom population 126f
    see also White/Black Caribbean
        pupils
Against Human Dignity 33, 36, 37
age distribution by ethnic group
    125–7
anti-racist training 15, 46
anti-social behaviour 93
area based research 160, 222–3
Asha Centre 114–15

Asian communities 42–3
    and discrimination in the
        criminal justice system 43, 44,
        45
    United Kingdom population 126f
    see also Bangladeshi communities;
        Chinese communities; Indian
        communities; Pakistani
        communities
Asian offenders
    experiences of school 87
    main source of income 84
    and pre-sentence reports (PSRs)
        47, 48–9, 51–2
    sentencing 48–9, 106
    types of offences 67
Asian sex offenders 14
assessments of criminogenic needs
    62–3
Association of Black Probation
    Officers (ABPO) 12, 18, 53
attrition rates for programmes 177–8

Bangladeshi communities 42, 102
    economic activity amongst
        women 103
    unemployment among offenders
        84

225